HARMONIOUS MEETING

By the same author

MUSIC AND SOCIETY
STUDIES IN CONTEMPORARY MUSIC
FRANCOIS COUPERIN AND THE FRENCH
CLASSICAL TRADITION
MUSIC IN THE MAKING

THE SONATA PRINCIPLE
ROMANTICISM AND THE TWENTIETH
CENTURY
MUSIC IN A NEW FOUND LAND

HARMONIOUS MEETING

A Study of the Relationship between English Music,
Poetry and Theatre, c. 1600-1900

by

WILFRID MELLERS

DENNIS DOBSON
London

First published in 1965 by
DOBSON BOOKS LTD.
80 KENSINGTON CHURCH STREET LONDON W.8

© 1965 Wilfrid Mellers

Printed in Great Britain by
Clarke, Doble & Brendon, Ltd., Plymouth

To Peggy

PREFACE

This book is an exploration of the relationship between English music, poetry and theatre by way of a detailed commentary on specific pieces. It proceeds from the particular to the general, and its technique is essentially aural. The substance of the book was given, in class, to university students: from the piano, and with frequent reference to recorded or live performance. While I am now convinced that this is the only kind of discussion of music which has value, it is a kind which is, of its nature, difficult to trap in printed form. Part I of the book, for instance, involves much bar by bar commentary for which the usual method of music quotation would be totally inadequate; to append all the pieces complete, however, would have made the book prohibitively expensive, even if problems of editorial copyright could have been overcome. I have therefore decided to cite clearly the edition of each piece I have used, employing where possible editions which are cheap and easily accessible. Anyone willing to read so much close analysis would also be willing, I've assumed, to buy or borrow, if they do not already possess, the relevant pieces. The Henry Lawes Hymns and the two ballads of Hook—which are not available in modern editions—I have included as appendices.

Part II of the book would be more susceptible to the normal method of music quotation, but the Purcell and Handel vocal scores to which it mainly refers should all be readily accessible to any one interested enough to read the book. I have therefore given, again, specific references to the edition I have used; and would emphasize here that Part II, as well as Part I, must be read alongside the text of the music (and sometimes poem or drama) if it is to be comprehensible.

Something should perhaps be said about the relationship between the musical and the literary-theatrical aspects of the book. On the whole, Part I is written from a musician's stand-

7

point; and some of the poems referred to are worth discussing only because they have served as an impulse to music. Even with the most apparently perfunctory poem, however, a relationship between the poetic image and rhythm and the (potential) musical image and rhythm exists; there were reasons why a composer found these words, rather than others, apt for music. In some few cases a composer has successfully set words that are rich and complex in their own right; when this is so—for instance the Raleigh-Gibbons *What is our life?* and the Donne-Humphrey *Hymn to God the Father*—I have devoted equal attention to words and music, and tried to show that the interpenetration of words and music is not the same as a simple addition of one to the other. Raleigh's poem is both great and subtle, and so is Gibbons's music when played, wordless, on viols; but Raleigh's words sung to Gibbons's music is a third entity, greater and subtler than either of the contributory elements.

In Part I, I trace the process whereby music became inherently dramatic; in Part II, I start from poetic drama and trace the process whereby the literary-theatrical medium became increasingly musical. Since in Shakespearean drama and in the masque music was subservient to poetry and to physical movement, I start from the literary and theatrical aspects. I don't attempt a historical survey of music in Shakespearean drama (on which subject much work has been done in recent years) nor of music in the masque. I rather choose certain themes and try to demonstrate how, in developing, these themes demanded an increasing degree of musical expression. Even in works such as *Comus* and *The Tempest*, wherein the literary element predominates over the musical, the basic themes are those which, of their nature, were to lead to the assimilation of poetry by music. By the time we come to Chapter 4, and to the relevant works of Purcell and Handel, we have reached a point at which dramatic organization is inseparable from musical: as is evident, I hope, in the 'amphibious' nature of my commentaries. After Handel, the dramatic-musical analysis thins out somewhat, because the relationship between the two elements loses its inner tension. It is at this point that literary-musical criticism begins to shade off into sociology. When art is vital, its intrinsic significance is inseparable from its social significance; it is representative because it is human. Only when art is in decadence do we consider it as

8

socially symptomatic, for without thinking about it we've become less concerned with what it means to us, now, more concerned with what we think it might have meant to the people who created it.

For the most part I've been preoccupied, in this book, with works of art which are still meaningful to us in the twentieth century, and I'm more interested in the meanings they have for us than in the meanings they may have had for contemporary audiences: though I suspect the subconscious meanings remain fairly constant while the social implications change. Since the pieces were chosen for their general significance as well as for their intrinsic merits the book amounts, in a sense, to a history of part of the 'mind of England'. But it aims at understanding and only implicitly at evaluation; makes no attempt comprehensively to cover any ground; and digs up no unknown factual information. My greatest debt is to the students—extra-mural to the University of Birmingham, intra-mural in the University of Pittsburgh—with whom I investigated these primary sources.

The title, Harmonious Meeting, is from an anonymous poem set by Pelham Humphrey. It refers both to the technical relationship between music, poetry and theatre and also to the general relationship between art and life: 'A Feast of Musick is a Feast of Love'.

UNIVERSITY OF BIRMINGHAM,
December 1963

CONTENTS

ILLUSTRATIONS

13

Part 1

FROM MASS TO MASQUE

1

HUMANISTIC ELEMENTS IN THE LITURGICAL MUSIC OF WILLIAM BYRD

Agnus Dei from the five-part Mass
Ave Verum Corpus

The last years of the sixteenth century and the first two or three decades of the seventeenth century are probably the richest period of our cultural history. This physical and spiritual vitality would seem to have sprung largely from the transitional position of the era: from the fact that it represented a fusion of, and at the same time a tension between, two views of the world. There was a growing concern with the individual consciousness, with the humanist's belief in the power of the Will to control its own destiny; men boldly explored the furthest reaches of the physical universe, the darkest depths of the human mind. Yet they could have the strength to do so only because they came as a climax to centuries of creative evolution: because they inherited conceptions of order and morality which belonged to the Christian hierarchy of the Middle Ages. We can see this even in the technique of the most directly representative medium of the time—the Shakespearean theatre: for recent research has revealed that the theatrical conventions within which Shakespeare's profoundly exploratory art manifested itself were not so much the beginning of modern theatrical technique as a development from the conventions of medieval drama.

The career of Christopher Marlowe, no less than his art, illustrates this tension between two worlds. His first play, *Tamburlaine,* expresses with magniloquent power the Renaissance ideal that the individual will may control destiny and become God. The swing of the 'mighty line', the sensuous decoration of the imagery, the incantatory effect of the rhythms and refrain-like repetitions, suggest that in the first part of the play at least Marlowe believes in Tamburlaine's earthly glory and intends us to do so. In the second part of the play there is a hint of irony because Tamburlaine is proved to be not, after all, a god but fallible and mortal; indeed, he is sick and dies in his bed, rather than in the midst of some martial exploit. So we are not altogether surprised when, in *Dr. Faustus*, Marlowe offers a thoroughly medieval criticism of the humanist view. The theme of the play is the same as that of *Tamburlaine*, except that Faustus seeks spiritual as well as merely material power. This makes the play much more deeply disturbing, because it deals with the threat of spiritual pride within us all; whereas we do not really deceive ourselves when we indulge in Tamburlaine-like illusions of grandeur. Faustus is, to varying degrees, all of us; and to an extreme degree he is Marlowe himself, the intrepid atheist. He cannot help feeling like that; yet at the same time all his inherited beliefs and his innate intelligence tell him that Faustus is damned. One of the consequences of pride is stupidity; tush, there's no such thing, says Faustus—to the devil who stands in front of him.

Marlowe never resolved the dilemma he presents so forcibly in *Faustus*. In *The Jew of Malta* both the self-assertive egoist and the old Christian order are presented with sardonic bitterness; in *Edward II* the God-King is finally deflated and presented as an object at best of pity, at worst of contempt ('Would you stifle your sovereign with puddle-water?') There is an allegorical appropriateness in the legend that Marlowe 'died swearing'.

Most of the other dramatists deal in different ways with the same theme. The plays of Jonson deal with the impact of self-assertive egoism on an ordered society. But Jonson makes little attempt to understand his monsters; he regards them as instruments of evil, whether horrible or ludicrous, who destroy civilization—civilization being, for him, the old manorial order. Thus Jonson, for all his acute understanding of what was happening in his time, is essentially an elegiac writer, as Marlowe is not. Webster, on the other hand, does sympathize with his egoists; at least he regards them at once with horror and fascination. He admires their courage; he is not sure whether the time has not come when the old world *ought* to be destroyed, even though he does not know what is to take its place. This is why all his creatures die in chaos. Their souls are driven they know not whither. Faustus knew very well where his soul was going.

It was not a pleasant place, but he was horribly clear about it. Webster's mist-clouded melancholy represents a further stage of disintegration.

The one man among the dramatists who achieved a re-integration of the inherited Christian ideas of order and the new humanist impulses of the time was Shakespeare: indeed, this is one way of describing his supremacy. In Hamlet he creates a hero-villain whose problem itself involves a conflict between an inherited Christian ethic and the desire or need of the individual to take the law into his own hands. Hamlet does not resolve the dilemma; but Shakespeare does, through the sequence of plays from *Lear* to *The Winter's Tale* and *The Tempest*. And although he does not sympathize with his more extravagant representatives of humanism—those who reduce morality to 'I am that I am'—he does understand the desires, or terrors, that drive them.

Now at their finest the composers of Shakespeare's time achieved precisely what Shakespeare achieved—a fusion of a medieval inheritance with all that was most creative about the humanist belief in the personal consciousness. We can see this most forcibly in the career and work of William Byrd, possibly the greatest of English composers, certainly the most Shakespearean in the range and depth of his experience. Even at a superficial level we can observe in Byrd's career a meeting of two worlds: for though he worked for and was revered by a Protestant Queen, he himself adhered to the old faith and, at the height of his powers, composed three Masses—in three, four and five voices respectively—for the Catholic liturgy. Admittedly, this was after Elizabeth's death, and the masses were performed only in the private chapels of Catholic families. Yet these works are not in any way anachronistic when seen against the background of Elizabethan polyphony: which fact itself suggests that the Reformation was not a sharp fight between opposing creeds. It would be truer to say that the Reformatory conflicts of the sixteenth century, like the Civil War of the seventeenth, were merely one external symbol of a change in consciousness that entailed, inevitably, changes in social structure. There is no sharp division between old and new but rather an interpenetration—as there is, we have seen, in Shakespeare.

If we are to understand how this interpenetration functions

in Byrd's music we must first look at one of the greatest, and latest, achievements of English liturgical music in the old Catholic world. In Dunstable's motet, *Veni Sancte Spiritus*,[1] the vocal lines are smoothly flowing, moving mainly by step or by pentatonic minor thirds, so that they preserve the ethereal, non-dramatic quality of plainsong. The harmony the concourse of lines makes tends to be more triadic than the harmony of a late medieval master such as Machaut: it has a euphonious sensuousness typical of Renaissance humanism. But this harmony is not structural; the motet is organized on medieval—on linear and rhythmic rather than on harmonic—principles. The whole structure is dominated by the dogma of the plainsong cantus firmus, which is played instrumentally in three sections. Each voice part, in each section, repeats more or less exactly the metrical pattern—but not the intervals—of the previous section. Since there is virtually no repetition of *phrase*, and no regularly periodic beat, the lines seem to flow on timelessly, while being subservient to plainsong dogma and to a ritualistic science or magic of numbers. There is even doctrinal significance in the fact that threefold repetition of the cantus firmus progressively decreases the time-values by one third. Such music is not fully intelligible apart from a liturgical act. It is meant to induce a state of receptivity in the listener, and we must think of it in association with the ritual and pageantry of the gothic cathedral. It is not meant to be expressive in a 'personal' sense; indeed no attempt is made to set the words in such a way as to make them apprehensible either intellectually or emotionally; they are an accepted ritual which induces music. In this case three different (though doctrinally related) texts are sung simultaneously!

Contrast this sophisticated, ritualistic structure with a piece of 'Reformed' church music—written about a hundred years later—like Farrant's familiar *Lord, for Thy tender mercies' sake*.[2] The language is now English, instead of a hieratic Latin; and since the four vocal parts move homophonically together, in a rhythm that follows the declamation, we hear the treble as 'top', maintaining the burden of the words. There is nothing here

[1] Hinrichsen Edition. Edited by D. Stevens.
[2] Novello MT 29. This anthem is still frequently sung—and ascribed to Farrant—in parish churches. Scholarly opinion now thinks it is by Tye or the elder Hilton.

comparable with the independent use of different texts and rhythms in Dunstable. The style is not so much ritualistic as intimate. We do not participate in the mysterious and wonderful myth of European Catholicism; we gather together with Tom, Dick and Harry, in town and village churches throughout England, to speak to God in our own way.

This intimate quality is found equally in melody and harmony. The contours of the lines are reticent, the movement being mainly step-wise and regular; the harmony acquires its pathos from its mingling of simplicity with richness. Thus on the words 'Lay not our sins to our charge' there is the slightest rise in emotional temperature as the music modulates sharpwards to the dominant; then the immediate reflattening of the seventh that comes, in the treble, on the word 'forgive' is like balm. The next clause—'to decline from sin and incline to virtue'—remains consistently in the tonic; we do not need to stray when we have found our true home. It leads into a vestigial hint of canon— of the old contrapuntal oneness—as we 'walk with a perfect heart', in more flowing crochets. But there's a suspicion of tension in the passing dissonances that the crochets create: for we have admitted that our hearts are sinful. The four-part spacing of the chords, the regular movement, the lack of modulation, render even chords of the ninth and thirteenth suave and heart-easing, rather than passionate. From the final clause even these passing dissonances are banished: so that the anthem involves an increase in tension, within its quietude, as its supplication becomes more personal; and a resolution as we hand over our burden to God. This also means that the anthem implies some kind of temporal sense—a beginning, middle and end—such as is not relevant to Dunstable's motet.

Of course, this harmonic style is common in Catholic church music too, especially after the decrees of the Council of Trent had insisted on the 'humanizing' of ritual. It is not, however, an accident that it should have been so popular in England with the composers of the Reformed Church; nor that such a 'perpendicular' style of composing—as compared with Dunstable's 'horizontal' organization—should coincide in date with the phase of English architecture known as Perpendicular.

Now the greatest music of the Elizabethan and Jacobean age— this is true whether the music be written for the Reformed

Church or, like Byrd's Masses, for Catholic chapels—achieves in musical technique a compromise between the extremes represented by Dunstable's motet and Farrant's anthem. In Byrd's Masses we find nothing so simple as Farrant's block harmonies; each line preserves independence in a habitually contrapuntal style. Yet the harmonic texture of Byrd's music is much denser than that of either Dunstable or Farrant: for the interplay of his lines is so devised that they create not merely a sensuously pleasing euphony, but a poignant dissonance on the expressive words of the text. Such harmonic intensity means, too, a modified conception of rhythm. The composer has to think simultaneously of the melodic beauty of his lines, and of the emotional possibilities of tension and relaxation between the chords that these lines create. Such alternations of tension and relaxation are impossible without what we would call a strong and a weak beat. So, just as the composer thought of his music on a melodic and harmonic plane simultaneously, he thought of it also on two rhythmic planes at once. There is the individual rhythm of each line; and there is the collective rhythm of the harmony. The free melodic rhythm preserves the music's inner vitality. The collective harmonic rhythm gives the music its sense of direction and momentum.

To sing this music is to realize that the full beauty of the individual part can be appreciated only by the singer; while the effect of the whole concourse can be fully appreciated only by the listener. For the technique combines 'oneness' and 'togetherness'. Each line makes sense by itself, grows lyrically from the implications of the words, with its own rhythmic contours and its own climaxes. Yet it makes a togetherness with the other parts; and the growth of the whole, the climaxes in the texture, are a mean of the contributory climaxes. Moreover, the harmonic structure, being dependent on gradations of tension, implies a sense of periodic time and therefore of the 'togetherness' of the dance. Medieval monody and most medieval polyphony had been essentially a religious act. Sixteenth century polyphony, especially in its maturest form, as in the later music of Byrd, has become at once a religious and a social act: which is another way of saying that it is both mystical and humanistic.

We can see this even in the most solemn moments of Byrd's most traditionally liturgical music. Consider, for instance, the

Agnus Dei from the five-part Mass.[1] The form of this Agnus, as of the whole Mass, is freely fugal, in the sixteenth century sense. Fundamentally, it is an incarnation of Oneness, not an expression of human feeling: indeed a single theme dominates not only this movement, but the complete Mass. Thus the opening phrase, the address to the Lamb of God, is the same as the Kyrie theme at the Mass's beginning. Entirely without metrical stress or harmonic implications, it is simply a stepwise undulation below and above the fifth: a suspiration as inevitable as the pulse or heart-beat, god-like because it seems equated with the mysterious source from which life flows. With the words 'qui tollis peccata mundi', however, we turn from the contemplation of Godhead to our sinful selves. A chromatic note, contradicting the quiet, vocal modality, appears in the soprano to consummate the cadence; and this sharp third conflicts with the natural third in the tenor, who has just entered with the theme. Another chromaticized cadence, C sharp to tonic, creates a sobbing chord of the augmented fifth when the alto undulates from E natural to F. As a result this opening clause, despite the level, timeless serenity of its component elements, effects a gradual increase in tension; the slow rise of the melodies, the increasing dissonance, culminate in a cadence on the dominant of the dominant, the stressed suspended fourth being lingeringly resolved. From this point of heightened consciousness, the music descends. The words 'miserere nobis' are set to a simple declining scale; but, entering in canon, the parts do not droop simultaneously. One is held while another falls, so that passing dissonances of minor ninth and minor second pierce our nerves. The music has acquired, within its apparent tranquillity, a humanistic pathos as we contemplate our weakness, as we live and suffer, crying for God's mercy.

The declining phrase brings the music to rest in the relative major. So far, it has been scored in three-voiced fugue. The text is now set twice more, first for four voices, then for five; and each repetition describes the same melodic arch and creates a similar equilibrium of tension, but in a more richly emotional, because harmonically denser, form. Thus in the four-part setting the original undulation is extended both up and down; the 'qui tollis' is pointed by the bass's octave leap; and the scalewise 'miserere' grows more tenderly sensuous since it is sung in parallel thirds

[1] Stainer and Bell. Edited by E. H. Fellowes.

or tenths. The lingering, chromaticized cadence now has a suspended seventh in the tenor, so that the music seems almost to melt with compassion. This is not, of course, self-pity, but pity for human fallibility: as is revealed by the music that follows the first appearance of the dominant seventh chord. An augmented version of the 'miserere' undulation in the bass clashes fiercely with the suspended F natural of the alto; there is a hardness, a severity in the acceptance of suffering, which is only partially lulled by a restatement of the dominant seventh cadence, this time with a sharp third.

The three-part section had, with passion suppressed beneath the almost unruffled surface, modulated sharpwards. The four-part setting offers assuagement, and modulates flatwards to the subdominant. The relaxation of that G major triad is, however, only transitory. The sharpened third is immediately cancelled by the minor third as the third repetition of the text opens in five-part setting. The parts move, for the first time, note for note; the massive sonority, the more dance-like lilt which at the same time follows the natural syllabic inflexion of the words—all these give the music an almost declamatory, even operatic quality: so that although the work is conceived liturgically its climax is incipiently dramatic. (Consider, for instance, the dotted rhythm figure in tenor and bass.) Then, with the words 'dona nobis pacem', the steadying, repeated Fs of the bass restore us to the softly undulating, stepwise movement of the contrapuntal style, and to its timeless obliteration of metre. But the appeal for peace cannot obliterate the awareness of suffering; so the slow arches of the melodies, quiet as breathing, beginning warmly in the relative major and returning to an archaically modal tonic minor, create the closest, most acute passing dissonances and suspensions in the movement. The suspended seconds of the final cadence are a stab of pain. Minor second resolves on to major second; and that on to the major triad which, in the context, sounds indeed like the peace that passes understanding. The full effect of this can, of course, be apprehended only when we hear the Agnus as apotheosis to the whole Mass.

So we have in this Agnus music of a religious sensibility, conceived as a devotional act. The modal, non-harmonic nature of the individual lines, the fluidity of the rhythms, release us, as does plainsong, from the burden of personality. Yet at the same time the dissonant texture which the overlapping parts create imbues the music with a sense of suffering; and this dissonance —the concept of the suspension itself—is inseparable from an awareness of periodic Time. Humanism, of its nature, involves an apprehension of man's mortality. Byrd's greatness lies in the fact that he can perceive this while still seeing man in the light of eternity: in relationship not only to his own passions (which however deeply felt must be snuffed out like a candle) but also in relationship to God. It is thus strictly accurate to see in Byrd's Agnus a quality of tragic pathos which can be called Shakespearean. Whether, as some think, Shakespeare died formally a Catholic is unimportant. But it is important that the themes of his last plays, with their obsession with rebirth, dying-into-life, and incarnation should manifest a profoundly humanist recreation of Catholic doctrine. One could not pay Byrd a higher tribute than to say that his achievement, in the technique of his Masses, strictly parallels Shakespeare's achievement in his (exactly contemporary) final plays. Both deal with the grace man may wring from his joys and sorrows; both have the painful serenity of faith not accepted, but attained.

In his Masses, then, Byrd employs a traditional polyphonic style, refelt and rethought in more harmonic terms. Occasionally he uses the simple homophonic style we associated especially with music, such as Farrant's anthem, conceived for the ordinary (Reformed) Parish Church. It is interesting that when he does so the immeasurably greater emotional richness of Byrd's music as compared with that of a composer like Farrant is inseparable from its fusion of new and old techniques. For it is the relative independence of his part writing, even in this manner, that makes the harmony so much more disturbed and disturbing: and the serenity paradoxically achieved so much the more rewarding.

There are many examples of this style in Byrd's Gradualia, which are strictly liturgical Catholic works dedicated to 'you who delight at times to sing to God in Hymns and spiritual songs the Offices of the whole year'. One of the most justly celebrated instances is the four-part setting of the Corpus Christi hymn, *Ave Verum Corpus*,[1] which comes from the second book of Gradualia, published in 1607: and which deals specifically with

[1] Stainer and Bell, Church Choir Library, No. 520. Edited by E. H. Fellowes.

Incarnation. The four parts begin moving note for note, in the same intimate style as the Farrant anthem, though they follow the spoken inflexion of the words more sensitively. In the first two bars, however, the quiet, sonorously spaced texture suffers a disturbing nervous tremor. The treble's F sharp creates the warm major third on D, suggesting a modern G minor rather than the transposed Aeolian mode; but then this F sharp is immediately contradicted by the modal F natural in the bass. This beautifully indicates how false relation—to which the English polyphonists were so partial—is a technical epitome of the fusion between two worlds on which we have commented. For the introduction of the sharp third comes from the Renaissance humanists' preference for the sensuously satisfying richness of the major third, while the minor third is a survival of the old melodic thinking in terms of vocal modality. In the second bar the sharp third returns in the treble, emphasized by a 'weeping' ornamented cadence. The tenor's tied C makes a warm dominant seventh chord (like the 'miserere' in the Agnus Dei of the five-voice Mass): which resolves through B flat to A, only to turn back to B natural. The whole of this opening clause thus hovers with precarious tenderness between the major and minor triads of both the tonic and dominant of G.

In the next clause—'natum de Maria Virgine'—birth is symbolized by more flowing movement, in the bass's six-two against the other parts' three-one; by leaping octaves; by the softly dissonant suspension of the bass's B flat; and by modulation oscillating between the relative major (B flat) and the tonic (G minor). This suppressed excitement urges the music sharpwards towards the dominant of the relative; but the sharp seventh E natural is again neutralized in the next bar by the tenor's E flat on 'cruce'. The reference to the cross has introduced a faint hint of counterpoint—a phrase in close imitation beginning with a lift up a third, then fourth, then fifth, followed by a droop down the scale. The increasingly independent movement of the voices, combined with the persistent harmonic ambiguities, wonderfully conveys the mystery that is both sensual and spiritual. In the dissonance, the hesitant rhythm, we feel Christ's physical suffering, as a man; while at the same time we apprehend in the music's ultimate calm, how Christ became, in dying, our hope of eternity.

On the words 'cujus latus perforatum' we shift abruptly from the dominant of G minor to F major, and then flatwards to B flat. The speech rhythm, as well as the tonality, is here free, so that the music seems at once more urgent and more intimate. It leads to a kind of refrain, now lyrical rather than declamatory, on the words 'O dulcis, O pie, O Jesu', in an antiphonal dialogue between one voice as solo and the other three voices in consort. The solo phrase is an expansion of the rising thirds and fifths which had first appeared on the word 'cruce', thus insisting on the paradox that identifies suffering and salvation. Each tender exclamation involves a false relation between major and minor third.

Back in the tonic, we appeal to Christ to have mercy upon us. The false relations become still more piercingly pathetic, the bass singing its modal F natural *simultaneously* with the tenor's sustained F sharp. The word 'miserere' is sung in ripe parallel thirds by alto and tenor, lifting up a third and then declining; the interplay of the quasi-solo voices with the concerted voices is an almost dramatic effect, as though now one, then another human creature were making his personal appeal to Christ. The refrain and 'miserere' are then repeated in an intensified form. The 'O dulcis' phrase now stretches yearningly up a minor sixth and falls through a third; but this time the tritonal six-three chord, followed by a stabbing suspended seventh, leads into an extended plagal cadence. Here again the archaic, modal feeling is modified by the suspended dissonance of D natural against the alto's E flat. We should feel this almost physically (should sing it as though it hurts) for it takes us back into the presence of Christ on the cross. It is precisely because the music makes us so vividly aware of Christ's suffering as a man like ourselves that the final, slowly resolving major cadence can suggest so infinite a beatitude.

Byrd's *Ave Verum Corpus* is a piece of devotional music that is half way to becoming human drama; even more than the Agnus Dei from the five-voice Mass, it balances the claims of heaven and earth, spirit and flesh. Orlando Gibbons died only two years after Byrd, but was born twenty years later. Since his attitude to the world was consciously elegiac—'more geese than swans now live, more fools than wise'—he approved of Byrd's kind of music and in some respects cultivated a deliberate archaism in his own style. None the less, that gap of twenty years cannot be ignored. 'Progressive' elements which in Byrd's music exist beneath the surface become patent in Gibbons's; and this is so even when he seems to be writing in a severely contrapuntal, old-fashioned style.

2

'PROGRESSIVE' ELEMENTS IN MUSIC
OF THE REFORMED CHURCH

Orlando Gibbons: *Hosanna to the Son of David*
Thomas Weelkes: *O Lord, arise*
William Byrd: *Lullaby, my sweet little baby*

At first sight, Gibbons's anthem, *Hosanna to the Son of David*,[1] looks like an extremely complex piece of traditional vocal polyphony. Yet it does not sound like mid-sixteenth century polyphony. That the text is in English has, of course, something to do with this; and we must remember that the (to us) time-hallowed phrases of the Authorized Version were in Gibbons's day contemporary literature, and not so far removed from contemporary speech. Yet neither the English text, culled from the gospels of St. Matthew, St. Mark and St. Luke, nor the jubilant theme, is what makes the essential difference. What has happened is that *physical energy* has become the dominant characteristic of the music; and physical energy implies dedication to fulfilment on this earth, rather than in a world of the spirit.

The seven-part texture is itself a source of power; and although the entries seem to be independent, continually overlapping in close stretto, they are in fact harmonically organized, mainly in a simple oscillation of tonic and dominant. The basic simplicity of the harmony, the relative lack of modulation, reinforce the sense of earthy stability. Moreover, although if each part were barred separately there would be many irregular measures and changes of time signature, each part is driven in a swaying triple dance metre that exploits cross accents between three-two and six-four. Indeed, the ostensibly traditional features have all become 'progressive'. Thus the theme, prancing up a fifth (symbol of stability and power) and then surging up the diatonic

---

[1] Oxford University Press, TCM, No. 39. Edited by E. H. Fellowes.

major scale to the octave, emphasizing the sharp seventh, now suggests a vigorous physical gesture; while the close fugal entries convey an almost breathless exuberance. Even the cross accent is not an equilibrium between 'melodic' and 'harmonic' rhythm, as in Byrd, but a deliberate exploitation of the exciting effect of contrasted dance measures. Again, the occasional modal flat sevenths that occur in melodic arabesques become a source of energy, for they habitually conflict with the sharp sevenths of the cadences. In Byrd's *Ave Verum* false relation exquisitely incarnated the Incarnation: a mingling of flesh and spirit; here in Gibbons's anthem the archaic feature—the vocal flat seventh that takes us back to the timeless, floating figurations of plain-song—has itself become a source of disturbance within the strong simplicities of 'modern' diatonic tonality. It is still more interesting that when the text refers to 'peace in heaven', the closely wrought counterpoint (on a single theme) stops for the first time; and the concept of peace is expressed by way of a series of homophonic cadences treated by inversion and anti-phonally, modulating to the dominant and back. They almost resemble the ceremonial movements of a masque dance, one group of angel-dancers bowing to another: so that the traditional functions of 'divine' counterpoint (in which the Many is resolved in the One) and 'human' dance (which imposes the domination of Time and mortality) have changed places. At the words 'Glory to the highest' the contrapuntal texture resumes, to sweep on with unbroken momentum to the end. But the entries grow ever closer, the conflicting dance rhythms more elaborately interlocked, the false relations sharper, the sonority more powerful: so that by the time we get to the tremendous final cadence, after the stretto introduced by fortissimo basses, we feel that this is not only a resplendent paean to God's glory; it is also homage to man's potentialities and to the beauty of the visible universe.

A comparable, but much subtler, case is Weelkes's anthem *O Lord, arise into thy resting place*,[1] also in seven richly sonorous parts, and with words from the Authorized Version (Psalm CXXII) and the Te Deum. Here the fugal theme opens in more traditional style. Beginning with three repeated notes, like liturgical intonation, it rises up a minor third, followed by a

[1] Oxford University Press, TCM, No. 63. Edited by E. H. Fellowes.

melismatic quaver scale on the word 'arise'. It sounds—compared with the thrust and bounce of Gibbons's rising theme—quietly hopeful, even pleading. It is also—compared with Gibbons's unambiguous diatonic major—traditionally modal, leading up to the flat seventh. The first section reaches consummation with an archaic, quasi-pentatonic 'nota gambiata' cadence on to the major third, for the words 'resting place'. Then follows, however, an antiphonal passage, similar to Gibbons's masque-like 'peace in heaven', repeating the words 'resting place' in a series of cadential false relations! It is restful, because the music keeps swinging to stillness on the major triad; yet the perpetual oscillations between major and minor third—reminding us, perhaps, of the swing of the pendulum measuring Time—make it also sad, because the peace seems illusory. It is as though the music were saying: the major triad is very restful; but it is also, to men of the Renaissance, sensuous, and for that reason likely to be soon disturbed. Human beings are restless creatures: so it is doubtful if the peace of God is for them.

Certainly from this point onwards the music grows cumulatively not only more exuberant, but also more perturbed, even agitated. We begin positively, with a modulation to the relative major. But the words 'thou and the ark of thy strength' are set fugally to a phrase which, though it begins with three repeated notes like the opening theme, is now thrusting, rigid, suggesting the screwing up of courage. The melodic interval of a diminished fourth gives a sinewy intensity to the texture, while triple dance rhythms in the individual lines begin to exacerbate the steady, march-like duple rhythm of the harmony.

All this increasingly *human* energy provides a transition from God's eternal strength to its effect upon us His people, needing salvation. On the surface, we are not here much concerned with human fallibility. We are not, like Byrd in his setting of the words 'miserere nobis', asking God to have pity on us because we are miserable offenders; on the contrary, we are asking him to save his people and to bless his inheritance, especially his priests and saints, among whom, no doubt, we would like to think we are numbered. Yet beneath the surface we are certainly aware of our sinfulness and are at the same time unashamed, praising God, indeed, for giving us strength to accept our imperfections and our mortality. With the words 'Save thy people' the cross

31

rhythms grow more obtrusive as the music swings positively to the dominant. Even when we return to the tonic and to a duple rhythm for the priests who are God's representatives on earth, the momentum is not relaxed, since the harmony is intensified by chromatically altered notes (consider the augmented fifth chord on 'clothed') and by renewed false relations. Then the modal minor is replaced for a while by a resonant diatonic major, as the saints sing in joyfulness—in rich parallel tenths and a lilting dotted rhythm that suggests dance movement and even string technique. The dancing diatonicism hints, perhaps, that the saint's merriment is an earthly matter; certainly the final alleluyas give an odd twist to celestial bliss. For the triple dance measure returns, combined with the most audacious and un-compromising false relations and with interlocking nota gam-biata figures that create between them a whirlpool of counter-rhythms and chromaticisms. It is significant that the old-fash-ioned nota gambiata—like Gibbons's flat seventh—should be responsible for some of the most acrid dissonances, as its flat sevenths clash with the sharp harmonic sevenths of the cadences: and also for the curious melting effect of 'added sixth' chords as the falling pentatonic phrase curls upwards to the *major* third or sixth. Since the cadential dissonances seem always to resolve on to other dissonances the effect of this passage, though tremendously exciting, is hardly consummatory, let alone con-solatory. It may be, in a sense, a paean of joy; it certainly suggests the hurly burly of the world, all the excitations of joy and sor-row, of pride and strife and remorse, that flesh is heir to. The final protracted major cadence, growing from the swirling quavers, is a human rather than a heavenly triumph.

The 'progressive' pieces that we have so far cited are all quick and, at least superficially, jubilant. Modernity is not, however, necessarily obstreperous: as we may see if we return to William Byrd and consider his famous *Lullaby, my sweet little baby*[1] which, published in an earlier generation (1588), is not the less forward-looking for being quiet in dynamics and slowish in tempo. The piece was originally written for solo voice with the accompaniment of four viols; both in this form and in the later version for five voices the song is essentially domestic music in-

[1] Stainer and Bell, The English Madrigal School, Vol. XIV, No. 32. Edited by E. H. Fellowes.

'Be still, my blessed babe': Mother and Child
Andrea Solario's *Virgin of the Green Cushion*

tended not, of course, for the Roman rite nor even for the Reformed Church, but for the home. Its domestic character is implicit not merely in Byrd's inclusion of the choral version among his *Psalms, Sonnets and Songs* (which are preponderantly secular), but in its atmosphere and theme. It is based on the Nativity story which, even in the Middle Ages, had encouraged artists in all media to stress human tenderness and compassion, rather than a more abstract mysticism. The cult of the Virgin Mother, especially in Catholic countries, was not an exclusively Christian symbol but was everyman's search for the mother-image; and although the Babe was the godhead incarnated, he was also our own futurity, a promise of life's renewal after the winter's dark. (See Appendix A for a comparison and contrast.)

The deeply moving quality of Byrd's Lullaby springs more, perhaps, from this generalized, seasonal significance—this precarious, post-Renaissance equilibrium between death and life—than from the traditional Christian associations, though these are, of course, present. We begin, anyway, with the physical reality of movement in time—a rocking. But though the piece opens with imitative points, we don't listen to it contrapuntally; we feel the rocking, dotted duple rhythm of the falling minor thirds, and subconsciously we recognize that the falling minor third is an interval that roots us to the earth, that has been traditionally associated with sleep and, still more, with the final sleep of death. Against the rocking, the tenor sings long, still, reiterated As in semibreves. These soon change to a triple rhythm which, poised against the duple-rhythmed swaying, tries to make the rocking stop: at which point the child would fall asleep—would be liberated from the pull of the earth and of time and, indeed, from death itself, since he would be no longer *conscious* of mortality.

Perhaps this is why the initial rocking isn't ultimately death-tending. The tonality, for instance, looks like D minor; but the Dorian sharpened Bs make the D minor triad act as a plagal approach to the dominant, A minor. This sharp, upward lift to the tonality exerts an influence on the re-established D minor, changing it to the relative major, F, as the singing mother addresses her 'sweet little baby'. The sopranos establish the new, positive key by contradicting their cadential C sharp with C natural and then rising up the scale, with sharp seventh, to the new tonic; then the fulfilled form of the 'sweet little baby' phrase transforms the earth-rooted minor thirds of the lulling into an exquisitely smiling cantabile phrase, *rising* in pentatonic minor thirds, and falling through a major third. This phase complements the death instinct of the initial lulling with the life instinct of the baby's sweetness and the mother's caress. And we are in the presence of a real baby and a real woman: the Babe and the Mother, but also ourselves and *our* mother. The quicker syncopated cross rhythms on the words 'sweet little' (especially the alto's quaver tremor and the tenor's undulating arabesque that transforms minor thirds into a pentatonic cooing) literally act the baby's stirring. Moreover, *because* the baby is real and human, whatever else it may be, it is born, like us, to suffering and death: so we realize, as the piece proceeds, that the stirring is not only the baby's physical presence, but also an unease beneath the apparent quietude.

The climax comes—with a disturbing octave leap, followed by a wistful nota gambiata cadence with a modulation to the dominant—when the mother asks the child 'What meanest thou to cry?' She tries to soothe the infant's disquiet with a falling lulla phrase, not this time drooping in minor thirds, but by step, down the scale, though the interval of a fifth. The descending stepwise movement is a physical gesture, a smoothing of the brow of care, as though she were asking him to forget the pain of being human; and the texture becomes simply sensuous, as the lulling scales fall in parallel sixths and tenths and the tenor returns to its long, still, reiterated As. But he cannot escape his humanity; the trance doesn't work, and syncopations and cross accents grow more obtrusive as the falling scales change back into falling minor arpeggios—an extension of the falling minor thirds of the original rocking. The descending arpeggios sound a knell, dust returns to dust, earth to earth: note how the bass emphasizes the falling minor triad by repeating it in augmentation. Yet the life-instinct of the mother-child relationship is not finally banished. The false resolution of the dominant of D minor on to an F major chord reintroduces the tender 'sweet little baby' phrase, soaring above the knell: though this time the modulation to the relative major is equivocal, being abruptly contradicted by the tenor's sharpened B, and by a peculiarly painful false relation between the tenor's upward-thrusting C natural and the treble's ornamented C sharp. This C sharp also clashes with the first alto's passing D natural: so that in the penultimate bar A, B, C natural, C sharp, D and E are sounded almost simultaneously. The final major triad seems strangely poignant, even frail, as it follows so uncompromising a statement of the paradox of human existence.

So the First Part of the Lullaby presents us with the Mother and Child, and evokes—but does not comment on—his disquiet. The Second Part goes on to explain the reason for the baby's unease, and in so doing becomes incipiently dramatic, even narrative. 'Be still, my blessed babe', the mother sings; but the music tells us that he can't or won't. The basic movement is more animated than in the First Part (triple, instead of duple); the minor thirds now rise rather than fall; and the close entries in stretto develop the tolling knell idea of the First Part's conclusion. The stretti also intensify the anxiety, for although all the parts swing in regular periodicity, they enter without reference to the bar metre, creating complex counter-rhythms. The irregular entries also disturb the harmony. The 'Dorian' B naturals persistently suggest tritonal relationships, while the minor thirds of the tolling phrase continually clash with the cadential major thirds: the false relation with which the First Part had rather unexpctedly ended becomes the initial impetus of the Second Part. Moreover, the music is physically descriptive: we feel the baby's struggle against the mother's supporting arms as the agitated syncopations of the alto act his wriggling—and introduce a passing B natural that, in the D minorish tonality, has the melting, weeping effect of an 'added sixth' chord.

So far we have experienced directly, have been involved in, the babe's distress and the mother's sorrow. But the point is not merely physical description, for this baby's fate concerns us all. So the music moves from physical description to drama, as the text tells us that the baby 'mourns' because the 'cruel king' has sworn to shed the blood of innocence. This cruel king is, of course, specifically Herod but is also the burden of human guilt; if the Child is, in potentia, all of us, so too we all have Herod within us, and we live in so far as we can control the death instinct, the urge to kill and destroy. Here the music acquires much greater energy. False relations between tenor and alto persist, but become subservient to vigorous cross accents, scalewise rising crochets like the thrust of a sword, and an expansion of the tessitura both low and high (blood is shed from a high A). Paradoxically, this gathering momentum—provoking modulations to the relative major F, then to the dominant of the relative C, then to A minor and ultimately to A major—is positive in effect, since we know that this babe, triumphing over the cruel king's wrath, *can* be our redemption; we suffer and die—or He suffers and dies for us—in order to live. Note how subtly the word 'thy' (in the phrase 'for thy sake') is emphasized by the offbeat melismata in alto and tenor, and by the tenor's slow As, as the ferocity is discounted by the Child's tenderness, in an exquisite nota gambiata cadence that carries us to the dominant radiance of A major. The climax comes when the text explicitly relates the two Kings—of life and of death—who are within us: 'a King is born, they say, which King this King would kill'. These words are set to a phrase, in resonant A major homophony, wherein the falling minor thirds have become positively assertive, moving from death to life. But then we remember that the promise, for mankind, is not yet fulfilled because 'wretches' (which means the Herod within us) still 'have their will' over the babe that is within us too:[1] so the final refrain turns the falling minor thirds once more into a lament. At first the 'O woes' are luminous, almost ecstatic, in their sharp A major, carrying over the visionary triumph of the climax. But the falling thirds have already acquired a declining wistfulness; and become unambiguously funereal as the tonality moves earthwards, from A to D, and then back to the original D minor. Perhaps significantly, the words 'when wretches have their will' are set to the same falling scale (but in dotted rhythm) as the mother had sung, in the First Part, to encourage forgetfulness. The false relations return, thick and heavy (consider the tenor's descending chromatics and the clash between the first alto and the second alto's melisma); while

[1] The subsequent stanzas of the poem—which are printed in the complete edition of Byrd's works but not in the sheet-form edition of the separate numbers—establish the relationship between the two Kings even more directly. The final stanza refers to the Second Coming, looking forward to a time when wretches will have their will no longer: when the destructive impulse will be banished and the life impulse flower eternally. Byrd's music wouldn't, of course, fit this evocation of the heaven of the millenium, and we may doubt whether the other stanzas were meant to be sung. Even one stanza, with the da capo, makes a sizable piece.

36

the strained interval of a diminished fourth in the treble produces, harmonically, a 'weeping' augmented fifth chord. Only the major third in the final tierce de picardie reminds us that the babe is blessed, and that we may be blessed through him.

So the story is told, by implication at least, and we return to the physical presence of the Virgin Mother who sings to her Child, repeating the lullaby *da capo*. We hear it afresh, of course, now we know why the babe stirs and cannot sleep. This piece is not a liturgical ritual but an aspect of human experience. Though it moves us deeply because that experience has religious implications, it is the human truth, rather than the religious implication, that Byrd starts from. The piece offers a dramatic complement to the musical image of Incarnation that Byrd presents us with in his *Ave Verum Corpus*. In a sense this is more obvious in the original version for solo voice with viols: for in this form the piece is identical in style with the songs that Byrd and other composers wrote for the Elizabethan theatre. But in both versions the drama is latent, not overt. Byrd does not seek for operatic projection; his human immediacy and awareness can still be absorbed, if need be, into the context of a mystical act.

3

THE MADRIGAL AND 'ELIZABETHAN EXUBERANCE'

William Byrd: *Though Amaryllis dance in green*
Thomas Weelkes: *Thule, the period of cosmography*

In Gibbons's *Hosanna to the Son of David* and in Weelkes's *O Lord arise* we have seen how traditional ecclesiastical polyphony was being metamorphosed into a 'humanistic' assertion of power. Gibbons's anthem is entirely optimistic, buoyant. In Weelkes's anthem, especially in the swirling chromatics of the conclusion, there is also a hint that reliance on the ego inevitably involves turbulence, anguish, even terror, as well as joy. In Byrd's *Lullaby* we have seen a composer responding to the human pity and terror which some aspects of the Christian story may itself invoke: responding, moreover, in terms that are incipiently dramatic and in a convention that is as appropriate to the home as to the church. This indicates how it was not unnatural that these 'modern' impulses should find more comprehensive expression in secular music than in church music. The elements that make up English madrigalian style are those inherent in the pieces of Gibbons, Weelkes and Byrd referred to above; but both their positive and their negative features are more extravagantly developed.

The two poles of human experience, though sharply differentiated in madrigalian style, are also complementary. The positive pole, which we may associate with the Elizabethan ethos, is extrovert and exuberant: the optimistic zest for life and adventure, a proud belief in the power of the individual will. The negative pole, which we may associate with the Jacobean aftermath, is introvert and melancholic: the pessimistic consciousness of death and the eternal worm, such as pervades the mortuary splendours of the sermons of Donne. These two aspects are not—as we have seen in discreet form when we discussed Byrd's Lullaby—sharply distinguished and are indeed interdependent: for the more vividly one is alive the more sensitive

38

one becomes to the certainty of life's cessation. Nor is the distinction to be viewed in a narrowly chronological sense, since there is 'Jacobean' melancholy in the Elizabethan age and 'Elizabethan' exuberance in the Jacobean. In musical terms, we have seen, the positive pole is associated with the growing importance of dance metre and of diatonic tonality: while the negative pole is associated with the disruptive effect of dissonance, especially chromaticism and false relation. The two poles had to come together, just as the Renaissance humanist had to reconcile his zest for living with his awareness of death and suffering. We will first examine two secular pieces which are directly concerned with the 'Elizabethan exuberance'; then a madrigal which is concerned with the split between optimism and melancholy; and then a number of madrigals which attempt a reconciliation and a new synthesis.

Our first example is from the older generation. Our commentary on Byrd's Agnus Dei and *Ave Verum Corpus* has suggested that no man was ever more deeply aware of the weight of human sorrow than he; yet in his church music he was able to assuage the burden with an assurance of peace. Most of his secular vocal music dates from a dozen or more years earlier than the devotional pieces mentioned above. In mood it is comparatively light-hearted, for a man of his generation preferred to put the best of himself into church music and would not have found the passionate introspection of the Jacobean madrigalists congenial. Here is the text of his *Though Amaryllis dance in green*:[1]

> Though Amaryllis dance in green
> Like fairy Queen,
> And sing full clear
> Corinna can, with smiling cheer:
> Yet since their eyes make heart so sore,
> Hey ho, chill love no more.
>
> Love ye who list, I force him not,
> Sith God it wot,
> The more I wail
> The less my sighs and tears prevail.
> What shall I do but say therefore
> Hey ho, chill love no more.

[1] Stainer and Bell, Byrd's *Psalms, Sonnets and Songs*, No. 12. Edited by E. H. Fellowes.

Superficially, this looks like an anti-love poem. Yet if we think of it in relation to the Petrarchan and Spenserian convention of the Wailing Lover we can take it as a song on behalf of life. The tradition of courtly love—harking back to the troubadours of the Middle Ages—involved a deliberate confusion between worldly and spiritual values. The Lady was to be adored, but only at a distance; moreover, she was apt to turn into the Virgin Mary, a symbol of mystical idealism rather than of fleshly fulfilment. So this charming little poem says in effect: Amaryllis and Corinna may dance and sing so enchantingly that watching them gives me a hint of heaven. But if they are to be only pie in the sky, beyond my reach, causing me nothing but anguish and frustration, why then, I'll have none of them, I'll love no more. Both the tripping verbal rhythm—with its delightfully fluctuating line lengths—and Byrd's music make this last clause the merriest affirmation of living in the present, without before and after. Not for a moment can one believe that such dancing joy can be destitute of love. We reject Petrarchan idealism only in order to live, love and be happy, as well as we can in a mutable and fallible world.

Though Amaryllis dance is often cited in history books as an example of the rhythmic flexibility typical of Elizabethan music. So it is. Its flexibility is, however, distinct from that of Byrd's Agnus Dei, in which the rhythm of each line is melodic, growing from speech inflexion and natural vocal contour, with no obtrusive accents. In the madrigal the rhythms are wonderfully varied; but they are all dance rhythms, sharply accented; and the multiplicity of opposed rhythms which are brought into conformity is itself a source of excitement. The technique is a more extravagant form of that manifested in Gibbons's *Hosanna to the Son of David.* That anthem said in effect: how marvellous that we can all in our separate individualities praise God so vigorously, while at the same time becoming one in the act of worship. This madrigal says: how jolly that we can all dance and sing in our own individualities, while at the same time creating concord out of variety. We will preserve, and rejoice in, our separate identities, though we know that we can be merry in the present moment only so long as we are together. If we were alone, we would think of things we would rather forget. The things we would rather forget are not present in this madrigal, or are pre-

40

'Hey ho, I'll love no more':
Hilliard miniature of young man with cloak and roses

sent only by implication. We know they exist from other madrigals—and, of course, from our own experience.

The basic rhythms in *Though Amaryllis dance* are triple; and Renaissance triple rhythms are always associated with physical dance movement and with abandonment to the here-and-now. As in Gibbons's *Hosanna*, excitement is generated by persistent oppositions between six-four and three-two: but is further intensified by syncopations within this rhythmic paradox. Thus the three lower voices start off with a bar of quick three-two, followed by a bar of six-four, with an irresistibly catchy, almost tipsy effect; it is difficult to avoid moving one's body, as well as one's lips, to the phrase. For one bar the words 'like fairy Queen' seem to be introducing a note of regal dignity: the melody soars in a proud, regular three-two, the bass flows in crochets. In the next bar, however, the six-four rhythm comes back in all the parts except the alto, which also introduces a sharpened F on the words 'sing full clear'. The suggested modulation sharpwards to the dominant does not happen, however. In soprano and bass, in the tonic C major, Corinna 'sings full clear' a cantabile phrase in three-two. But each lyrical phrase breaks up into a cross accent of six-four and sometimes into a jerkily syncopated three-two. So the music manages to be positively buoyant, yet at the same time ironically witty. The pretensions of Love are deflated; yet the process of deflation becomes itself an ecstatic stimulation.

This is particularly the case in the last clause of the verse: 'Yet since their eyes make heart so sore'. Soprano and bass sing in lyrically flowing minims, as though the alternation between three-two and six-four were growing into sustained melody, instead of being a rhythmic excitation. But while this is happening the inner parts grow still more jazzily syncopated. The tenor has a three-two plus six-four plus three-two metre which begins, however, on the last minim of a bar! The countertenor has a rumba rhythm in crochets, three plus three plus two. It is justifiable to describe this as syncopation, though of a subtlety exceeding that of jazz. In Byrd's Agnus Dei the rhythmic irregularities are never, in the strict sense, syncopated, for one is not *conscious* of a beat for the accents to be 'off'. Here one is conscious, if not of a beat, of several beats. The fun consists in our not being sure which, at a given moment, is dominant.

41

In this verse, then, a lyrical tune lilts along, but repeatedly breaks into dancing cross rhythms. It is as though we were trying to say something but cannot quite get it out because we break into titters of mirth. If this seems to be frustrating, the frustration itself becomes a kind of vitality. There is a similar quality in the tonality of the passage. It starts unambiguously in the Ionian mode, identical with our modern C major and traditionally associated with dance music because its major seventh makes possible the formation of clear harmonic cadences. (The medieval church disapproved of the Ionian mode *because* it was associated with dancing; they called it the modus lascivus.) From this C major the music is always trying to dance sharpwards. The first F sharp is, however, immediately cancelled by a flat F and the cadence into the dominant does not occur. Next time the F sharp appears it manages to produce a dominant cadence, though the music returns to the tonic in the next bar. None the less, the buoyant, 'sharp' feeling is enchanced when the verse ends on, if not in, the supertonic D : for D is the dominant of the dominant.

The refrain, 'Hey ho, I'll love no more', goes back in fifths from D to G to C. Despite the words it sounds more spontaneously gay than the verse, partly because the phrase is short, echoed in bell-like stretti through the parts : more because most of the rhythmic ambiguities are now ironed out. The firm minim followed by semibreve on the words 'No more', the quaver melisma at the cadence, are triumphant : hurray, having thrown over this wailing pretentiousness we haven't a care in the world; we can pop in an occasional six-four cross rhythm in sheer exuberance, laughing at ourselves while we laugh at those haughty, unreal young women. There are few passages in Elizabethan music of such unsullied worldly gaiety as this refrain. It touches us the more because we know that Byrd knew more than most about both the darker regions of the human heart and the heavenly aspirations of man's spirit.

A more comprehensive example of 'Elizabethan exuberance'— the humanist's positive zest for life—is provided by Weelkes's *Thule, the period of cosmography.*[1]

> Thule, the period of cosmography,
> Doth vaunt of Hecla whose sulphureous fire

[1] Stainer and Bell, The English Madrigal School, Vol. XII, No. 7. Edited by E. H. Fellowes.

Doth melt the frozen clime and thaw the sky;
Trinacrian Etna's flames ascend not higher;
   These things seem wondrous, yet more wondrous I
   Whose heart with fear doth freeze, with love
      doth fry.

The Andalusian merchant that returns
Laden with cochineal and china dishes
Reports in Spain how strangely Fogo burns
Amidst an ocean full of flying fishes:
   These things seem wondrous, yet more wondrous I
   Whose heart with fear doth freeze, with love
      doth fry.

The verse has not high poetic merit; yet its slightly grotesque
wit is serious and its theme is grand. For the Elizabethan's delight in the wonders of the physical universe is explicitly related
to his preoccupation with his own mind and senses. Exploring
Nature and exploring the self are the same activity, both opposed
to antique theological dogma. The 'I' is, of course, a specific
lover, racked by the extremities of feeling: hot desire for the
beloved, cold fear lest she repel him. But the I is also Elizabethan
Man in a generalized sense. The love that fries him is the passions human beings are prone to as they live in the fulness of
their senses; while the fear that freezes him is the ills that flesh
is heir to—especially the consciousness of death that ends all
exploration and all delight.

The two stanzas of the poem are treated as a double madrigal.
The structure of the second part is identical with that of the
first, except that all the elements are intensified. Though the
opening is contrapuntal, it is a fugued dance; the interest is not
in the melodies as such, nor in the polyphony, but in the dancing
dotted rhythm. The long notes on 'Thule', appearing in each
part, sound like a clarion call: which summons up a dance of the
voices in close stretto, all bouncing up the scale, unambiguously
diatonic, with the simplest tonic-dominant harmony, and modulating firmly to the dominant major. The animation is increased
by dancing leaps on the word 'vaunt'; they sweep us into Hecla's
sulphureous flames, when the four upper parts break into two
sets of parallel thirds, whirling in contrary motion, while the two
lowest voices sustain the fifth in semibreves. This is a colouristic

effect that has nothing to do with traditional polyphony; indeed, it is an illustrative device of a type common in baroque music, wherein the wonders of man's mind and senses are likewise in tune with the glories of the visible world. To 'illustrate' Nature is to fulfil oneself. The sulphureous flames sound still more exciting when they are repeated with the rolling thirds between pairs of the highest and lowest voices, with the pedal notes in the inner parts.

The flames tend, too, to disturb the simple tonality. There is a hint of relative minor in the first rolling, while the repeat carries us towards the subdominant of the relative. The flat seventh on the word 'frozen' stills the movement, makes us catch our breath. Then the sky thaws with a return to dancing, upward-tending imitation, taking us (with a jazzy syncopation, like a chuckle, at the cadence) back through the tonic to the dominant major. A momentary change to quick triple measure, on a sonorous dominant triad, leads to the phrase about Etna's flames. This returns to the contrapuntal dance and the simple tonality—tonic major with a strong dominant flavour—of the opening. Then, on the word 'wondrous', the flat seventh that had frozen us comes back much more significantly, long sustained, relaxing gently to the sub-dominant major: but is almost immediately contradicted by the sharp seventh as we swing to the relative minor. This initiates a musical synonym for the paradox of simultaneous freezing and frying. The rhythm breaks and broadens; and the final clause—relating the wonders of Nature to the greater wonder that is I—abandons fugued dance for a solemn ceremonial antiphony. This balances flat sevenths and subdominant in the lower voices (for the freezing) against sharp sevenths and dominant in the upper voices (for the frying). The tone here is much more serious, more involved, than anything in the previous part of the madrigal: for, like his poet, Weelkes does not pretend that being fully alive is all a bed of roses, important though both beds and roses may be. Even in the final 'frying' cadence there is an equivocal false relation, the flat third of the dominant being conspicuous in the tenor. The major third wins the day, however. The last chord is not only traditionally major, but also optimistically on the dominant.

The second part of the madrigal begins again with a fugued dance for the Andalusian merchants. The harmony is simple, and once more there is a persistent tug sharpwards to the dominant. The dance rhythms are, however, much more complex than they were in the first part. Numerous cross accents—triple metres against duple—give a sprightly audacity to the witty line about the cochineal and china dishes. What the merchants 'report' is an extravagant intensification of the first part's 'sulphureous flames'; for they tell us 'how strangely Fogo burns'; and the strangeness provokes an extraordinary sequence of melting chromatics, oscillating between dominant minor and the subdominant of the dominant. Chromaticism which, as we shall see, becomes a musical synonym for the disintegrative effect of passion, is here used positively, as a symbol of discovery. These oddities happen in a New World, so it is not surprising that we feel lost and rudderless: consider, for instance, the queer, wandering line of the first tenor part. Yet being lost is exciting as well as, perhaps rather than, frightening. We are aware, here, of the implicit identification between exploring the wonders of Nature and exploring our own violent passions.

The chromatics sink to rest on the major triad of the subdominant: which is then treated as the dominant of the dominant. The turbulent undercurrent disappears, to be replaced by a witty delight in both physical and sensuous agility: the flying fishes leap in a dancing fugato of scales in contrary motion. This is not merely illustration; it is also a musical equation for a physiological state, producing a tingling of the aural nerves similar to (and perhaps accompanied by) a prickling of the scalp. The dance is 'frozen' once more by the appearance of the flat seventh on the word 'wondrous': all these exotic extravagances and this pyrotechnical display are nothing compared with the paradox of my frying-freezing ego. The last clause, which repeats the words of the first part, repeats the antiphonal music too, except for the final cadence. The first part had concluded optimistically in the dominant, after some vacillating false relations. This time we fall to the subdominant, then to the subdominant's relative (with chromatic third in the alto), then apparently back to the dominant (with sharp seventh in the bass). Abruptly and unexpectedly the dominant chord, instead of being final, reverts to its dominant function; and with an old-fashioned nota gambiata in the second tenor, we reach a brave but curiously unresolving cadence to the tonic. All through, the music has seemed to be eagerly seeking the dominant, or relaxing to the sub-dominant; even at the end, the tonic sounds like half-way house, rather than home. The last cadence sums up, in shorthand terms, the precarious balance between frying and freezing—between the joy and the fear within exploration—that has been typical of the piece.

4

THE MADRIGAL AND 'JACOBEAN MELANCHOLY'

Thomas Weelkes: *O Care, thou wilt despatch me*
John Ward: *Hope of my heart*
              Out from the vale of deep despair

In the wonders of Thule there is perhaps a faint hint of the dark undercurrent of passion that is the negative pole of humanism expressed in Weelkes's *O Care, thou wilt despatch me*,[1] the text of which is a simple statement of this opposition.

> O Care, thou wilt despatch me
> If music do not match thee,
> Fa la la la la
> Fa la la la la.
>
> So deadly dost thou sting me,
> Mirth only help can bring me,
> Fa la la la la
> Fa la la la la.

This Care which is about to despatch me, to break my humanity, is the ego in darkness, the melancholy of the personal life. On paper the texture of the opening looks vaguely fugal, the theme being an undulation up and down around a single note, as is the the theme of Byrd's Agnus Dei. The upward undulation is, however, chromaticized; and the effect of the music lies not in the fugal interweaving, but in the harmonic intensities created by that single chromatic alteration. Thus at the beginning the answer by inversion in tenor and bass creates the sobbing chord of the diminished seventh. The entry in the alto makes a sensuous dominant seventh with the suspended tenor C; the entry in the soprano forms a stabbing diminished fourth with the chromaticized major third of the tenor; while the bass's second entry

[1] Stainer and Bell, The English Madrigal School, Vol. XI, Nos. 4 and 5. Edited by E. H. Fellowes.

4

builds up a climax of suspended major sevenths. All this cumulative dissonance tells us that the personal life is about to disintegrate under the intensity of its passion. Then comes the balancing clause: one thing can stay the disintegration, and that is music. So music takes the place of God, and the old fugal discipline—resolving the Many in the One—reappears. But the music does not sound in the least like ecclesiastical polyphony because the metre is symmetrical and dance-like, and in that sense of the earth, earthy. Indeed, the canonic style, the simple harmony, the absence of passing dissonances as compared with the acutely dissonant texture of the first section, suggest a round-dance. We sing-dance in canon to assert our human togetherness; but the oscillating false relations (similar to those in the ambiguous 'resting place' of O Lord arise) prove how little we are self-deceived. So simple a togetherness is not really an answer to the terrors that individually beset us. So our fa la refrain—habitually associated not with 'spiritual' counterpoint but with the earthily homophonic ballet—sounds dimly forlorn; and we are not surprised when Care comes back with redoubled ferocity.

The theme on the words 'so deadly dost thou sting' is again the chromatic undulation both ways up; but now the entries follow so closely one upon the other that the music becomes a string of dissonances on each strong beat. Diminished seventh is followed by major seventh, then augmented fifth, then minor second, culminating in a 'deadly stinging' false relation—a simultaneous clash of the alto's cadential F sharp with the soprano's soaring F natural. To such vehemence of personal suffering there can be no valid reply. This time we do not pretend that music can be an answer; we merely say 'mirth only help can bring me', there is nothing to do but laugh it off, pretend it is not true. Perhaps it is not an accident that the deadly false relation that forms the climax on the word 'sting' had first been hinted at in the refrain. However this may be, when the dance-fugue starts again, now in tripping quavers, the fa las ring desperately hollow.

Weelkes wrote a second part to this madrigal, which repeats and intensifies the pattern of the first part. In the first section, setting the words 'Hence Care, thou art too cruel', there is now hardly a pretence of fugal organization. The effect depends on the harmonic surprise of chromatic alteration. Chords of G major,

48

'With love I fry':
Hilliard miniature of man with flames

C minor and E major follow in sequence as the soprano rises chromatically from D to E; each harmonically unrelated chord delivers its shock to the nervous system. Then the music declines through a series of frustrated cadences. It seems to be resolving into D, but a sharpened A in the tenor turns it into B minor. Resolution into B major is destroyed by the substitution of G natural for F sharp, producing a sobbing augmented fifth; and then chains of suspended sevenths keep us painfully hovering before the cadence into G is ultimately achieved. In this extraordinary passage the personality seems to be swept from its moorings. The effect is already operatic. One can imagine the top line declaimed by a solo voice (with appropriate physical gestures) while the other parts were played instrumentally; and it would be easier to play than it is to sing.

The appeal to music, 'sick man's jewel', to bring relief is made in a phrase that declines slowly down the scale. The fa la refrain continues the descending scales, now in pathetically tripping quavers, as the tremulous false relations recur. With the words 'his force had well nigh slain me' the scale is inverted; paradoxically, it thrusts upwards, landing on dissonances on each strong beat, for in this piece the negative, destructive force is stronger than the positive. Significantly, when the dance-fugue comes back for the last time ('but thou must now sustain me') it has lost its quaver lilt. Its crochet movement, its three repeated notes on 'sustain me', have a relentless, rigid quality, while the syncopation in the soprano, thumping on to the word 'sustain', is fiercely desperate. The metre, over the anchor of the pedal note in the bass, is almost like a funeral march; the fa las have become a lament. It would seem that to such destructive passion there is no answer but a numbness of the spirit.

Of course, there had to be an answer to the disrupted sensibility. The nature of it is intimated in a madrigal of Ward, *Hope of my heart*,[1] which is closely related to Weelkes's O *Care*. Weelkes's madrigal was in two contrasted sections, both repeated: the contrast being between declamatory passion and an attempt at contrapuntal order. Ward's madrigal does not have the repetition, but again falls into two complementary sections, the first on the whole declamatory and homophonic, the second contra-

[1] Stainer and Bell, The English Madrigal School, Vol. XIX, No. 17. Edited by E. H. Fellowes.

puntal. The counterpoint is again a response to the melancholy of the declamation: only whereas Weelkes's contrapuntal fa la refrain is no more than a dream-answer to the realities of melancholy, Ward's contrapuntal dance, accepting things as they are, is an affirmation created from sorrow.

> Hope of my heart,
> O wherefore do the words
> Which your sweet tongue affords
> No hope impart,
> But cruel without measure
> To my eternal pain
> Still thunder forth disdain
> On him whose life depends upon your pleasure?

The poem, like the text of O *Care,* is a conceit and a paradox: the hope that turns out to be no hope. The opening declamatory section divides the singers into two antiphonal groups. The held G minor triad stresses the word 'hope'; yet the phrase belies the word, since it moves down the scale in thirds, sighfully syncopated across the barlines. Although the second soprano starts afresh with the high D, now poised over a rich five-part texture, the hopeful phrase cannot be sustained. It droops again, and all the voices utter heavy chords on the exclamation 'O'. What looks like being a sturdy relative major (B flat) proceeds to the dominant minor, and the triad-exclamation is left desolate on the empty fifth, with neither major nor minor third. Then the music begins to move forward on the words 'wherefore do the words which your sweet tongue affords'. Though there is a trace of counterpoint here, the purpose of the imitative entries is not contrapuntal order but the creation, through a regular pattern in syncopated dotted rhythm, of a series of dissonant suspensions on each strong beat. The imitative points, the syncopations, the sensuous dissonances (minor sevenths and major seconds) excite us as we think what her sweet tongue *might* mean; but though we modulate rapidly through this passage, we proceed in a cycle of *falling* fifths from D to G to C. So we are not surprised when the tenor enters on his agonized high A, with the words 'No hope imparts'; slows down the movement to minims; and swings us back through G, with a suspicion of E minor, to A.

Then, at the words 'cruel without measure', a chromatic G

sharp appears in the crochet movement of the second soprano, is echoed by the other parts, and leads into a series of dissonant suspensions to create the text's 'eternal pain'. These suspensions are both longer sustained (in minims) and more acute (major sevenths and minor seconds) than the previous series on 'your sweet tongue'. They culminate in a savage false relation in which the first soprano rises to a cadential third G sharp, and then abruptly leaps to the G natural above. So, after the deceptively noble opening on the word 'hope' (which turns out to be ironic), the madrigal has thus far built up an inexorably cumulative tension, expressed in ever acuter dissonance and in increasingly wayward modulation, checked only by the rigid metre, and by the long held, almost instrumental pedal notes.

At this point, however, the word 'pain' finds resolution in a powerful major triad on A. This releases a new motive for the words 'still thunders forth disdain'. This is a fugato passage alternating between G and C, thundering in a dotted rhythm that implies bodily movement, the energy of the dance rather than the fluidity of vocal polyphony; indeed, it forcibly suggests Purcell and the technique of Restoration string music. The time-impetus in the thundering is contrasted with the eternity of pain in the sustained dissonances; so that although the words are, on the face of it, hardly cheering, the passage has a decisive positive effect. He is no longer indulging in his grief; indeed her disdain seems to become his anger. The martial note suggests that he is taking arms against his sea of troubles; so when the contrapuntal thunder leads into the final section that takes us back to the disappointed lover, it produces music that has a certain determined energy, as well as a dignified resignation. It is significant that the last clause no longer refers to 'me' but to 'him'. He can stand detached from his sorrow, as the words 'on him whose life' are set antiphonally, rather than contrapuntally, to repeated triads in sequences rising *upwards*. The upward tendency fights considerable odds: the broken phrase sounds as though one is gasping for breath, the repeated notes as though one is deliberately screwing up one's courage; and the upward sequences seem to be settling down in an unexpectedly flat (plagal, subdominant) C major, with painfully sharp passing dissonances (one chord sounds B natural, C and D simultaneously). Yet the crochet movement gathers a quiet power; and the final G major cadence,

51

though weakened by the prolonged subdominant approach, is not a sham. He has won through.

There is a further development of this association of self-discipline with harmonic and tonal—as opposed to contrapuntal—order in Ward's six-part *Out from the vale of deep despair*.[1]

> Out from the vale of deep despair
> With mournful tunes I fill the air
> To satisfy my restless ghost
> Which Daphne's cruelty hath lost.
> O'er hills and dales in her full ears
> I'll send my notes with bitter tears.

The verse, as so often, is paradoxical, saying two things at once. From one point of view, the vale is a metaphor; he is in the dumps, and indulging his misery. In so far as the vale is a real valley, however, he is climbing out of his misery, leaving self-indulgence behind as he reaches the sane spaciousness of the hills. Similarly, he is a restless ghost because without her he is as good (or as bad) as dead; yet he can find a kind of strength in pouring out his woeful tunes to Nature because he knows that Nature, being inhuman, cannot be *expected* to respond. By a subtle shift he equates his Daphne with Nature: since her mythological prototype was turned into a tree it is hardly surprising that her ears should be dull. So he learns to make a virtue of necessity.

At the opening the parts are beautifully singable, yet the texture has an instrumental resonance; it is not an accident that the Jacobeans were so partial to six-part writing. The regular minim movement creates a passionate suspension on each strong beat, while the regularity of the metre and the sustained pedal note in the bass imply an iron control. At the words 'with mournful tones I fill the air' self-discipline is symbolized in the long static Ds in the soprano. In one sense they are realistic; we hear his voice soaring out of the valley, echoing through the air. But in so far as they are an inverted pedal note, anchored, unmoving, without melodic flow, they are psychological rather than realistic; they hold on, as it were, for grim life. The other voices fill the air with mournful tunes in symmetrical homophonic sequences; and we seem to be winning through because—despite the metrical rigidity—the whole passage is repeated a third higher, in

[1] Stainer and Bell, The English Madrigal School, Vol. XIX, No. 21. Edited by E. H. Fellowes.

the relative major. Then the pedal note joins in the solemn dance and we return to the tonic.

At the words 'to satisfy my restless ghost' there is more independence of part-writing, because he is concerned with the nature of, as well as with discipline over, his inner life. His ghost wanders to a rising scale; but the scale usually flows in thirds or tenths, richly sensuous; while the sharp passing dissonances and the long notes in the bass do not allow us to forget the psychological effect of the suspensions and pedal notes in the first section. So at the climax of the rising scales we return to the original minim movement, and come to the point: which is that Daphne's cruelty has created this misery, depriving me (as well as herself) of humanity. Recollecting her cruelty, we live through our anguish again. The major triad that seems to assuage the 'restless ghost' is dismally disturbed by the minor third entering in the bass; and this leads to a passage in which we no longer have merely the suspensions sanctioned by tradition: we have cumulative double and triple suspensions that attain an almost ferocious anguish. (The ultimate dissonance on 'cruelty' telescopes the chords of C minor and B flat major, and sounds five consecutive degrees of the scale simultaneously.) Yet again the regular movement, the sustained bass notes, the control of tonal direction, give the music dignity as well as force. The richness of the texture, reminding us of seventeenth century string style, becomes almost a positive affirmation.

So we can conquer our personal suffering and commit our sorrow once more to the hills and dales. The last section begins like a free recapitulation of the opening, only with the material in the reverse order. The antiphonal echo-effects on the words 'o'er hills and dales' are based on the 'mournful tunes' motive, suggesting the projection of grief into physical movement: while 'I'll send my notes with bitter tears' returns to the initial minim movement. Syncopated accents are now, however, more prevalent; there is a conflict between the regular duple metre and triple measures provoked by the inner agitation. The bitter tears also create a peculiarly uncompromising false relation and a series of dissonant passing notes—including major and minor ninths—on the strong beat. Again, however, this instrumental, almost Purcellian intensity is controlled by the long pedal notes and the strongly marked harmonic progression of the bass; and the final cadence is dignified, almost peaceful, with the second soprano reaching upwards to the major third while the first soprano descends. The ultimate major triad sounds brave but a bit uncertain, because the G minor-major tonality of the last section has been tinged (as is the concluding section of *Hope of my heart*) with a chastened, plagal, subdominant feeling.

5

THE JACOBEAN ELEGY

Orlando Gibbons: *What is our life?*

In the course of our commentary on both 'optimistic' and 'melancholic' madrigals we have seen how a different approach to human experience slowly established itself during the first two decades of the seventeenth century. It did so because a highly developed humanism of its nature implies introspection. Introspection, if it does not lead to the destruction of spiritual values, must lead to their re-assessment: so the search for a new kind of order which we have examined in the work of Weelkes and Ward was not basically a technical matter, but was rather the start of a spiritual renewal. No one could live continuously at the level of passion expressed in Weelkes's *O Care*: that would be as inconceivable as a whole community of Gesualdos! So Melancholy must induce a mood of acceptance; suffering must be borne with dignity and a stiff upper lip. Weelkes's 'operatic' violence, in *O Care*, resembles the rhetorical ferocity of the heroes and heroines of Webster, whose souls are driven they know not whither, because they have lost their belief in an inherited Law. They hysterically try to believe in themselves because they have nothing else left to believe in. At a slightly later date the heroes and heroines of John Ford also believe in little except the validity of their own passions; Ford even implies a sensual recreation of Mariolatry, in that physical beauty in woman is to be worshipped as a symbol of virtue and itself justifies any behaviour that the passions may demand. But the heroes and heroines of Ford live and die not 'in a mist', but with their eyes wide open. They know that submission to their passions will let loose chaos: yet are unwilling, or unable, to escape their fate. They accept their suffering as the price they must pay for being a law unto themselves. If their self-sufficiency leads only to disillusion, they will at least escape bombast, and make a good end.

This attitude is very close to the mood of Ward's most characteristic madrigals; and there is a relationship between Ford's highly personal, elegiac verbal rhythm and the ceremonially solemn, sonorous texture of Ward's harmonic polyphony. Both manifest the will to endure without achieving the serenity that comes of acceptance. An explicitly 'philosophical' statement of this changing approach to man's experience is offered in Gibbons's 'spiritual madrigal', *What is our life?*[1] Perhaps it is not an accident that so impressive an instance of a 'new' Jacobean polyphony should be married to a poem by Sir Walter Raleigh which is, in its own right, a profound and complex exploration of an essential Jacobean theme. That few madrigals have texts of such subtlety is hardly to be regretted, since the human intelligence cannot attend to too many things at once. In this case, however, there is so rich an identity between the poetic and the musical image and rhythm that one feels that poem and music grew almost simultaneously from a crucial development in the human consciousness. Certainly Raleigh found in Gibbons a composer with genius to match his own: certainly the complexities of the poem lend themselves magnificently, and perhaps by conscious intent, to symbolism in musical terms.

The poem, though not religious in the strict sense, is concerned with what one might paradoxically call the religion of humanism. It is about the eternal realities of life and death, and is built around a metaphor fundamental to seventeenth century humanism: the comparison of man to an actor, strutting and fretting his hour upon the stage, exhibitionistically presenting his experience, surrounded by darkness.

> What is our life? a play of passion,
> Our mirth the music of division;
> Our mothers' wombs the tiring houses be
> Where we are dressed for this short comedy.
> Heaven the judicious sharp spectator is
> That sits and marks still who doth act amiss.
> Our graves that hide us from the searching sun
> Are like drawn curtains when the play is done.
> Thus march we, playing, to our latest rest;
> Only we die in earnest, that's no jest.

[1] Stainer and Bell, English Madrigal School, Vol. V, No. 14. Edited by E. H. Fellowes.

The poem begins with a question—what is life?—and continues with a paradox. It is a 'play of passion'. Passion is earnest, the essence of our humanity, our striving natures. In so far as the metaphor is musical, 'play' means that by conscious volition we live through our experience; and there is probably a hint of the Christian Passion in the background, for God became Man for us and, since the Fall, life is inevitably suffering, a purgatorial process. But in so far as 'play' means a theatrical presentation it implies that our lives are only a simulachrum of reality. There is even a suggestion of the frivolous sense—we are 'playing at' life, rather than living. A similar equivocation appears in the second line—'our mirth the music of division'. The technical meaning is that our mirth,[1] our creative joy and energy, burgeons like divisions on a ground—the dividing of a theme into ever smaller note values, ever more exuberant 'graces'. But division also means the state of being divided: *not* being whole, *not* flowing creatively; and this gives to the mirth an air, if not of frivolity, of incipient frenzy. Similarly, in the next couplet our mothers' wombs are tiring places where we are dressed up in flesh: which suggests that the dress is tawdry, a pretence, like the actors' costumes. It *is*, of course, because in time it will fall off; but the poem remains ambiguous as to what will be left when the flesh is no more. Is it our eternal souls that are dressed in flesh? or merely the bare bone? When the play is over, do we see nothing but a deathshead? Probably, the word 'tiring' contains also a hint of *growing tired*: so that, in the typical seventeenth century manner, our wombs become our tombs. We begin to die as soon as we are born; 'you grow old while I tell you this'. All flesh is grass.

In the next couplet we turn from us to God, called Heaven. If we are the actors he is the audience. He is judicious, as we might expect; but also 'sharp' as he sits and marks who doth act amiss. This is probably a technical pun again: for the sharpened note, according to the principles of musica ficta, 'corrected' the 'false' note in the imperfect fourth or fifth, the tritone that was

---

[1] The word 'mirth' is probably not used here in its modern sense: or at least the modern sense is subsidiary to the sense in which the word is used in fifteenth and sixteenth century devotional books. Sir Thomas More— or Hamlet when he said he had 'lost all his mirth'—meant by the term a condition of equanimity, sanity, spiritual calm consequent upon faith.

traditionally associated with the devil. Yet there is an equivocation even here, for while the line might mean that God gives us good or bad marks according to the morality of our acts, it could also mean that he is judging merely the conviction of our acting, our performance of a part. Do we put up a good show: which perhaps means, ultimately, are we unafraid. The word 'still' reflects on this, for its meaning is partly temporal (he's still sitting there, always has been and always will be), and partly physical (he sits still as a stone statue, because he is impervious to our sufferings). In the next couplet, however, God seems to become equated wtih the Sun, the physical source of life rather than a mystical abstraction. This is why it is so important that we should cast out fear. We have to accept life, for it is all we have; yet life is terrifying even while it is creative. Nature grows and blossoms in the sun; and the sun also breeds maggots in a dead dog; it 'searches' us out, pierces through our pretences, creates us only to reduce us to the whiteness of the skeleton. So the grave becomes the 'drawn curtains' that, when the play is done, shut us off from the sun, the source of life, and also the God-audience. We are left alone on the stage, presumably in darkness, without before or after. This is a very strange development: for the implication is that when we die, God cannot see us any more and we cannot see Him. This is exactly the opposite of the traditional Christian attitude that sees God not simply as the source of life, but as a metaphysical Absolute.

Then comes the final couplet, with its curiously sturdy, positive rhythm. The word 'marching' has almost as much energy as the earlier 'searching'. We no longer just go on acting. We *march*, banded together in a sort of ritual ceremony: seeking social togetherness to protect us from the cold and the dark. We are 'playing'—performing on our instruments and in that sense making our destiny; or if merely 'acting our parts' at least we know we are acting, and that we shall never get anywhere except to our 'latest rest', which is silence (a musical pun again). The only thing we do know is that we die 'in earnest', however we have lived, whether or no our life has any meaning. All we can do is to accept this with courage. There may be a hint of the legal sense of 'in earnest': we die in the flesh 'in earnest' of future bliss. But of course that is not the main meaning, which is conditioned by the tone of the grim joke. The spirit of the poem is no longer Christian, but stoic; and in the context the Christian implication of the last line, if it is there at all, sounds ironic.

In setting this poem as a 'spiritual madrigal' Gibbons appropriately adopts a style that, beginning severely fugal, looks as though it belongs to the old 'theocratic' world. The theme enters in the second soprano. The long note on *What?* stresses the question; the rising sixth introduces an element of yearning: we don't know the answer and, not knowing, cannot be at rest. Then, for the 'play of passion', the line declines through a series of decorated suspensions: playful because they are decorated, tense because they create dissonance. This is a strict musical synonym for the paradox of the words.

The answer follows in close stretto, in the first soprano. It is, however, a modified answer, for the line now falls through a fifth instead of a fourth, and rises a fourth instead of a sixth. This means that whereas the first entry makes a leap upwards and then declines, the second entry forms melodically a continuous descent. The first entry is full of tense yearning: what is our life? It is essential we should know. The second entry is wistful and resigned: what is our life, after all; a bubble in eternity. The entries in tenor and bass emphasize the question by prolonging the 'What' through two bars; and the opening clause ends when the bass settles on the dominant and all the other parts droop downwards, forming dissonances on each strong beat. Despite the fugal texture, this music relies on periodic harmonic stress—on a regular bar-rhythm and on the passage of Time that inevitably conditions the humanist's approach to experience. Its technique is as close to Ward as it is to Byrd: which is one reason why it sounds so effective when performed with instrumental doubling on viols.

The opening has been tense, but droopingly elegiac. The question is now asked positively. While some parts continue to fall, in others the scale is inverted; moreover, it rises up the sharpened sixth and seventh, discounting archaic modality, creating a luminous six-four chord on the word 'passion'. This leads into the next clause: the mirth that is the music of division. The movement becomes crochets instead of minims, mirth being suggested both by the more rapid lilt and also by elaborate cross rhythms. But the rhythmic contrarieties—triple dance measures against the harmony's duple movement—are also 'division', a dislocation which is reinforced by the extravagant emphasis on the unimportant word 'of'. There is something a bit strained, excessive, about the gaiety: which is connected with the fact that this counterpoint of rhythms is an equivocation between different Time-dominated metres. No more than in Weelkes's *Thule* have the lines the apparently timeless fluidity of Byrd's Agnus Dei.

Throughout this clause and the next couplet about our mothers' wombs there is little trace of 'vocal' modality. The key-sense gravitates, again with an increase of positive energy, around the relative major and the dominant of the relative. At the word 'dressed', however, the dancing lilt (the vanity of the world) begins to give way to old-fashioned fugato. Stretto entries seem to put on flesh as the sonority grows richer. But the appearance of fugato really prepares the way for God, the judicious sharp spectator. He enters with a bold leap of a descending octave, followed by a rigidly metrical rise up the scale, with consistently tonal *sharp* sevenths. His effect, in the music as in the poem, is very odd for a divine being. The entries in stretto seem remorseless, implacable, especially since the chromaticized notes create savagely accented chords of the augmented fifth and, as climax, a suspended major seventh. This takes us back to the tonic minor, and to the 'sitting and marking' episode, set in note for note crochets, except for an occasional nagging misplaced accent. This God, compared with the Lamb of Byrd's initial phrase, seems an ill-tempered schoolmaster.

He seems to have the last word. One cannot argue with him; there is a cadence on to the major triad. But at the words 'our graves' a most mysterious alchemy happens. The fifth of the triad of D becomes the third of the triad of F, with a single chromatic alteration from F sharp to F natural. The bass descends by a whole tone from F to E flat, while the soprano rises chromatically from A to C, the movement being now triple, note for note, but in solemn minims. A tremor of fear runs through the music as we contemplate our end, the one fact of which we can be certain. The fear brings back the elegiac mood of the opening, but softer, more wistful, with interweaving chains of suspensions that are a musical equation for the metaphor of the drawn curtains. This passage is a permutation of the descending, 'resigned' version of the opening phrase. Its suspensions fall consistently, gently, being mostly major ninths or seconds or minor sevenths—whole tone rather than semitone dissonances. It is as though we long to sink into the dark of death to escape the terror of the searching sun.

Yet this elegiac resignation is not sensuously indulgent; in the context it serves only to screw up courage for the final confronting of life and death. At the words 'thus march we' there is a sudden change to triple rhythm with false relations that parallel those that occurred on the triple rhythm provoked by our graves. But whereas the oscillation on 'graves' had slowed the movement down to minims, that on 'thus march we' quickens it to crochets, setting the movement going with almost desperate, if suppressed energy. The general effect of the succeeding passage is of a processional masque-dance, which speaks for human solidarity against the threat of Time. We are always conscious of the threat because of the agitated cross-accents that upset the duple march; yet it seems that human endurance is winning as the momentum grows in power and the music modulates from tonic minor decisively sharpwards to the dominant. This affirmation is, however, counteracted by the bass. The 'march' theme is an extension of the rising fourth and descending scale of the opening clause, with the scale now in a driving dotted rhythm. Having arrived at the dominant, A major, the bass proceeds downwards until it arrives at C *natural* and then B flat: thereby deflating the tonality and the mood of affirmation. Then it thrusts slowly up the scale from the low A, in massive semibreves, on the words 'only we die', creating an excruciating dissonant seventh when it reaches B flat. The final cadence is powerful, with, of course, the major third. But it is a testimony to human courage, remote from the simultaneously human and mystical apprehension of Byrd.

6

JOHN WILBYE AND THE SERENITY OF DISILLUSION

Oft have I vowed
Draw on, sweet night

Gibbons's *What is our life?* stresses man's self-reliance, his ultimate will to live, but no more than Ward's melancholic madrigals does it attain a new serenity in place of the peace man
forfeited when he affirmed his independence of God. Perhaps
only one composer of the Jacobean era—John Wilbye—reached
such a haven; and this achievement on behalf of the human spirit
is inseparable from the fact that his greatest work contains within
its apparently traditional technique a new conception of tonality
and form. This we will examine in two of the finest madrigals
from Wilbye's collection of 1609.

The poem of *Oft have I vowed*[1] is based on the familiar cliché
of the frustrated lover:

> Oft have I vowed how dearly I did love thee,
> And oft observed thee with all willing duty.
> Sighs I have sent, still hoping to remove thee,
> Millions of tears I tendered to thy beauty,
>
> Yet thou of sighs and silly tears regardless
> Suff'rest my feeble heart to pine with anguish;
> Whilst all my barren hopes return rewardless,
> My bitter days do waste, and I do languish.

Yet while the poem is apparently without faith or hope, the
music subtly modifies our response. It may be true that 'no
pleasure here but breeds a world of griefs'; it is not true that we
have no choice but to 'loathe that life that causeth such laments'.
Wilbye's music is instinct not with loathing, but with regret for
potentialities unfulfilled, as they always must be, given the im-

[1] Stainer and Bell, The English Madrigal School, Vol. VII, No. 20. Edited
by E. H. Fellowes.

perfections of our temporal existence. So the madrigal becomes an elegy not merely on a particular Tom or Harry desiring hopelessly a particular young woman, but also on the seventeenth century humanist desiring the earth and the moon, wanting to be self-sufficient, while knowing that his senses are unappeasable.

The madrigal opens quietly, even unobtrusively, with the avowal of love. The simplicity of the rhythm, the rising line in parallel thirds, even the discreet imitation, would suggest (if we had not read the poem) a gentle confidence: which becomes firmer when the music modulates to the relative major, and the 'loving' phrase, rocking symmetrically between tonic and dominant concords, is emphasized in almost hypnotic repetition. The apparently 'positive' direction is continued as we move sharpwards to the dominant of the relative, and little contrapuntal entries act the observing of the beloved: our eyes gaze towards her as the 'points' enter discreetly, one after the other. But as soon as our attention is directed at the object of our passion there is an unexpectedly disturbing development. The second soprano contradicts the prevailing diatonicism with a diminished fourth, F sharp to B flat—which then wriggles uneasily to B natural for the cadence in the tonic. This cadence, moreover, has the third doubled in the bass instead of the root note: which is probably not, as Fellowes suggests, a misprint, for the uncertainty of the cadence—after that ambiguous soprano line—is the point. The quiet confidence of the opening is illusory.

In any case the curiously unresolved cadence releases, with unexpected energy, a contrary idea. From the simple vowing of love we switch to the facts of experience; life and love are, in themselves, neither simple nor consoling, but a perturbation and an agony. The 'sighs' enter on a C minor triad, the E flats making a diminished fourth with the soprano's nervous cadential B natural. The return of the parallel thirds and of the regular clauses in dotted rhythm is in the tonic minor, not the relative major, and the repetitions now convey a numbing despair; the 'hope' cannot break through. With the reference to 'millions of tears' the music splinters into rhythmic fragments; the triple-rhythmed tears phrase creates crazily distraught syncopations, the lines waving pell-mell in the air like frenetically flapping hands. Only the pedal D in the bass saves us from disintegration; and suggests, perhaps, that the frenzy of the tears is in part a rhetorical gesture which is not, after all, completely beyond our control.

That we can control our despair becomes evident in what follows. To begin with, when we turn to the woman who is regardless of our sighs, we seem defeated. The bare fifth on 'thou' suggests both his desolation and her indifference; the broken rhythm and dislocated syntax—with the word 'of' separated on either side by rests—is both his panting exhaustion, after the whirlpool of his tears, and also her callous frigidity. The suspended major seventh on 'tears' is his agony; but in the repeat the melismatic decoration on 'silly' is the futility of his passion. This almost simultaneous statement of human aspiration and of human inadequacy leads to a synthesis: which becomes an alleviation. He says she suffers his feeble heart to pine in anguish, and the bass descends in chromatics, while the other parts form lamenting suspensions on each strong beat. But the effect of this is not the same as that of Weelkes's chromatic disintegration: indeed, it is not disintegrative at all, but ordered, with an architectural control in its handling of the dissonances that anticipates Purcell, or even Handel and Bach. And so, although he speaks of his feebleness and anguish, and although the bass's upward chromatic E flat creates the most painful dissonance in the piece, yet the recognition of his hope's barrenness becomes a kind of sensuous pleasure. The texture is rich yet luminous, voluptuous yet controlled.

When the chromatics have subsided, the last section opens in the relative major with an augmentation and inversion of the original 'vowing' phrase. The phrase droops now, instead of rising: yet it has a harmonic vitality that it did not have at first, because it has now accepted the pain that is experience. So it can lead, by way of softly declining suspensions, to the tonic *major*. The words say 'my bitter days do waste'; yet the music, lyrically singing, radiantly spaced, is as far removed from bitterness as could well be. The effect of the major lyricism is, indeed, almost Schubertian, or even comparable with the E major end of Delius's *Sea Drift*; and as in the case of Schubert and Delius, its ecstatic sweetness is nostalgic. It yearns for the bliss of innocence, after 'the pain of consciousness'; but the sweetness makes the pain bearable. So when the chromatics return in the final 'languishing' cadence, the suspensions are all whole-tone, meltingly ten-

64

der. Though the ultimate bare fifth testifies to the hollowness of worldly hopes, the whole of the final protracted cadence over a dominant pedal expresses a heartfelt pity for the illusory nature of man's joy. As the music 'languishes' it achieves its most exquisitely ordered consummation.

Related to this ability to achieve an ordered serenity out of disillusion is the fact that the madrigal manifests, embryonically, formal principles distinct from those of the polyphonic motet. The opposition between the 'vowing' and the 'sighing and weeping' in the first section creates thematic groups that have some of the qualities of a sonata exposition. The chromatic middle section is a harmonic development from both ideas (the parallel thirds and the dissonant syncopations); while the third section, beginning like an inverted recapitulation when his vows and tears are *sent back*, achieves a synthesis. So the piece deals, exploratively, with the growth of experience within the mind; we are not the same at the end of it as we were at the beginning.

This tendency towards a modern 'dualism' is more developed in another Wilbye madrigal—*Draw on sweet night*[1]—in which the theme of the poem itself is a dichotomy: the contrast between the turbulence of the individual spirit and the apparent serenity of Nature.

> Draw on, sweet night, best friend unto those cares
> That do arise from painful melancholy.
> My life so ill through want of comfort fares
> That unto thee I consecrate it wholly.
>
> Drawn on, sweet night. My griefs when they be told
> To shades and darkness, find some ease from paining,
> And whilst thou all in silence dost enfold,
> I then shall have best time for my complaining.

This is based on a typical Jacobean paradox. Night is a sweet friend because it obliterates, or seems to obliterate, care and pain; the religious metaphor ('consecrate') suggests that Night is conceived as a kind of Nirvana that brings forgetfulness of self, rather than as a Christian heaven. Shades and darkness in the external world are ease, relaxation, compared with the shades and darkness within the mind; what night offers is oblivion

[1] Stainer and Bell, The English Madrigal School, Vol. VII, No. 31. Edited by E. H. Fellowes.

('silence'), and one may calmly sing one's lament into the night precisely because Night cannot reply (just as Nature and the dull ears of Daphne cannot hear Ward's disconsolate elegy).

The words 'draw on, sweet night' are set serenely in rich parallel thirds, flowing in conjunct motion. The tonality is a clear, unambiguous D major; a touch of dominant and then of subdominant serve to emphasize the tonic's equilibrium. Yet even during this luminous tranquillity a passing G natural, grinding against the sustained F sharp of the triad, hints at the pain within; and at the words 'unto those cares' a sustained inner pedal note clashes acutely on the major seventh and minor second with one of the flowing parts. In the individual lines there is no perturbation, though the harmony stabs into our nerves. The words 'painful melancholy' are expressed by way of a procession of dissonant suspensions, culminating in a lush dominant seventh, and then dominant ninth. It is interesting to contrast these suspensions with the comparable passage, dealing with Daphne's cruelty, in Ward's *Out from the vale*. Ward's suspensions are rich, yet powerful, anguished, even acrid; these of Wilbye are painful, but cloying, almost voluptuous. There is in them an element of sensual indulgence: for he is half in love with easeful death, and the Jacobean death-wish takes the place of a religious affirmation.

In the context, the purpose of these suspensions is to build up a climax to the first section; and to lead into what one might almost call a 'second subject', when the poem switches attention from the impersonality of Nature to the passions of the Ego. We cannot, after all, subside into oblivion, so the increasing tension of the harmony resolves into a clear dominant-tonic cadence only for the tonic minor to be—at the words 'my life so ill'—abruptly substituted for the expected major. This is a development from the by then traditional device of false relation; but in the context of Wilbye's tonality and structure it sounds more like the dramatic use of alternating major and minor typical of eighteenth and nineteenth century music.

The section which we have called the 'second subject' contains two elements. The first is a phrase, in the tonic minor, for 'my life so ill', rather agitated in effect, despite the stepwise movement, because the melodic rhythm is triple while the harmonic rhythm remains duple. Ironically enough, this phrase, having modulated to the stability of the relative major, stops still on the word 'fares'. It is repeated in sequence, taking us back to the tonic minor: and leading to the second constituent of the 'second subject'—a phrase rising a fourth and then falling down the scale in dotted rhythm. This phrase, prompted by the word 'consecrate', is a cliché of ecclesiastical polyphony. The religious metaphor suggests both a more sustained modulation to the relative and a more consistently imitative texture. But we do not find a divine consolation in the polyphony, for the rhythm has none of Byrd's celestial flow. It is metrical, dance-like; indeed is perhaps, in its regularity, more earthy than the sensually indulgent opening. So the music can return, inevitably, to the tonic major, for the exposition to close with a modified repetition of the opening clause (and words), with the dissonance now banished.

After hovering between the major and minor third—with an almost Schubertian nostalgia—the final cadence of the 'exposition' finds inverted resolution in another dramatic surprise—a cadence on the dominant of A. What one might call the 'development' takes up the rising scale figure from the exposition and presents it in comparatively short, gently undulating phrases in a number of different keys. The texture is three-part, divided antiphonally between low and high voices; and the phrases, unlike those of traditional sixteenth century polyphony, are self-enclosed: luxurious, almost secretive in their close part-writing and low registration, suggesting the lulling relief from care that night offers. The bass and alto emphasize with long notes the word 'my'; and the enclosed, ingrowing nature of the clauses perhaps implies an illusory quality in the peace. Anyway, the almost hermetic quietude is disturbed by soft but piercing suspended seconds and sevenths in nagging syncopation; these make us aware of the 'paining' to which Night (we hope or imagine) brings ease. Despite the stepwise movement, the shades and darkness faintly agitate the texture and harmony with a cross rhythm; and the chromatically intensified suspension on the word 'paining' is anguished, evaporating into a hollow fifth.

With the words 'in silence dost enfold' we desert the short, self-enclosed, antiphonal sections and return to continuous linear and harmonic evolution, in the tonic. This give the music something of the feeling of a sonata recapitulation. Though there is no literal repetition, the tranquillity of the opening is re-established, but is imbued with the subtly disturbing feelings we have experienced during the course of the madrigal; as in a real sonata recapitulation, we re-hear with new ears and senses. In an intense hush the repeated notes and rising scale (with sharp seventh) of the fugato theme steal in imperceptibly until a climax is reached, in rich six-part texture, on a melismatically heart-easing cadence on the word 'enfold'. It seems as though we are to lap ourselves in the security of Night, as we did at the beginning. But then, immediately after the cadence, there is a dramatic change that exactly complements the switch from major to minor at the entry of what we called the 'second subject'. The fugato theme enters in close stretto; but the three repeated notes are no longer followed by an ascent up the major scale. Instead, they rise through a minor third, to descend down the minor scale, with flat sixth, sometimes in cross rhythm on the words 'I then shall have best time for my complaining'. The fugato entries are in close stretto, and the repeated notes, often in minor thirds, have a suggestion of ominousness as well as fortitude. The melismatic 'enfolding' phrase turns into a gloomy 'complaint' in the soprano's lowest register; and the minor tonality, with its oppressive flat sixths, is maintained until the final chord, when a tierce de Picardie appears only after the sustained preparation of a dominant pedal. So the madrigal has begun in an indulgent sensuality, using Night as a balm for personal suffering; then it has opposed the knowledge of suffering to the desire for oblivion; and finally it has achieved a synthesis between evasion and acceptance. The final major triad, after the 'minor-seeking' recapitulation, admits that the peace attained can be but transitory; but the peace is real, and a more positive achievement than the dolorous if noble stoicism of *What is our life*.

In thus dealing with the *development* of experience *Draw on, sweet night*, even more than *Oft have I vowed*, marks a tendency away from fugal polyphony, which is the basic musical equation for Oneness or the state of Being, towards the later sonata principle, which is the musical equation for dualism, growth through conflict, or Becoming. More than any of his contemporaries, Wilbye revealed prophetically the path that music and the human spirit would have to explore not in the next decade but many generations ahead. The experience with which he was concerned is inevitably contained within the humanist's belief in the self, though its implications were not to become apparent for another hundred and fifty years. In those years man created another idea of Oneness which was man-made, rather than God-given. That was aristocratic autocracy, of which the central artistic image was the opera. It is interesting, however, that the twilight of the old technique should, in Wilbye, contain within it the dawn of the future; and that working at a time when values were threatened and confused, Wilbye should have anticipated some of the problems of belief and unbelief with which we still labour.

7

THOMAS CAMPION AND THE SOLO AYRE

Author of light
When to her lute Corinna sings
Follow thy fair sun
It fell on a summer's day

We have seen how, in the madrigals of Ward and still more of Wilbye, a new kind of musical structure, apposite to a new kind of experience, was in process of evolution. This new technique often implied, and sometimes literally involved, instrumental resources; ultimately it was to seek fulfilment in the humanistic (rather than divine) ritual of opera. But in order to provide the basic elements of operatic music there had to be, alongside the development in ensemble techniques, a complementary development in solo song. Such a development was in any case natural in a society that stressed the humanly expressive power of words. Thomas Campion, equally celebrated as both poet and composer, and the leading theorist among the writers of ayres, emphasized the solo song with lute accompaniment precisely because in pieces for a solo voice music and sweet poetry could agree without the absurdities sometimes occasioned, in the madrigal, by contrapuntal treatment. At the most rudimentary level, the words in a solo song could be heard, not merely by the singer, but also by others who cared to listen. The lute, a sensitive but quiet instrument, could add its expressive commentary on the words as sung by the soloist. But there was no danger that the lute would become too obtrusive. The words would be immediately comprehensible; their human significance would be perhaps more directly 'realized' when they were sung rather than spoken.

In conformity with the spirit of the humanist movement Campion—like the Pléiade group associated with Ronsard in sixteenth century France, and like the Italian experimenters who worked for Count Bardi in the early years of the seventeenth century—

imagined that in thus making music the overflow of poetry he was reviving the principles of classical antiquity. He even went so far as to try to systematize the setting of words by a literal equation of long and short syllables with long and short notes. Yet though his theory may seem pedantic, his practice is another matter. Basically he followed traditional notions of the relation between music and words. He resembled the French in that he wanted the musical rhythm to derive directly from the inflexions of the text as spoken, since music was 'la soeur puisnée de la poésie'. He resembled the Italians in that he wanted the lyricism of the musical line to be convincing in itself. When the complete fulfilment of this ideal was achieved—in the later work of Dowland and to a lesser degree Danyel—it entailed, as we shall see, some sacrifice in theoretic consistency. We should, however, start with Campion, if only because he was equally talented as poet and composer and perhaps for that reason the most conscious experimenter in the possibilities of music for a solo voice. From his work we can obtain an idea of the general principles by which Elizabethan composers tackled the setting of a text. We will begin with the simplest, because most 'systematic', example; proceed to some subtler cases from Campion's own work; and so lead on to the fulfilment of the ayre—which is also to some degree the relinquishment of Campion's theory—in the mature work of Dowland.

Unlike the madrigal, the ayre was normally strophic, the same music serving for several verses of the poem. Of course we do not know precisely how a man such as Campion set about writing an ayre. We may guess, perhaps, that he wrote the first stanza of his poem and then composed the music for it: unless, indeed, the music grew almost simultaneously with the words. This music must reflect the meaning of the text, so that thus far the music has been moulded by the poem. It is probable, however, that the poem will be incomplete in one stanza; and any further stanzas the poet writes must now fit the conventions of the already existing music. In the first verse the music is conditioned by the poetry. In the second verse the poetry must be conditioned by the music.

The song, which is of a religious nature, is in two stanzas.[1]

[1] Stainer and Bell, The English School of Lutenist Song Writers. Thomas Campion's First Book of Ayres. Edited by E. H. Fellowes.

Author of light, revive my dying sprite;
Redeem it from the snares of all confounding night.
Lord, light me to thy blessed way,
For blind with worldly vain desires I wander as
      a stray.
Sun and moon, stars and underlights I see,
But all their glorious beams are mists and darkness
      being compared to thee.

Fountain of health, my soul's deep wounds recure.
Sweet showers of pity rain, wash my uncleanness pure.
   One drop of thy desired grace
The faint and fading heart can raise, and in joy's
      bosom place.
Sin and Death, Hell and tempting Fiends may rage;
But God his own will guard, and their sharp pains
      and grief in time assuage.

The first stanza depends on a characteristic Renaissance equivocation between World and Spirit. What the long sweeping rhythm
suggests is a powerful awareness of the glories of the visible
universe: 'confounding night' and 'worldly vain desires' turn
out to be symbolized by the splendours of sun, moon, stars and
underlights. It would seem to be pious duty, rather than inner
conviction, that says these wonders are mists and darkness in
the sight of God. In the second stanza the religious element is
much stronger, because Campion is now thinking of the purgatorial process, in personal terms. This immediacy is conveyed,
for instance, in the beautiful rise in rhythmic impetus as the
fading heart is 'raised'. So in this stanza the ambiguous equation of the glories of the cosmos with worldly vanity disappears;
the opposition is now unequivocally the powers of evil, sin,
death, hell, and the fiends. This shift in emphasis provides Campion with his only problem in setting the poem strophically.

The opening apostrophe to the divinity is set to the noble interval of the falling fifth—the most stable of all interval relationships after the octave. The bass line rises to suggest the revivify-
ing process of the flooding of light: but rises chromatically, so
that light leads inevitably to its polar opposite, darkness and
death. The highest note of the bass (E flat) makes a harsh dissonance with the lute's suspended seventh; above it, 'dying' is
expressed by a drooping phrase, syncopated across the bar-line to

create a little catch in the breath, with a tremulous semiquaver melisma. Thus this first line is a beautiful example of music's power to convey, through inherently musical means, two contradictory ideas—birth and death—at the same time.

In the next line, the reference to redemption suggests a clear diatonic phrase, built on a firmly rising fourth, in the relative major; whereas 'all confounding night' is set again to a strained syncopation and a perturbing melisma. 'Lord, light me to thy blessed way', is set in hopefully rising thirds, with a cross rhythm that carries the movement eagerly forward. But the cross rhythm then becomes, not hopeful impetus, but broken hesitancy; the melody really does 'wander as astray', swayed by worldly vain desires, fumbling and stumbling like a blind man. 'Sun and Moon' significantly recalls the opening address to the Author of Light, being a decorated version of the falling fifth. Thus it is at once a point of musical structure and illustrative: obscurely revealing, indeed, because it seems to equate the Author of Light with the Sun and so makes the ostensible identity between the sun and earthly error still odder. The leaping sixth and the cross rhythm of 'but all their glorious beams' convey the poet's rising excitement, prancing up to the high D with what we might take for resplendent affirmation. Then the line descends an octave when the 'glorious beams' turn out to be mists and darkness, which are set chromatically, of course, because chromaticism destroys tonal stability and the natural order. But the passage begins low and rises, because it is an ascent from the uncertainty of the mists to the certainty of God's love. The major triad at the end is thus, though conventional, also symbolic.

Having created this music, flowing so inevitably from the text, Campion then writes another stanza which nearly fits the music. Instead of 'Author of light' we have, for the noble fifth; 'Fountain of health'. For the syncopation, melisma and dissonance we have 'deep wounds' instead of 'dying sprite'. 'Sweet showers of pity' take the place of redemption; and 'uncleanness' that of confounding night. The faint and fading heart serves the same purpose as the blind wandering eyes; the heart-beat threatens to stop before it presses up through the sharpened seventh to the major triad on 'raise'. The only snag comes in the next line, when sin and hell are so inappropriately identified with the sun and moon: unless one thinks that this is in the profoundest sense logical, since only through the agency of the devil is the purgatorial process possible. In any case the chromatic ascent and major triad is perfect for the last line's assuaging of 'sharp pains and grief'.

The technique of musical allegory that Campion uses in this song harks back at least as far as the fifteenth century. With Campion, however, musical allegory is being translated into emotional realism. It is significant that the element of rather naive systematization is not present in his secular songs even when—as in *When to her lute Corinna sings*[1]—both the poetic and musical imagery are based on a conscious stylization.

> When to her lute Corinna sings,
> Her voice revives the leaden strings,
> And doth in highest notes appear
> As any challenged echo clear.
> > But when she doth of mourning speak,
> > E'en with her sighs the strings do break.
>
> And as her lute doth live or die;
> Led by her passion, so must I.
> For when of pleasure she doth sing,
> My thoughts enjoy a sudden spring;
> > But if she doth of sorrow speak,
> > E'en from my heart the strings do break.

The two stanzas of this poem bear much the same relationship to one another as do the two stanzas of *Author of light*: the first makes a general statement, the second reveals its personal application. Each stanza is based on a dichotomy between the opening quatrain, which is positive, and the concluding couplet, which is negative. The first two lines carry the music—as Corinna's singing revives the leaden strings—from G minor into the relative major, and then sharpward into the dominant, with an ornamental resolution to make the revival more reviving. A dancing lilt appears with the words 'and doth in highest notes appear', with repeated quavers prancing up through an octave. The phrase about the challenged echo excites this merry confidence by way of a cross rhythm; and the section ends, after eight

[1] Stainer and Bell, The English School of Lutenist Song Writers. Thomas Campion's *Songs from Rosseter's Book of Ayres*, Part I. Edited by E. H. Fellowes.

symmetrical bars, with a clear modulation to the dominant major. The second half of the musical structure, which sets the couplet with some verbal repetition, is asymmetrical, as broken and disturbed as the quatrain is assured. The change comes with the chromatic E flat that enters the lute part on the word 'mourning', taking us back to the tonic minor. Then the sighs are set in a fragmentary dialogue between voice and lute, the verbal inflexion being literally broken as we pant for breath, yet in *rising* sequences, so that our agitation cumulatively increases. At the climax the strings 'break' in a descending arpeggio, echoed by the lute. In the excitement, a bar is dropped out of the eight-bar period. After an empty silence the voice rounds off with an ornamental cadence, repeating the words 'the strings do break'. The ornament is a quiver, almost a literal break in the voice.

The second stanza repeats this poetic and musical pattern exactly. The word 'passion' has the ornamental arabesque that in the first verse suggested revival. The cross rhythm for the challenged echo becomes the spring of joyful thoughts, prepared by the octave leap on 'pleasure'. In the second stanza the word 'heart' gets the stress that her sighs had originally. The music is not different; but we hear it more sympathetically because we now know that the conceit is not merely musical. It is not just the lute strings that are breaking, but also the strings of my heart.

This song is a fairly direct, if in effect subtle, example of poetic-musical form. Campion's lyrics are sometimes much more complex in their apparent simplicity; and when the verse's equivocations are complex the musical imagery is likewise richer in effect.

Like so many Elizabethan lyrics *Follow thy fair sun*[1] is based upon a paradox.

> Follow thy fair sun, unhappy shadow.
>> Though thou be black as night,
>> And she made all of light,
> Yet follow thy fair sun, unhappy shadow.
>
> Follow her whose light thy light depriveth.
>> Though here thou liv'st disgraced,
>> And she in heaven is placed,
> Yet follow her whose light the world reviveth.

[1] ibid.

75

Follow those pure beams whose beauty burneth,
    That so have scorched thee,
    As thou still black must be
Till her kind beams thy black to brightness turneth.

Follow her while yet her glory shineth.
    There comes a luckless night,
    That will dim all her light;
And this the black unhappy shade divineth.

Follow still, since so thy fates ordained.
    The sun must have his shade,
    Till both at once do fade,
The sun still 'proved, the shadow still disdained.

The basic idea is that the beloved is compared to the sun, which is the source of light and life; she is great creating Nature and therefore not so far from God (compare *Author of light* and Raleigh's *What is our life?*) The lover is the shadow. He is black and melancholy, presumably because the sun is indifferent to him: and also because apart from her, the sun, he has no existence. She is made all of light, and even if she is not God would seem to be a god: whereas in his blackness there is a taint of sin too, perhaps a suggestion of lost innocence. She is beyond moral judgment, he is a miserable sinner. She is in heaven and her light brings life to the world; but he, as shadow, lives 'disgraced', cut off from both heaven (her) and earth.

In the third stanza, however, there is a shift in the metaphor. Her 'pure beams' have burned him up, blackened him, not like a shadow but like charcoal. At least he now has material existence; and there is a further suggestion that black charcoal may turn to bright diamond, which is a treasure, solid and real, not an illusory shadow. So in the fourth stanza the shadow grows stronger. For a moment we even think he might *be* stronger, last longer, than the sun: for he points out that she is not really impervious to time and change; the sun's glory will be dimmed by night, when she and he will be equal. His final thrust is that the 'sun must have his shade, till both at once do fade'; they need one another, just as good cannot be conceived except in reference to evil. This is true despite conventional estimates of the relative worth of sun and shadow. There is a slightly sinister smugness, perhaps, in the shadow's turning of the tables.

This equivocal quality comes out in the music, which is again strophic. The first phrase is set simply and diatonically; a gentle arch that suggests how inevitable it is that the shadow should follow the sun. The long notes on 'though thou' stress the conditional clause; the slowly declining scale landing on the chromatic F sharp on the word 'black' has a resigned, inevitable pathos, rather than intensity. The answering phrase for 'and she made all of light' rises up the scale, to balance the shadow's descent. But it rises not diatonically but chromatically; and from the chromaticism springs an equivocation parallel to that of the words. Though we aspire towards the light, the aspiration is also a perturbation; and when we get to the high D we immediately fall through an octave. Abruptly, the sharp third of the cadence is cancelled by the minor third; and the rising chromatic scale literally 'follows' us through the instrumental bass, giving a nervous tremor to the harmony, culminating in a stress on the word 'unhappy'. The cadential resolution, as the phrase declines, has a trembling ornamental dissonance on the word 'shadow'.

The words of the other stanzas fit the musical images provoked by the first stanza, though sometimes with ironic implications. In stanza 2 the chromatic F sharp on 'black' appears on the word 'disgraced'. The ascending chromatic scale goes up to heaven. Here the words do not seem to be equivocal, but the music tells us that they are, and thus prepares us for the subsequent stanzas. By the time we get to stanza 4 the rising chromatic scale has become a *dimming* of light: which is what it really was from the start, since, though it rises upwards, its chromatic nature implies uncertainty rather than fulfilment. The long note and melisma on the word 'shade' beautifully convey the touch of self-satisfaction at the end of this stanza. The uncertainty thus admitted to remains in the last stanza, where the ascent becomes a fading. We are left with the shadow, as at the beginning, faintly self-indulgent.

A no less subtle example of the strophic song, with an equation between the poetic and musical image, is an apparently light piece, It fell on a summer's day :[1]

> It fell on a summers day,
> While sweet Bessy sleeping lay

[1] ibid

In her bower on her bed,
Light with curtains shadowed,
Jamie came. She him spies,
Opening half her heavy eyes.

Jamie stole in through the door;
She lay slumbering as before.
Softly to her he drew near;
She heard him, yet would not hear.
Bessy vowed not to speak;
He resolved that dump to break.

First a soft kiss he doth take;
She lay still and would not wake.
Then his hands learned to woo;
She dreamt not what he would do,
But still slept, while he smiled
To see love by sleep beguiled.

Jamie then began to play;
Bessy as one buried lay,
Gladly still through this sleight
Deceived in her own deceit.
And since this trance begun,
She sleeps every afternoon.

Superficially, this looks like a ballad; but its slightly arch wit is poles apart from the folk spirit. Since the poem is highly sophisticated, the music is appropriately artful. Though it begins with a simple, folk-like phrase for the conventional opening gambit, there is artifice even here: for the second half of the vocal phrase is in canon (a love-pursuit?) with the bass; while the flattened F that harmonizes sweet Bessy gives us, as it were, an unobtrusive, delicate nudge or wink. The little shock of the false relation is sweetly sensuous (she's a gentle creature); yet there is a tang, too, of pleasurable excitement. In the next phrase the dancing, hesitant, irregular rhythm creates the chequered shadows and Bessy's playful sleepiness, the hazy summer's afternoon; this is a case where the musical rhythm complements, rather than intensifies, the extremely subtle verbal rhythm. In the poem these exploratory subordinate clauses lead with a bump into the trenchant words *Jamie came*. So in the music he comes after

78

a double bar. His rhythm is regular; pressing onwards, with little imitative points: for it is a chase, albeit a love-chase. On the word 'came' there is a false relation exactly similar to the earlier one for 'sweet Bessy'. The pleasurable excitement exists, after all, for them both, for she's in the game, and 'spies' him as part of the imitative chase. When she 'opens half her heavy eyes', however, we are taken back to the dreamy heat of the afternoon. There is a most delicate cross rhythm to stress the word 'half' and a lovely arabesque—at once drowsy and knowing—on the word 'heavy'.

This pattern of imagery is repeated with delicate precision in each stanza. In stanza 2 the F natural in the bass of bar 3 refers compassionately to the deceit in Bessy's 'slumbering'. The hesitant cross rhythm that had been the chequered shade becomes Jamie's cat-like approach, Bessy's hearing and not hearing. The imitative passage conveys her 'vow', his resolution. The cross rhythmed stress comes on the word 'resolved'; while the arabesque becomes the breaking of the dump. In stanza 3 the F natural suggests both the shock of the kiss and Bessy's quivery stillness. The hesitant rhythm becomes Jamie's wooingly exploratory hands, Bessy's dreaming and not dreaming. The regular movement of the imitative passage becomes the deceptive quiet of sleep; the archly stressed word is 'love', the arabesque becomes a beguiling. In the last stanza the F natural false relation deliciously buries Bessy in sleep, in bed, in love, while the cross rhythm acts the being deceived in her own deceit. The imitative phrase becomes associated with the development of delightful habit, with a tender chuckle, too. The stressed word is 'every': which points the joke to round the song off. The arabesque on 'afternoon' becomes a cooing; it is impossible to sing it other than comically.

In all these songs the poems are devised so that both imagery and rhythm can be complemented in musical terms, and the parallelism works in each stanza. The strophic convention would seem to imply rigid stylization; yet the songs are remarkable for the unexpectedly rich meanings that emerge from the interlocking of words and music. Though the songs are generalized, lyrical and narrative rather than dramatic, they reveal a personal situation beneath the generalizing convention. This mating of the general with the particular is more potently evident in the work of a much greater composer than Campion, John Dowland. It is significant that the ayres of Dowland are less dependent than those of Campion on the words; and that the texts he set were often, though not always, of inferior poetic merit. In a piece like *It fell on a summer's day* Campion has written a poem that is charming, subtle, and complete in itself. He has created musical images and rhythms which precisely parallel the delicacies of the poem, making a complementary experience; but the music does not 'improve' the poem, and is not intended to. Campion is, above all, the poet-composer. In the case of Dowland, however, the poem often exists to release the musical impulse. Even when the poem is good (as in the two beautiful fountain songs) it is so in a pervasively musical way; and when once we have heard the words sung to Dowland's music we can no longer read them without echoes of his haunting lyricism. We will first examine a simple strophic song of Dowland which seems, superficially, to approximate to Campion's manner; then we will turn to three of Dowland's greatest, maturest expressions of Melancholy : pieces wherein the ayre has ceased to be merely a lyrical poem 'musicked'.

8

FOUR AYRES OF JOHN DOWLAND

Shall I sue?
Flow my tears
I saw my Lady weep
In darkness let me dwell

Dowland's *Shall I sue?*[1] is an unpretentious song, set in a simple strophic form.

Shall I sue? shall I seek for grace?
Shall I pray? shall I prove?
Shall I strive to a heavenly joy
   With an earthly love?
Shall I think that a bleeding heart
Or a wounded eye,
Or a sigh can ascend the clouds
   To attain so high?

Pity is but a poor defence
For a dying heart;
Ladies' eyes respect no moan
   In a mean desert.
She is too worthy far
For a worth so base,
Cruel and but just is she
   In my just disgrace.

Silly wretch, forsake these dreams
Of a vain desire;
O bethink what high regard
   Holy hopes do require.
Favour is as fair as things are,
Treasure is not bought;
Favour is not won with words,
   Nor the wish of a thought.

[1] Stainer and Bell, The English School of Lutenist Song Writers. John Dowland's, *Second Book of Ayres*, Part II. Edited by E. H. Fellowes.

Justice gives each man his own.
Though my love be just
Yet will not she pity my grief,
    Therefore die I must.
Silly heart, then yield to die,
Perish in despair.
Witness yet how fain I die
    When I die for the fair.

Like so many of Campion's lyrics, this is an expansion of a single literary conceit: the contrast between heavenly joy and earthly love. It goes back to the medieval convention of chivalrous love; the beloved, associated with the divine as opposed to the human, is to be worshipped, but only at a distance, for she is an ideal beyond the reach of temporal mortality. As in Campion's *Follow thy fair sun*, however, this archaic concept is given an odd twist in the later stanzas. Puns on 'worth' and 'favour' introduce an ambiguous note, and there is a hint that the conventional Wailing Lover has learned to regard himself ironically. 'Justice gives each man his own'; he seems to admit that he has got, in some sense, what he deserves. There is a certain coolness in the precise elegant movement as the 'silly heart' perishes in despair; this may be irony or simply a lack of enthusiasm for the heroic gesture.

Now we have seen that the words of the several stanzas of Campion's strophic songs tend to follow the same pattern of imagery and rhythm and, broadly speaking, the same emotional contours. The considerable shift in tone and mood throughout the stanzas of this lyric means that it is not really suitable for strophic treatment. That Dowland should none the less treat it strophically is indicative of his more 'musical' approach. Since the shifts of meaning do not lend themselves to music he uses the words of the first stanza mainly as the impetus to a tune, and although the structure of this tune is evolved from the structure of the lyric, it differs from most of Campion's tunes in being complete in itself. It is still a marvellous melody if you take the words away: remarkable for its memorability, which gives it an almost popular flavour, yet richly satisfying in its sophisticated structure. Campion achieves such lyrical inevitability but seldom: and then in a style which is so close to folk-song as to suggest some conscious or unconscious adaptation of traditional material (consider, for instance, *My love hath vowed*).

At the beginning of Dowland's tune short phrases grouped in sequence suggest the suing and seeking. The opening phrase, falling scalewise through a third, is then inverted and augmented in time value. It aspires yearningly up the scale till it reaches a climax on the words 'heavenly joy', modulating towards the stability of the relative major, and then to the dominant of the relative, the sharp seventh emphasizing the ascent to the high F. Then, when the brief suing and seeking phrases have been thus integrated into this liberated climax, we descend abruptly in a short subsiding phrase for 'an earthly love'. The second half of the stanza musically mirrors the first, as do the words. But this time the sigh ascends to the clouds on a high G instead of F; and the sense of release as the phrase droops down to the tonic becomes the more affecting. The cross rhythm, suggested by the 'wounded eye', is not just an illustrative detail; it is also a rhythmic means of enhancing the animation as the line approaches the climacteric G. The harmonization of this G with the E flat chord, rather than the tonic, deepens both our awareness of the G as the goal of the melody and also the sense of wistful regret when the line once more declines. In the first half of the stanza we feel the descent from the modulatory F to the tonic as a kind of assuagement. In the second half, in the descent from the high G, there is also a hint of something like resignation: an admission that, after all, we cannot hope to attain the heavens.

Dowland's music has thus grown out of his apprehension of the words' meaning; and translates into musical terms the verbal equilibrium between heavenly aspiration and earthly acceptance. But the translation into musical terms is complete; this is not simply a poem musicked. So, having arrived at this melody, Dowland thinks, rightly, that it is good enough to stand on its own feet. In the second stanza there is nothing to parallel the crucial contrast between heaven and earth in the first stanza; there is no poetic reason why the melody should take the form of that soaring ascent and declension. Only in minor details—for instance the reference to 'worth so base' complementing the first stanza's 'wounded eye'—is there accommodation between music and text. The third stanza, on the other hand, verbally

83

mirrors the musical structure, 'high regard' taking the place of heavenly joy. The last stanza has nothing to parallel the celestial yearning of the tune, though it refers to death in both the declining final phrases. The cross rhythm is effectively associated with the words 'perish in despair'.

In this ayre, then, Dowland writes a song which resembles Campion's in being simply lyrical, unpretentiously strophic, and on the whole impersonal in approach. It differs from Campion's in the musical vitality and self-sufficiency of the melody. As Dowland's art matured, it became increasingly rich in musical substance; and the richer it grew the more introspective was his range of experience. Or it would be truer to say that the more passionately melancholic his awareness of the suffering ego, the more inevitable it was that he should substitute for the strophic ayre's 'commentary' on a poem a musical technique responsive to the texture of experience, as it is lived here and now. We will comment on three 'melancholic' songs that reveal this development at different stages of maturity.

The first of these songs is the most famous of all Dowland's compositions—Flow my tears[1], the 'lacrimae' which is so promiscuously referred to in drama and literature. The haunting, almost obsessive, effect of this song on the contemporary imagination—in an apparently wide social context—cannot be explained away simply by reference to melancholic fashion. It was a summation of the humanist's death-consciousness, of his introverted awareness of the pain inherent in being human; and it makes that pain bearable, partly because it is expressed lyrically, partly because it is objectified in the ceremonial movement of a dance. For Flow my tears is a pavane in the conventional three strains, each with repeat. A dance is a corporate act, and the stately ritual of the movement lends dignity, even a kind of tragic universality, to what might seem to be the self-regarding melancholy of the words.

The initial phrase, 'Flow my tears', droops stepwise down the scale through an interval of a fourth; the flowing is sad, yet free. Strain comes into the music with the leap of a minor sixth on to the word 'fall', reinforced by the lute's dissonant suspended seventh: from which point the line falls again scalewise, but this time through a diminished, not perfect, fourth, so that the

[1] ibid. Part I.

84

tension is sustained. With the words 'Exiled for ever let me mourn' the mind turns inwards. Beginning with a falling fourth (the interval, not the stepwise progression), balanced by the lute's rising fourth, the intervals close in; rising and falling minor *thirds* descend low in the register of the voice. At the reference to 'night's black bird' the falling thirds are intensified by false relations between G major and E major triads and by a thrusting cross-rhythm on the word 'infamy', again accompanied by a suspended seventh. The diminished fourth (G sharp to C natural) enters the vocal line itself to introduce the cadential clause; the stress on the tritonally harmonized word 'live' and the final lute melisma (again beginning with a diminished fourth) give an increase rather than a decrease of animation to the acceptance of night and solitariness. The words, in the repeat of this strain, slightly modify the musical effect. After the descending scale for 'down vain lights', the leaping sixth makes the melody 'shine', only to put out the light when the line droops to G sharp. The closing in of the thirds beautifully suggests the singer's hugging himself in the darkness; while again the false relations and the intensified cadence give suppressed energy to the evocation of 'despair' and 'shame'.

This prepares us for the paradox of the second strain. The words say 'Never may my woes be relieved'; but the music, modulating abruptly from the A major tierce de picardie that concludes the first strain to C major, is much more positive, even animated, in its celebration of woe. The original scalewise descending fourth creates a rich 'added sixth' chord of C major and the major cadence on 'relieved' fulfils the implications of the word, rather than the sense of the phrase as a whole. At the phrase 'since pity is fled' we return to the tonic minor; but the cross accent preserves the almost dramatic energy of the music which, at the 'and tears, and sighs, and groans' phrase, becomes physical action. And although the phrases are broken, panting, and return to the minor thirds, these thirds no longer droop in dark self-involvement; they rise sequentially, are extended through a fifth, and almost become a kind of affirmation at the resolution on to the dominant, with a lute melisma which is not, this time, dissonant. The repeat of this strain makes this affirmation explicit, for it says that fear and grief and pain are now my *hopes*, since hope is gone; he will make a virtue out of the acceptance of despair. In this repeat the proud C major phrase beautifully expresses the highest spire of contentment: from which the cross-rhythmed phrase throws my fortune painfully down to the minor. The (almost comic?) immediacy of this poetic image gives fresh vitality to a literary cliché: which vitality is directly expressed in the music.

The final strain returns to the reflective rather than dramatic mood of the opening; it should probably return to the original speed, which the second strain will have considerably increased. The opening clause inverts the stepwise fourth, which now rises, since living in darkness is to be accepted as bliss. He condemns light in a declamatory cross-rhythmed phrase involving false relation and suspended seventh; while in the final clause the descending fourths become a kind of liberation. Dissonantly syncopated across the bar-line they are, in their lyrical and rhythmic freedom, almost 'happy'; certainly they give a different sense to the stepwise descent through a diminished fourth from the word 'happy' to the word 'hell'. The abrupt transition from the E major triad on 'hell' to the C major triad on 'Feel' becomes pridefully assertive. There is almost a defiant toss of the head in it: which is emphasized by the lute's final dissonant melisma.

This inversion of values, whereby sorrow becomes bliss, is the ostensible theme of the next 'melancholic' song on which we will comment, for the extremely beautiful poem of *I saw my Lady weep*[1] is a conceit, identifying what ought to be opposites.

> I saw my lady weep,
>   And Sorrow proud to be advanced so
> In those fair eyes where all perfections keep.
>   Her face was full of woe;
> But such a woe, believe me, as wins more hearts
> Than Mirth can do with her enticing parts.
>
>   Sorrow was there made fair,
>   And Passion wise, tears a delightful thing;
> Silence beyond all speech a wisdom rare.
>   She made her sighs to sing,
> And all things with so sweet a sadness move
> As made my heart at once both grieve and love.

[1] ibid.

86

> O fairer than aught else
> The world can show, leave off in time to grieve.
> Enough, enough your joyful looks excels;
> Tears kills the heart, believe.
> O strive not to be excellent in woe,
> Which only breeds your beauty's overthrow.

My lady is so beautiful and so noble that she makes sorrow (which is apt to be disfiguring) proud: passion (which is beyond reason) wise: and tears (which are wells of grief) a source of delight. Sweetness and sadness are identified, as my heart both grieves and loves.

But that this is not *merely* a conceit is revealed in the verse's subtle movement: the simple, regular statement of the first line, the stress the movement gives to the word 'proud', the gradual increase in momentum as the lines grow longer, ending in the word 'keep' (to which the sharply defined rhyme gives an eternal 'perfection'). The following short line, consisting entirely of words of one syllable, again slows down the movement. The Lady is a real woman, yet she acquires here a sculpturesque gravity. We *see* her motionless woe, as though she were a weeper on a tomb; and so she becomes all of us and, as we look, our hearts stir with pity and passion for her, for all mortality. The movement of the following long line is given greater urgency by the conversational parenthesis ('Believe me'). From our contemplation of the universal Weeper we return to a world of personal feeling. For this is not a chivalric or Petrarchan abstraction but a specific Lady, whose flesh and blood we see, whose senses we feel. And because we are aware of her as a living, breathing creature the lover, who is ourselves, is no less real.

In the second stanza the movement is equally sensitive. The rhythm naturally stresses the paradoxical words: sorrow, fair; passion, wise; tears, delightful. In the short line 'she made her sighs to sing' the slow music vibrates, the rhyme words echoing. Speech accent here turns into music and leads into the slow ceremonial dance of the last couplet, in which sweetness and sadness are identified. There is a third stanza, in which the lover-poet invites the lady to 'leave off in time to grieve'. Her joyful looks are even lovelier than her melancholy ones; tears kill the heart and sorrow will only destroy her beauty. The stanza is exquisite in itself but is extraneous to the poem. It not only breaks the spell but is inconsistent even with the prose sense of the previous stanzas, the whole point of which lies in the identity of opposites. Perhaps the third stanza is better omitted.

Dowland allows these words to generate a musical structure which is complex and, in the last resort, independent of the words, for the song is again a pavane. The solemn movement of the dance, however unobtrusive, is marvellously appropriate to words which objectify intense personal feeling in a ritual-like physical movement. The lute prelude, which introduces the song, at once establishes the indrawn, self-communing atmosphere and also the quietly 'ceremonial' movement. The bass descends in regular semibreves, while the melody rises a semitone only to droop through sighing suspended sevenths. Then the voice enters with the same phrase as the lute, only with the note values protracted. The immensely long initial note on the word 'I' centres the song's melancholy in the ego; and the suspensions that the voice makes with the lute part are much more acute than they were in the instrumental prelude. They cling, reluctant to resolve: yet urge the music forwards because each dissonance 'resolves' on to another. The enormous arches of the melody, as compared with the Campion songs, counteract any disintegrative tendency in the dissonance; and the musical shape overrides verbal accentuation. The high E expresses pride, yet occurs on the unimportant word 'to'; what matters is the sweep of the phrase and its modulation to the relative major on the word 'advanced'. Sorrow becomes, in the woman's beauty of body and spirit, a positive value.

The modulation, as usual, concludes the first part of the pavane. There is then a lute interlude which, moving in crochets, is a freely diminished version of the original undulating phrase. This physical movement in time leads too to an increase in emotional intensity. A chromatic rise in the vocal line on the words 'in those fair eyes' provokes a sequential modulation sharpwards, thrusting upwards: but is immediately deflated by a stabbing 'neapolitan' descent to B flat, and a cadence flatwards into the subdominant. The final cadence peters out in a bare fifth on D; after all the positive excitation he perhaps sees her 'perfection' as in a sense inhuman, like the sculptured Weeper. But he soon responds to her again as a woman, as flesh and blood. A single chromatic alteration lifts us surprisingly from D minor to E minor, with chromatic passing notes and suspensions in the lute part. The sweep of the line grows more urgent. Though it suggests the speaking voice in its flexibility and immediacy, the speaking voice is here sublimated to lyrical passion. Words are repeated, almost rhetorically, as the line rises; and the dissonances in the lute part are also cumulative, attaining a sobbing dominant thirteenth. With the text's reference to mirth, the music's increasing agitation breaks into triple dance rhythm. But the lilt is only momentary; the phrase droops on to the dominant, which echoes unresolved.

The first section of this song, up to the modulation to the relative, contains eleven irregular bars. The second section is an enormous unbroken paragraph of thirteen bars, urged forward by passion, left suspended in mid-air. In melodic, harmonic and rhythmic structure this ayre is no longer, like Campion's songs, an 'architectural' mould into which the words are, however sensitively, fitted. We begin to live through the pressure of experience, to *feel* the surge of passion rising within us, followed by something that might be resignation if it were not left unfulfilled. For this reason the song cannot be as successful as Campion's as an example of strophic form. The poetic ambivalence of the second stanza parallels that of the first, and some details fit the music better than those of the first stanza: for instance, the high E at the end of the first clause (when the music modulates to the relative) now effectively occurs on the word 'tears', off the beat. But in all three stanzas there are details that have to be *made* to fit; and Dowland's conception has really outgrown the strophic form. Because the poem was thought and felt musically the other stanzas can be fitted to the music adequately enough. Yet repetition is hardly justifiable artistically, for the sung pavane is complete in itself, and to repeat the unresolved cadence is bathetic. In his late work Dowland did in fact relinquish the strophic convention; and perhaps it is no accident that in Dowland's last and greatest songs the words are usually in themselves insignificant. In *In darkness let me dwell*,[1] for

[1] Stainer and Bell, The English School of Lutenist Song Writers. Dowland's A *Pilgrimes Solace* and A *Musicall Banquet*. Edited by E. H. Fellowes.

instance, the words are a melancholic cliché; yet they generate the maximum intensity in purely musical expression.

> In darkness let me dwell, the ground shall sorrow be;
> The roof despair, to bar all cheerful light from me;
> The walls of marble black that moistened still shall
>   weep;
> My music hellish jarring sounds to banish friendly
>   sleep.
> Thus wedded to my woes, and bedded to my tomb,
> O let me living, living die, till death do come.

Again, we open with a prelude for lute, creating mood and atmosphere. A slow rising third descends down the scale, forming quietly weeping suspensions and dissonant passing notes; then rises up though the sharp sixth and seventh till its yearning is appeased in an ornamented cadence that is almost like a spattering of tears. Then the voice enters, low in its register, lingering in the darkness, its stressed F natural forming an anguished diminished seventh with the chromaticized cadence in the lute. The line slowly climbs (but with flat sixth and seventh) to the tonic A on the word 'me'. The melody note, harmonized with a suspended major seventh, is protracted, and resolves on to the major third faintly, limply, when the lute harmony is complete. Already the emphasis is upon the Me; this lingering line and secretive harmony tell us that I, like Wilbye in *Draw on, sweet night*, am half in love with easeful death.

The 'dwell' echoes into silence. In the next phrase Dowland repeats the words 'ground' and 'sorrow', savouring them in a supple triple rhythm as the phrase droops down the scale. The low, repeated notes on 'sorrow', first harmonized as a consonance, then as an acute dissonance, recapitulate and intensify the effect of the previous cadence: we sink further into the loving cultivation of melancholy. Then the lute plays a diminished modification of the opening phrase, in the dominant minor; the chromaticized cadence in the bass creates the sob of an augmented fifth. The voice takes up the same phrase, itself creating an augmented fifth on the word 'bar': as though one shudders at the thought of light being shut off. The cutting off of light is symbolized by a tenuous cadence that thins out to unison As. Augmented fifths grow increasingly prevalent in the next phrase, and are combined with a melismatic decoration on the word 'weep', when the voice's B flat swings the tonality flatwards towards D minor, or even G. The melisma and dissonance suggest that weeping is a pain but also a 'grace', an ecstasy.

The lute prefaces the words 'my music, hellish jarring sounds' with some discreet chromaticisms. These make the music move faster, in crochets rather than minims: and hint at sequential modulations in descending fifths. The words 'hellish' and 'jarring' are often repeated: they make a false relation between the voice's G natural and the G sharp of the lute, and rise to almost operatic vehemence in quaver figuration that makes a suspended major seventh with the bass's F natural. With the words 'to banish friendly sleep' we return to the tonic, or rather to a lulling, ornamented cadence on the dominant: merely to recall what sleep is or was serves to remind us of the luxurious indulgence of the opening. This mood is continued in the next line 'Thus wedded to my woes, and bedded to my tomb': for here the texture is more dissonant than anywhere else in the song and at the same time, because of the spacing, more sensuous. False relations, augmented fifths, suspended ninths: these dissonances resolve, or fail to resolve, the one on to the other. As climax, on the word 'tomb' the false relation of F sharp and F natural is transformed into a lush dominant seventh to C major, in place of the expected resolution in G minor. C major takes us to its relative, which is the home tonic A minor; and from the traditional identification of tomb and womb, death and life, bursts another cry, half desperate, half ecstatic, 'O let me living die'. The sustained, almost metreless lyricism here breaks into repeated quavers, with something of the direct immediacy of operatic recitative. This rising excitement leads into the phrase 'till death do come': which starts on the highest note of the song and falls through two fourths, the second of which preserves the music's inward anguish by being diminished. Gradually the passion subsides as the bass flattens the sixth and seventh and the word 'come' is harmonized with a frustrated cadence—the chord of the sixth, F, instead of the tonic. (This is exactly the same frustration as occurs in the prelude to Wagner's *Tristan*.) From this point, the lute sinks slowly to the tonic, painfully approached by the diminished fourth. Then the song concludes with a whispered repetition of the opening phrase, its penultimate note sustained still longer and more lovingly over the dissonant major seventh until it echoes into silence, still awaiting the release of death. This is an almost dramatic, if not operatic, effect: when will the cadence be completed, the axe fall?

One could hardly imagine music more passionate than this song and in a sense its passion is highly personal: a complement to the introspective melancholy of Hamlet or to the self-analytical love poetry of Donne, especially in the elegiac mood of the *Nocturnall upon St Lucies Day*. Yet just as Gibbons's melancholy in *What is our Life?* is controlled by a traditional contrapuntal discipline, so Dowland's melancholy is absorbed—even when passion threatens to splinter into operatic recitative—into sustained vocal lyricism. The song is a through-composed pavane with a musical structure derived from the words, much subtler yet no less satisfying than the instrumental dance. Perhaps it could have been written only at this particular epoch, for it profits equally from the old polyphonic tradition (the lute part is much more contrapuntal than anything in Dowland's early work), from the harmonic and formal experiments of the madrigalians, and from the declamatory techniques of the Italians. Fiercely passionate yet not dramatic, at once personal and with a tragic impersonality, it bears within its maturity the riches of past, present and future.

It is, indeed, illuminating to compare *In darkness let me dwell* with manifestations of the love-death theme occuring three hundred years previously and subsequently. We have remarked that there is a sense in which Dowland, singing to his own lute, looks back to the troubadours. They too sang of frustrated love, for the Beloved they celebrated was always unattainable and usually unapproachable. She was at one and the same time the Dark Goddess of Gnosticism, the mother-image, and the Virgin Mary or the Eternal Beloved; and while their monodic, non-harmonic lyricism sought for the sublimation of Eros, there was a profound melancholy in their art which differentiates it from the complementary monody of plainsong. In liturgical plainchant, sublimation becomes ecstasy; in troubadour music sublimation involves, too, regret for the senses' non-fulfilment. In moving paradox, the melancholy inherent in troubadour song is inseparable technically from the greater structural significance of dance movement —and therefore of temporal progression—which is displayed in it.

Three hundred years later, Dowland's free, flexible, stepwise-moving vocal lines have much in common with the 'sublimatory' element in troubadour music. But the awareness of the pain of consciousness—of the suffering that complements the joy in the sensual present—is now overt in the polyphonic and harmonic, rather than monodic, texture. As we have seen, Dowland comes almost to accept the pain as pleasure, as a good to be desired because it is an affirmation of humanity. And although he often longs for darkness—for death as a release from consciousness—he does so with a curious tragic detachment. Paradoxically, the expression of his desire for death becomes a quiet acceptance of the will to go on living. We find this in Dowland's noble religious songs—such as *If that a sinner's sighs*—as well as in his love-songs and songs of introverted passion: for the religious pieces are never mystical, but are always concerned with guilt, and therefore with the burden of consciousness.

The ultimate apotheosis of this love-death theme, which is the heart of humanism, occurs three hundred years later in Wagner's *Tristan*. We have already paralleled the frustrated cadence in Dowland's *In darkness* to that in the prelude to *Tristan*; and Tristan's curse on 'Day' in the third act of the opera may be compared with the Lacrimae's condemnation of light. It was certainly no accident that Wagner revived and recreated this particular medieval legend. In Dowland the (harmonic) pain grows from the interweaving of (quasi-monodic) voices. Wagner, bearing so many more years' burden of consciousness, guilt, and frustrated sexuality, starts from the weight of harmonic passion: which proves too great to be borne. So the harmonic chromaticism splinters into a new polyphony and ultimately even seems to be seeking the monody of the troubadours. At the beginning of the third act Tristan-Wagner has drunk death (the love-potion) and has failed to fulfil his love in the conditions of the temporal and material world. Almost dead, he is awakened by the Shepherd's monodic piping, which seems eternally to undulate between godlike fifths and the perfect and imperfect fourths of the Tristan-chords' sexual yearning. Its oscillations around a nodal point seem—even more than those of troubadour monody—to be both Christian and pre-Christian, both occidental and oriental: to celebrate simultaneously the Light God and the Dark Goddess; and the effect of this vision of

Paradise Lost is to lead Tristan to live through his traumatic past, from earliest childhood and even pre-natally. Attempting to live again, however, he comes to make the admission that had been merely implicit, six hundred years earlier, in troubadour song: the ultimate ecstasy can be achieved only with the complete loss of consciousness. So only after his death can Isolde—who is no longer a separate being but the Anima to his Animus—enter the state of benediction as she too finds 'blessed unconsciousness'.[1]

Dowland too longs for nirvana, singing to himself of a melancholy that is eternal. But he still exists in the context of civilization in the sense that his lyricism—and often the ceremonial movement of the dance—calms his fever and ours too, if we care to listen. But Wagner involves us in a rite, invites us to become part of *his* consciousness, to be engulfed in it. Dowland sang with his own voice, to his own lute, in his own or his patron's home, a song lasting perhaps five minutes. Wagner employed an enormous orchestra (the nature of which he himself created) in a vast opera house (which he himself caused to be built) to present a music-drama lasting perhaps five hours, wherein the orchestra and we ourselves must become his yearning if the music is to mean anything. Though a personal statement, *In darkness let me dwell* is still an achievement of civilization. *Tristan* is the end of a civilization and of a phase of European consciousness; and we still do not know what is to succeed it. Yet the song and the opera deal with fundamentally the same experience. Each is overwhelming in its way; each is a supreme achievement of European history.

[1] The above account of an essential Wagnerian theme is not, of course, an estimate of his total achievement. Wagner also wrote *The Mastersingers*, which is full of social-religious implications; and *The Ring* itself was conceived as a gigantic mythological drama which concerned man's personal consciousness in relation to Society, Cosmos and God. None the less the point is that the cycle ends with the gods' *twilight*: there must be a dissolution of consciousness as a prelude to rebirth, just as the social realities of the First Act finale in *Tristan* have to be relinquished for the lovers to triumph in death.

9

THE CHORAL AYRE AND THE CAROLINE ANTHEM

John Dowland: *Me, me and none but me*
Come, heavy sleep
Thou mighty God

Martin Peerson: *Man, dream no more*

While the quintessence of Dowland's work is in *In darkness let
me dwell*, which is a quest for nirvana, he remains a social composer, in a sense that Wagner was no longer. This is most
obvious in the lute ayres that Dowland arranged as part-songs;
and it is significant that he did not treat in this domestic and
social manner any of his more introverted melancholic songs—
not even the Lacrimae, which was his most widely celebrated
composition. Two of the choral ayres may be commented on as
examples of the way in which Dowland made even his typical
love-death theme socially amenable.

> Me, me, and none but me, dart home, O gentle Death,
> And quickly, for I draw too long this idle breath.
> O how I long till I may fly to heaven above
> Unto my faithful and beloved turtle dove. ([1])

In this song, as in his most melancholic ayres, Dowland starts
from the Renaissance ego-obsession—Me, Me and None but Me
—and asks for death as a release. While longing for 'sublimation', however, he sees his translation to 'heaven' as a sensual
fulfilment with his beloved turtle-dove, who is presumably unapproachable here and now, because dead. And the music offers
—sensuously, not mystically—the fulfilment that life denies.
Limpidly in G major, instead of the traditional melancholic A
minor, the slightly agitated repeated triads that act the urgency
of the appeal dissolve into long sustained notes to invoke death,
the suspended minor seventh on 'gentle' being soft as a caress.

[1] Stainer and Bell. Edited by Thurston Dart and Nigel Fortune.

The rapidly reiterated chords return on the words 'and quickly', and lead into sharpwards modulations (from C to G to D to A) to create the tension necessary to sustain this 'idle breath': the more so since the tonal movement contradicts the suspension of the *melodic* movement on the words 'too long'. But from this invocation of the pain of living the music simply subsides a tone. The tension is not resolved; it is merely relaxed, almost, it seems, by conscious choice or volition. So the desire to fly to heaven and be united with his turtle-dove returns (without any grammatical modulation) to G major and to an exquisitely radiant, stepwise-moving texture, with only the most tenderly dissonant passing notes. The little cooing melisma for the turtle-dove is like balm; and although the poetic burden of the ayre is not very different from that of the melancholic songs, the musical effect is now explicitly a solace. Duality may be inescapable, we may never be one with our turtle-dove in the conditions of this life, but our imaginative vision of such perfect love may keep us going. It is by no means certain, incidentally, that the turtle-dove is a girl. The second stanza omits reference to her, compares the singer to the silver swan uttering his own death-knell, and desires 'from earth and earthly joys to fly', since 'he never happier lived that cannot love to die'. The love-death equation seems to involve here a tranquillity of soul, a resignation, that can become paradoxically a social virtue.

This is more directly, and at the same time more profoundly, evident in *Come, heavy sleep*.[1] Here the poem relates the death-wish to the sleep, the rest from pain, that we all can and must experience in our everyday lives.

> Come, heavy sleep, the image of true death,
> And close up these my weary-weeping eyes,
> Whose spring of tears doth stop my vital breath
> And tears my heart with sorrow's sigh-swoll'n cries.
> Come, and possess my tired, thought-worn soul,
> That living dies, till thou on me be stole.

The key is again G major, and the opening invocation, in long notes rising from the third to the fifth and falling down to the tonic by way of the second, is harmonized consistently in lucent

[1] ibid

'Tears kills the heart, believe': Weepers on a tomb

diatonic concords. The 'image of true death' phrase modulates sharpwards to the dominant, but subsides to the subdominant as the eyes are closed. The sealing of the eyes is marvellously suggested by the sustained, ornamentally resolved six-four suspensions, all tenderly concordant. The weariness and weeping are not physically illustrated, since we are concerned with the solace, not the misery. After a cadence on the major triad of the relative minor for the words 'vital breath' there are, however, false relations between the E major G sharps and the G naturals of the tonic major; while sorrow's cries provoke a faintly declamatory cross rhythm.

So the music's tranquillity becomes deepened as it becomes more aware of pain beneath the surface. The E major-G major dichotomy becomes the generative impulse to the living-dying refrain; and the sudden intrusion of the B major triad after the double bar deeply disturbs, while at the same time making the slow resolution into G major, over the quietly descending bass, the more affecting. Again the second stanza poetically makes the point that the music has made already. Sleep, 'child of death's black-fac'd night', is welcomed because it can charm the rebels in his breast, 'whose waking fancies do my mind affright'. Sleep helps us to face, day after day, the agony of being human; and death, being only our last sleep, should do likewise. The acceptance in this wonderful music is more than resignation; indeed its sad serenity can hardly be separated from joy, though it contains, in its luminously harmonic texture, no hint of mysticism. It is a simpler, but no less profound, complement to the 'serenity of disillusion' which we commented on in Wilbye's *Draw on, sweet night*; and the fact that it is a (more or less) homophonic part-song rather than a polyphonic madrigal, emphasizes its consolatory, and therefore potentially social, virtues at the expense of its personal intensity. Moving together, the parts affirm a common lot: whereas in madrigalian polyphony the parts tensely seek a unity from their separateness and multiplicity.

In the solo ayre the separate voice wails, as it were, alone to the moon; and we have remarked on the fact that Dowland did not make choral versions of his more passionately melancholic pieces. He did, however, make choral arrangements of some of the sacred songs from his last collection *A Pilgrimes Solace*, probably because he thought of them as being within the tradition of the polyphonic motet; and in these pieces the tension within the polyphony is perhaps greater than that in any specifically madrigalian music. This is because as solo ayres Dowland's religious songs are subjective songs of personal guilt rather than liturgical pieces. In preserving, in each line, the passionate intimacy that characterizes the solo part of the ayres, Dowland creates in his four-part versions a new kind of polyphonic texture. Though the traditional nobility of the motet survives, the melodic contour and rhythm of each separate line now grows from the meaning and inflexion of the words, as it would do in a solo ayre. As a result, the harmonic texture has extreme density; and the support of lute and string bass is an integral part of the effect. No music more powerfully combines psychological depth with an inherited religious sense: for it concerns my relationship with God, at this given moment, in this given situation; and at the same time tells us that my experience is not an end in itself. We will comment in detail on *Thou mighty God*,[1] which is perhaps the most imposing of these arrangements.

The relationship between God and the Self is the theme of the poem; and that the poetic statement is somewhat flat is no disadvantage, since it allows Dowland's music to imbue dry bones with life.

> Thou mighty God, that rightest every wrong,
> Listen to Patience in a dying song.
>
> When Job had lost his children, lands and goods,
> Patience assuaged his excessive pain;
> And when his sorrows came as fast as floods
> Hope kept his heart till comfort came again.
>
> When David's life by Saul was often sought,
> And worlds of woes did compass him about,
> On dire revenge he never had a thought,
> But in his griefs Hope still did help him out.
>
> When the poor cripple by the pool did lie
> Full many, many years in misery and pain,
> No sooner he on Christ had set his eye
> But he was well, and comfort came again.

[1] ibid

No David, Job, nor cripple in more grief;
Christ, give me Patience and my hope's relief.

The poetic and musical structure both take the form of a prelude and postlude, enclosing three narrative sections. The prelude and postlude concern what is happening to me, now; the narrative sections describe episodes from biblical history which prove that what is happening to me has happened to others before, perhaps even more painfully. But the divisions are not as obvious as that. My suffering is given dignity and impersonality by the broad span of the polyphony; while the historical anecdotes are felt with such immediacy that they become part of me. The past becomes present; and the present is absorbed into the past.

The prelude opens in declamatory style. With almost operatic vigour, we cry to God. The soprano enters alone on the firm major third; the other voices complete the chord, and the soprano slides up to the dissonant fourth and then resolves again on to the third. So even this initial appeal is at once noble and painful. On the words 'Thou that rightest every wrong' the bass rises powerfully, assertively, up the sharp sixth and sharp seventh; while the soprano falls down the scale from the high E. When we get to the word 'wrong' we land on a stabbing augmented fifth (which should be sung with a slight sforzando, as though it hurts), followed by a suspended major seventh. Both the alto and the tenor have here more energy, even agitation, than the soprano and bass; the tenor leaps a sixth, the alto holds its dissonances in a triple rhythm across the other parts' duple measure. The fallibility of man, the divine justice of God, are synthesized in this combination of contrapuntal power with declamatory rhetoric.

Overlapping the cadence on 'wrong', the tenor leaps an octave to cry 'Listen to Patience': beginning with a firm minim and then falling down the scale in quavers. The phrase is imitated in stretto by all the voices; and again, though the texture is continuous, the declamatory nature of the phrase gives the music dramatic immediacy. (Each entry is an individual voice, crying from the wilderness.) The bass still rises through the sharp sixth and seventh, but the other parts all droop, and the movement slows down. With a fluttering false relation between soprano and alto, we modulate momentarily to the relative major, with slowly subsiding suspensions on the word 'Patience'; we are reminded, perhaps, of the significance of this key-word in Shakespeare's tragedies. A protracted cadence on the words 'in a dying song' returns us to the dominant chord of A minor; soprano and tenor waver in sixths, while the voices literally die away one by one, until only an empty fifth between tenor and bass is left, and then finally only the bass's E. So the prelude. which had begun as an almost desperate personal appeal to God, ends in this resigned invocation of Patience. This is a curious introduction to a sacred song. We ask God to help us to endure the ills of the flesh but there seems to be no promise of metaphysical consolation.

The first of the historical illustrations—the Job story—now begins. An abrupt transition to E minor separates the narration from the prelude. Intentionally, the story opens unemphatically; the melodic phrases are less striking, less memorable, than those of the prelude. The inner rhythms, however, are more complex; and contrapuntal though the texture is, it has little resemblance to the texture of a Byrd Mass, let alone a motet of an early Tudor composer such as Fayrfax. Instead of Fayrfax's relatively abstract, timeless flow of sound, we have a sustained whole comprised of interlocking fragments, each of considerable emotional intensity, stemming directly from verbal accent and implication. Consider, for instance, the tenor's phrase on the words 'patience assuaged', with its vacillation between G sharp and G natural, its flattened B that wrings the withers, even while it brings relief. Consider, too, the tenor's cross rhythms on the words 'excessive pain'. He must sing them as though they were a solo part, for their effect is harmonic as well as rhythmic. Yet the total effect of the music must not be agitated, since the point is that the pain which the tenor momentarily, almost operatically, represents is assuaged by patience. This is suggested by the soprano's steady rise up the sharpened form of the minor scale, while the bass slowly descends: an inverted form of the noble opening to the prelude.

There is a similar fusion of pain and patience when 'sorrows come as fast as floods', and 'hope keeps his heart till comfort comes again'. The sorrows droop in sighing suspensions, the floods induce sharpwards modulations and thrusting cross rhythms in the alto. The soprano's Hope steals in with a cross rhythm that emphasizes the word 'kept'; while the bass brings hope in with firmer, slower note values, returning to the tonic and a consummatory major triad.

The second historical anecdote—that of Saul and David—begins in energetic fugato. The leaping sixth in the theme suggests physical movement, the murderer's destructive gesture. When we get to the 'world of woes', however, we leave physical action and embrace mental suffering. The soprano strains up the chromatic scale, reaching a suspended B flat that creates a piercing augmented fifth. Having subsided to A it then curls back to B *natural* and then to C on the word 'woes', each chromatic alteration adding a stab to the harmony. On the words 'did compass him about' there is a touching alternation between the soprano's cadential G sharp and the natural G in the falling melodic phrase.

The words 'on dire revenge' promote a return to physical action. The rhythm, though elaborately syncopated, is dance-like, the parts broken into arpeggio figures: the tenor, especially, moves in almost recitative-like quavers, with angular leaps. But this physical movement derives from the *word* revenge; the verbal sense is that David was above such moral crudity. So the grief turns to hope, and the leaping sixths carry us forward into lyricism: consider, for instance, the tenor's transition from a semibreve grief to hope a sixth higher.

The third story—that of the poor cripple—for the first time brings in the idea of spiritual comfort, as well as the mere capacity to endure. The fugato opening, with its intoned repeated notes, sounds liturgically solemn; but leaps of minor sixth and diminished fourth soon give density to the harmony. The alto's fluctuating rhythm, when she repeats the words 'many, many years', is a speech-accent, which the soprano transforms into cantabile lament. A piercing suspended ninth leads into a cadence on the dominant, with parallel sixths between soprano and tenor, recalling the prelude's 'dying song'. There is a break. Then, with an abrupt modulation to the subdominant, the words 'no sooner he on Christ had set his eye' are sung in sonorously spaced homophony. The soprano's chromatic B flat, the alto's tritonal E natural, and the tenor's ringing G on the dominant seventh of the chord stress the word 'Christ': while the soprano's syncopation on her repeated As enacts the steadying of his regard. He realizes, we realize, that something momentous is happening as he looks. Tenor and bass rise up the scale in parallel thirds; the cripple gets well to rising chromatics; and comfort comes again in slowly resolving suspensions, through which the tenor soars triumphant on his high G. The story closes powerfully, the soprano falling through an octave to thrust upwards through major sixth and seventh to the major triad. The victory intensifies the pain; or the pain becomes an ecstasy.

This is certainly the case in the miraculous postlude—the adjective is not fortuitous—which relates the David, Job and cripple stories to Myself, my own suffering. It also seems musically to epitomize the previous sections. It opens more or less the same as the third story, quietly reflective on its E minor triad that disturbingly succeeds the cripple's A major resolution. But the soprano again strives upwards, landing on the chromaticized B flat on the word 'grief' which is immediately sharpened to B natural, just as it was on the word 'woes' in the David story. This time, however, the dissonance is still sharper, for the B flat clashes with the tenor's suspended A. The tenor's leaping sixth and broken rhythm on the word 'cripple' recall his inner agitation in the Job and David stories. But now the soprano's yearning B natural, following her flattened grief, resolves upwards on to the chord of C major, and the piece ends with a direct reference back to the prelude's declamatory invocation. The bass rises up the sharpened minor scale, appealing to Christ, while the soprano descends diatonically, off the beat, from her high E. Though the dissonant suspensions on each strong beat are powerful, the total effect is at once noble and resigned.

The kind of dramatic polyphony that Dowland creates in *Thou Mighty God* is further explored in the work of a great, recently rediscovered composer of the next generation, Martin Peerson. Most of his bigger madrigals and anthems were scored for voices and viols 'with an organ part which for want of Organs may be performed on Virginals, Bass Lute, Bandora or Irish Harpe'. The viols mostly double the voice parts; the lute or keyboard instrument adds a skeletonic continuo which is occasionally independent of the voices, as are Dowland's lute parts to his choral ayres. Instrumental doubling was common, even habitual, in all sixteenth century polyphony, though the style of the music was vocal in origin. In Peerson, the instruments have become almost a necessity; they point the declamatory phrases, add bite to the harmonic acerbities.

Peerson's *Man, dream no more*[1] is a setting of a verse from a philosophical poem by Sir Fulke Greville, a man of the old tradition.

> Man, dream no more of curious mysteries,
> As what was here before the world was made,
> The first man's life, the state of Paradise,
> Where heaven is, or hell's eternal shade.
> For God's works are like him, all infinite,
> And curious search but crafty sin's delight.

In a sense, this is an anti-metaphysical poem: for although it admits that there are mysteries beyond our material lives, it relinquishes any hope of mystical experience. Man must be content to live as well as he can, here and now. As for the after-life, he will find out by and by.

The texture, at the beginning, is not contrapuntal, but harmonic. The tonality is half-way between modality and modern major-minor; and the key signature of one sharp means a basic D that hovers between major and minor, and between sharp and flat seventh. The tenor enters alone, his long note isolating man in the void. Then the other four voices come in together, and the second soprano immediately suggests uncertainty by sliding from minor to major third. She falls back on to the minor third on the word 'curious'; and her F natural, coinciding with the alto's sharp seventh, creates an augmented fifth sob: which is repeated, more forcefully because a fifth higher, in the next bar. This cadence into the dominant major is contradicted immediately by the minor third, when the next clause—'as what was here before the world was made'—enters contrapuntally. This counterpoint, however, is built on a brief arpeggiated phrase involving a rising sixth, in regular crochets. The texture is instrumental rather than vocal; and the leaps grow both bigger and harmonically more intense (consider the second soprano's augmented fifth version of the rising arpeggio). Such energy emphasizes, perhaps, the mental strife within man's spiritual

[1] Schott & Co. The Complete works of Martin Peerson. Edited by Marilyn Wailes.

quest: the more so because the section modulates rapidly from tonic to dominant and then, in the space of half a bar, to the dominant of the dominant. Ambiguous thirds are prevalent, and the cadence into E minor is approached by an augmented fifth.

For the next clause—'the first man's life'—we return to the tonic and a texture of close imitation. Again the phrase—a rising third followed by a little ascent up the scale—is brief and the treatment of it instrumental, in that the effect depends more on harmonic ambiguities than on sustained line. Again, the suppressed energy in the music stresses man's unsatisfied craving, rather than the 'mysteries' he is striving towards. Significantly, the setting of the next clause, referring to 'the state of Paradise', presents heaven simply as a cessation of the rather agonized movement of the preceding music. The bass, instrumental in character, falls through a diminished fourth to create another augmented fifth chord; then all the parts move ceremonially together to form a solemn full close in the relative major. Heaven is no longer celestial monody, a oneness, but a quiet human togetherness wherein, accepting our lot, we quest no more.

Paradise has slowed down the movement from crochets to minims. This slower pulse remains while we review the other ultimate mysteries—'where heaven is, and hell's eternal pains'. Yet despite the slower movement, the restlessness, the sense of unappeasement, comes back; apparently man cannot be content in his unknowing. The texture, though imitative, is still built from short phrases, arpeggiated rather than stepwise-moving, with angular leaps; there is even a minor ninth in the first soprano. And the overlapping entries muddle up heaven and hell. Hell's eternal shade descends chromatically, of course. The chromatics produce dismal sequences of augmented fifths and dissonant suspensions, as the voices descend into their lowest register; the bass's semibreves on the low A resound like a horrid knell.

When we reach the final couplet, however, an odd thing happens. We leave the mysteries to point out how God's works are like himself all infinite, and therefore inapprehensible by mortal creatures; and the words about God's infinity are set to the chromatic phrase that was originally associated with hell's eternal pains, but now inverted! First the three upper voices, then the lower voices, slide up in parallel chromatics. Now we have seen—in our commentary on Weelkes's O *Care*, for instance—how extreme chromaticism was associated with disintegrative sensuality; harmonic excitation of the nerves destroyed the old modal unity and continuity. The wavering texture of this section of Peerson's anthem also grows from his 'humanistic' passion. Still more than Weelkes's chromaticism it is singularly melancholy, for it implies that the personality, revelling in its joys and sorrows, is becoming rootless, directionless and, in the last resort, scared. Though it may seem strange that such music should now be linked not with sensual experience but with the metaphysical mysteries, this takes us to the heart of the Counter-Reformation. We may recall that composers such as Bull and Frescobaldi employed this advanced chromatic style in their organ music for the most sacred moment of Christian ritual—the Elevation of the Host. As Renaissance humanists, these men delighted in world, flesh and devil; but their delight tingled the nerves the more because they still knew God. The Counter-Reformers, no less than the Reformers, were determined that the devil should not have all the good tunes, exciting harmonies, brilliancies of virtuosity. Knowing that man was 'a proud and yet a wretched thing', they felt that he was at once fearfully frail and potentially divine. The Word become Flesh was the first miracle. Such strange dissolving chromatics as we find in this piece of Peerson hint at a more wondrous miracle: perhaps Flesh might become Word.

Of course, it does not happen: the wonder consists in man's imagining that it might. The point of the verse is exactly the opposite of what the music is saying in this passage: for Greville tells us that spiritual presumption is the work of the devil. So, after the chromatics, tonality is reinstated. The 'instrumental' dissonances are now, however, fiercer than before because, having experienced a blurred vision of what we might be, we are more aware of the anguish within our striving. In addition to the processions of augmented fifths, we now have, on the words 'curious search', savage false relations between alto and second soprano, and then between tenor and first soprano. Throughout these perturbations the bass again behaves instrumentally, with long notes defining the basic harmony, and leading into a firm cadence when the major third finally banishes the flat third of the augmented fifth. The parts are close together, warmly sustained. So we end with a minor triumph of the human will: thankful for small mercies, though the vision of that chromatic aspiration (man growing into god) is beyond our reach, now and always.

HENRY LAWES AND THE CAROLINE AYRE

We have seen that in the Elizabethan age poets naturally thought musically, and musicians poetically. Poetic rhythms were varied and supple and never entirely lost the inflexions of a speaking voice; yet they flowed spontaneously into lyrical music, and the Elizabethan lyric was itself almost a musical structure. The 'musical' nature of the convention means that the songs tend to be generalized in their emotional reference: while the presence of the 'speaking' voice means that the songs preserve a sense of personal involvement.

In the Jacobean period the lyric begins to turn into self-exploratory drama. In the lyrics of Donne and Herbert, no less than in the Elizabethan song-lyric, there is immense variety of metrical pattern. But the metrical ingenuity no longer serves a musical purpose. It rather acts as a discipline on complexity of feeling; the tension between metrical pattern and speech accent becomes inherently dramatic, as it is in Shakespeare's mature blank verse, though the drama is intimate and introspective. This kind of poetry was not often set to music (we have remarked that Gibbons's setting of Raleigh's *What is our life?* is exceptional) because the lyrical composer was not concerned with inner conflict. We have also observed that when music did seek a comparable fusion of personal intensity with tragic impersonality—as in Dowland's *In darkness let me dwell* or *Thou mighty God*—the composer tended to choose words that were conventional, serving merely to release the musical impulse. One can have intensity of poetic or musical experience, but not both simultaneously. There is a limit to the human mind's powers of assimilation.

Fundamentally, the poetry of Donne and Herbert, the music of Dowland, is a private utterance. The poems and music deal with the creator's own experience, whether in relation to his God, his mistress, or himself. Since poetry and music are activities befitting a gentleman, a few choice spirits may be allowed to overhear; but this does not imply a public audience. Even in ostensibly 'public' art—such as Donne's epithalamiums, the ceremonial odes of Jonson or Lord Herbert, or the masque songs of Dowland—the urbanity of the tone, the subtle intimacy of the rhythms, suggest that the public manner never loses contact with the realities of personal experience. Our social functions are inseparable from the kind of people we and our friends are intrinsically, for society is a communion of kindred spirits. One has not one face for the World, a different face for one's parents, wife, mistress—and one's mirror.

Between the Jacobean and the 'Cavalier' lyric there is direct continuity; yet the difference in spirit is unmistakable. For whereas the Cavalier lyric is still written by gentlemen for gentlemen, it is now conceived as a performance, to be appreciated as such. Even if tender as well as sensual, proud as well as insolent, it is comparatively extrovert, involving a number of conscious 'attitudes'. This means a coarsening of emotional fibre which is reflected in the rhythm. The accent of speech is still present; but speech rhythm itself now tends to rhetoric. We overhear Donne and Herbert talking to themselves or to their mistress or God. When Suckling writes:

> Quit, quit for shame, this will not move,
>   This cannot take her;
> If of herself she will not love,
>   Nothing can make her :
>   The divel take her,

he is a man speaking at a particular time and place; yet, what he says is savourless if there is no audience to enjoy its insolence. Indeed, the manner is perhaps more important than the matter. Similarly, though the metrical patterns are still varied and often intricate, their complexity is no longer—as it is in Donne or

Herbert—the result of a complexity of thought and feeling. There is a hint, again, of 'performance' in the metrical variety. It creates a lilt that carries one along buoyantly; yet though the buoyancy is a positive virtue it is not only simpler, but also less honest, than the more wavering rhythms of the Jacobeans.

The lilt is also, of course, more song-like than the rhythms of Donne and Herbert. As the poetry grows less introspective, a direct relationship between poetry and music, comparable with that cultivated by the Elizabethans, reappears. There are, however, two important differences between the Elizabethan and Jacobean ayre on the one hand, the Cavalier ayre on the other; and both are a musical reflection of the change within the lyric itself. The first is that the song-lilt of the Cavalier ayre is much more directly related to the social rhythm of the dance: physical movement is more obtrusive in Lawes than in Campion, not to mention Dowland's subtle melodic-harmonic movement, so delicately responsive to the inner emotional life. The second difference complements, and in a sense explains the first: it is that the Caroline ayre habitually, the Elizabethan ayre hardly ever, involves an element of rhetorical self-dramatization.

Some charming examples of the simple dance-song are provided by Henry Lawes's settings of Caroline poets who preserve, if not the intensity, the delicacy and urbanity of the earlier generation. Consider his setting of Aurelian Townshend's *Sufferance*.[1]

> Delicate beauty, why should you disdain
> With pity at least to lessen my pain?
> Yet if you purpose to render no cause,
> Will, and not reason, is judge of these laws.

The poem deals with suffering in this precisely gracious movement and with a sweetly reasonable detachment; and Lawes sets the words in sixteen symmetrical bars to an exquisitely tender melody in regular flowing crochets. The time signature is $3:4$; and the preponderance of triple rhythms is significant if we remember the Elizabethan's association of triple rhythm with dance ceremony. In this little song the level movement, the simple tonality (there is no modulation, not even at the half-way mark), the smoothness of the melodic contours, the absence

[1] Stainer and Bell, *Ten Ayres by Henry Lawes*. Edited by Thurston Dart.

of dissonance, reflect the urbanity of the poet's 'sufferance'. Only a recognition of social virtues makes it possible to accept mental anguish with such good manners. Of course the anguish is not acute: but neither is it insincere. The sincerity flows into the gentle pathos of Lawes's tune, the good manners into the cere-monial lilt of its dance rhythm. The subtlety of Dowland's rhythms and counter-rhythms, growing from personal feeling, would be inappropriate here. Wistfully resigned, we are content to dance away our sorrow, in communion with an elite of fellow-sufferers. There is a quality rather like irony involved in dealing with pain, at whatever level, in terms so amiably limpid. This links up with the grosser cynicism that characterizes many later Cavalier lyrics.

A Caroline poet to whom Lawes was partial is Herrick: nor is it fortuitous that Herrick should have treated the traditional seventeenth century themes as a charming game, rather than with dramatic immediacy. When Lawes sets *The Primrose*[1] his music has an artful grace comparable with that of the poem. Though simple, the song is highly sophisticated; and the sophisti-cation reflects ironically on the simplicity. There is an element of conscious artifice in the feeling as well as the technique: which is why this delightful song, if less obviously than *Suffer-ance*, is also a social piece. The artifices of feeling have no point unless they are shared.

> Ask me why I send you here
> This firstling of the infant year?
> Ask me why I send to you
> This Primrose all bepearl'd with dew?
> I must whisper to your ears
> The sweets of love are washed with tears.
>
> Ask me why this Rose doth show
> All yellow, green and sickly too?
> Ask me why the stalk is weak
> And yielding each way, yet not break?
> I must tell you these discover
> What doubts and fears are in a lover.

[1] Boosey and Hawkes, *Select English Songs and Dialogues of the 16th and 17th centuries*. Book II. Edited by Arnold Dolmetsch.

Musically, the simplicity consists in the rhythm, which this time is duple: and in the symmetrical disposition of the clauses, four bars of tonic minor modulating to dominant major for the promise of spring; four bars of relative major with dominant flavour to present the dewy flower, ending with a clear cadence; and four bars modulating back chromatically to tonic minor, to make the parallel between the spring flower and the tears of love. The rhythmic regularity and tonal symmetry are simpler than would be found in a Jacobean ayre; indeed, in the second stanza the delicate verbal rhythm that creates the stalk's 'yielding' is completely destroyed by the dance rhythm, and the word 'break' occurs inappositely on the firm cadence in the relative major. On the other hand, there is artifice in the rising phrase, with sharp seventh, that asks why I send you here: in the caressing ornamentation on the second 'ask' and on the 'bepearl'd with dew' phrase: in the chromatic ascent as he whispers in her ear about the sweets of love: in the broken cadential ornamentation when the sweets of love prove to be washed with tears. The second stanza repeats the same pattern, except that the tears of love are now not generalized but related to his own doubts and fears: for this reason the cadential ornamentation is more tremulously extended. Paradoxically, it is the simplicity of rhythm and tonality that make this song seem 'artificial' as compared with a song of Dowland, in which most of the same expressive devices of harmony and ornamentation occur. In Dowland the stabbing dissonance, the lyrical efflorescence, seem to happen spontaneously as the song creates itself. In Lawes, they are conscious refinements of feeling, conceits or 'graces' in both the emotional and technical sense. Again, Dowland's music is fundamentally a private art, Lawes's a public, however small and select that public may have been.

Lawes's rhythmic effects are not always, perhaps not often, as simple as that. His more complex rhythms depend, however, on metrical variety rather than, like Dowland's, on rhythmic flexibility. A delightful example is his strophic setting of another Herrick poem, *Amidst the mirtles*.[1] The poem is a dialogue between a shepherd, sad because he has lost his shepherdess, and Love, who says she is not really lost but is contained in all the flowers of the field. The shepherd plucks the flowers 'to make

[1] ibid. Book I

of parts a Union'. Then he realizes, 'of a sudden', all was gone; and Love points the moral, complacently remarking that joy and hope must wither like the flowers.

The time signature of Lawes's setting is 3 : 4, but the rhythmic structure is consistently 3 : 4 plus 3 : 2. This fits the metrical form of the poem neatly, though the effect is basically musical. The sophisticated lilt gives to the words a quality at once wistful and witty. The fluctuating rhythm—the second half of each clause being twice as long as the first—has a tremulous frailty that suggests from the start how joy must die, like the flowers. On the other hand, the consistency with which the formula is repeated habituates us to it. It does not disturb us, and is not meant to : for although we are aware of the inescapable fact of death in this mutable rhythm, hebetude makes it possible for us to dismiss it in a conceit. This is why Lawes hardly attempts, in this strophic setting, to 'illustrate' the little drama : apart from the softly falling chromatic bass, there is not even any musical change for the last stanza, unless perhaps, as Dolmetsch suggests, one sings it slower. But this is probably to miss the point. The song should lilt on in its gay-melancholy dance of impermanence, while suggesting that social artifice alone makes such physical and spiritual elegance possible. Together, we can make game of death, pretend we don't have to face him, as Donne, Herbert and Dowland faced him.

The same rhythmic formula—3 : 4 plus 3 : 2—appears in a setting of a fully-fledged Cavalier lyric of Suckling : [1]

> I am confirmed a woman can
> Love this or that or any man;
> This day her love is melting hot,
> Tomorrow swears she knows you not;
> Let her but a new object find
> And she is of another mind.
>> Then hang me, ladies, at your door,
>> If e'er I dote upon you more.

Here the rhythm, sung faster, conveys not a piquant tenderness but a jaunty insolence that matches the tone of the poem. Until the final couplet the alternating 3 : 4, 3 : 2 rhythm has reference to rhetorical speech-accent : consider how it stresses the words 'any man' and 'she knows you not', suggesting a raffish

[1] ibid. Book I

'Amidst the mirtles': title page of Herrick's *Hesperides*

gesture as the points are made. In the final couplet ('Then hang me, ladies') the alternating rhythm disappears in favour of a brusque 3 : 4. Aristocratic though it may be, this is in effect a pub chorus. It is a communal effort; the boys band together to dismiss the subject—and 'the ladies'—as beneath contempt. So in the later stanzas Suckling can go on to say that women have no existence except as instruments of sexual satisfaction for Myself. He does not even mean it, of course; it is no more than a pathetically bouncy male pride, exhibited for the approval of his cronies.

The exhibitionistic element in this song tends towards the other fundamental feature of Caroline song—rhetorical self-dramatization. Lawes's setting of Cartwright's A Complaint against Cupid[1] shows dance-song beginning to splinter into something like declamatory arioso. Without being operatic, it projects emotion theatrically; one can imagine it acted, as it is sung.

> Venus, redress a wrong that's done
> By that spriteful boy, thy Son;
> He wounds, and then laughs at the sore;
> Hatred itself could do no more.
> If I pursue, he's small and light,
> Both seen at once and out of sight :
> If I do fly, he's wing'd and then
> At the first step I'm caught again.
>
> Lest one day thou thyself may'st suffer so;
> Or clip the wanton's wings, or break his bow.

The invocation to Venus is poised, assured, on its descending fourth, harmonized with tonic and dominant. Dissonant passing notes and the phrasing of the words across the beat give stress to the words 'wrong' and 'done'. Cupid's spritefulness is expressed by the undulating chromatic bass, by the protracted rhythm, and by the break before 'son'; the chromatics indeed introduce a slightly sinister note, making Cupid not only spriteful but also spiteful—an ambiguity which is clearly in the poem too, since hatred is explicitly referred to in the next couplet. Spite seems to break sustained song into declamatory phrases. Cupid wounds to a rising fourth (an inversion of the original

[1] Boosey and Hawkes, Ten Ayres of Henry Lawes. Edited by Thurston Dart.

H

113

Venus interval); laughs scornfully in a rising *diminished* fourth; hates in a descending diminished fourth and in a cadential ornament vigorously modulating to the dominant. Then the pace quickens. We pursue the 'small and light' Cupid in a phrase broken by rests, in a feathery dancing texture, so that the music is insubstantial as thistledown as he skips into the relative major of the dominant. 'If I do fly [rising arpeggio], he's wing'd [leaping fourth, separated by rests] and then At the first step [break] I'm caught again [short phrases modulating flatwards to the relative of the original tonic].' All this love-chase is physical action in music, much more frivolous than the declamatory opening. The song ends, however, with a return from airy D and G major to the tonic E minor, a change to triple dance rhythm, and something that remotely presages the dance-arias with which Purcell rounds off his most vehement passages of arioso; there is even a final broadening of the 3 : 4 lilt into a hemiola 3 : 2. This sounds much tougher, more in touch with reality, than the love-chase; it comes, as we say, from the heart, from knowledge of what love may be like. But it is no more than a miniature consummation. Lawes has relinquished Dowland's identification of lyricism with emotional introspection, without achieving Purcell's dramatic action in musical terms. Caroline poetry and music both tend to 'play at' the old themes in a spirit of hedonistic persiflage. The new themes, which went to make the new techniques fulfilled in Purcell, were not yet defined.

This is suggested by the fact that Lawes lavished some of his most 'modern' techniques—notably operatic arioso—on poems that were not intended to be dramatic. The Spirit's song and to some extent the Lady's Echo song from *Comus* are cases in point, which we shall refer to in another context. Another example is the famous song *The Lark*.[1] One would expect a lark to be unambiguously lyrical. This one sings a kind of ordered arioso: his rhythms follow speech inflexion, as though he spoke human language and were participating in a human story. Of course there is not any 'psychological' drama in his declamation; but his ornaments are physical description, and the lyrical qualities of the music are directly related to this 'theatrical' presentation.

[1] Boosey and Hawkes, *Select English Songs and Dialogues*, Book II. Edited by Arnold Dolmetsch.

There is thus in Lawes's Lark, as in almost all his love songs, a quality that is theatrical rather than dramatic. The emotion is admitted to be in some sense illusory; and this admission is a part of the poet's fear of taking experience seriously. The wit of Donne, Herbert or Marvell—the recognition of 'other modes of experience that are possible'—degenerates in the Cavalier poets into conceit; and the technical conceit is also a kind of spiritual conceit—or pride—since it implies an amused detachment, a conscious superiority, springing from fear, to the realities of experience. This is directly paralleled by Lawes's sophistication. Both his and his poet's attitude would seem to imply—as compared with Donne or Herbert, Dowland or Danyel—a deliberate exclusiveness.

This may be why Lawes's most successful songs of the through-composed or declamatory type are his settings of poems that have a highly developed intellectual rather than emotional content. His partiality for the poems of Carew no doubt stems from the poet's mood of ironic detachment; though his passion may be genuine, it is always controlled by intellectual argument, so he is never fooled. The majority of Lawes's settings of Carew are through-composed; and in all of them the music serves to point the verbal rhythm of the poem, to underline the shifts in the argument. We do not find here, as we do in Dowland, a poem metamorphosed into lyricism: nor, as later in Purcell, a poem that becomes musical drama. We find a musically unobtrusive setting that exaggerates the manner in which a reciter would declaim the poem before an initiated audience. By giving relatively long notes to the important words Lawes clarifies the complicated syntax; at the same time he underlines the conceits, exhibits them for polite applause. The musical rhythm is not a natural speech rhythm; but it is a reciter's rhythm: that of an orator who is trying to 'get over' difficult language to an audience, and to impress that audience with his verbal ingenuity. In all these songs the music is the servant of the poetry in a manner that is remote from Dowland, or even Campion. Significantly, Lawes's lute or harpsichord accompaniments seldom indulge in expressive dissonances, not even in declamatory songs. The harmony supports the voice; but it does not attempt to intensify the words' meaning.

There was, however, one range of experience to which self-protective detachment seemed inapposite: this was Lawes's relationship to his God. As the servant of a hyper-sophisticated court he was habitually a secular rather than a religious composer. Yet he seems to have been a man of sincere religious conviction; and when he addresses his three noble Hymns to the Trinity[1] he creates declamatory music that is truly dramatic, rather than theatrical. There is no longer illusion or equivocation; he is dealing with real experience. Thus these arioso songs provide a link between the religious songs of Dowland on the one hand, and of Pelham Humphrey and Purcell on the other.

Dowland starts from contemplative lyricism: which he imbues with dramatic intensity. Lawes, in these songs, starts with the here-and-now of the speaking voice, with declamation: which he lifts—as he seldom does in his secular songs—to lyrical and even harmonic power. The first Hymn, to God the Father, begins with phrases that are declamatory but noble, over simple dominant and tonic harmony: rising high, with a modulation to relative major, as we invoke the quickening rays of God's light. But we call upon God in order that he may give life to my 'dead soul'; and whereas Dowland (or Herbert) communes with his God introspectively and meditatively, Lawes's approach to God becomes much more direct, even physical. The sudden descent of the vocal line on the words 'dead soul' suggests a physical shrinking; the leap and quickening rhythm on 'forbid me to despair' are a girding of the loins. Similarly, at the end the chromatic ascent from the grave to my 'cleansed soul' conveys not only release but also the anguish which such acceptance of death has cost me. Though the acceptance has been won through God's help, we remain, at the end, conscious of human fear and frailty.

The Hymn to God the Son shows this physical, tactile quality in the musical imagery in a more developed form: not unnaturally, since it deals with God's descent to human kind. Christ's suffering on the cross becomes our suffering ('thy sufferings too are by translation mine'): the big leap and rising chromatics, the tritonal chords, the suspended diminished sevenths, 'act' the 'sharp nails that pierc'd thy hands and feet'. In the third Hymn, to the Holy Ghost, the sense of physical tor-

[1] These songs, which are unpublished in a modern edition, are given as Appendix B.

116

ment is, of course, to some degree assuaged; but there is the same kind of physical enactment in the marvellous image of the dove's wings soaring scalewise over the wounded spirit: in the quiet cadential phrase that brings the 'bleeding heart's' diminished fourth to rest, 'folded in the arms of death': in the 'dropping dew' that carries us gently to the relative major: in the 'serene calm' of the low cadence in the dominant, before the final leap to the 'rock of faith' and 'assurance of the promised land'. This is a *personal* religious art not unworthy to be put beside the introspective poetry that Donne wrote about his struggles with his God, and hardly to be paralleled in music before Pelham Humphrey's great setting of Donne's *Hymn to God the Father*.

This piece shows the ultimate transformation—anticipated in Lawes's Hymns to the Trinity—of the lyrical solo song into operatic drama: being a religious song composed at a time when the mainspring of creative energy had gone into the apprehension of those *human* loves and hates that Lawes and his contemporaries tried to deflate by way of a civilized facetiousness. The poem takes us back to the point from which we started. If in Byrd's Agnus Dei from the five-part Mass we see the beginning of a new approach to human experience, unconsciously manifested within Christian tradition, here we see the consequences of that new approach, as they came to effect the basic techniques of music.

11

FROM AYRE TO ARIOSO

Pelham Humphrey: A Hymn to God the Father[1]

Probably no poet, not even Marlowe, has a more potent significance, as representative of the 'split sensibility' of Elizabethan
and Jacobean art, than John Donne. It is hardly extravagant to
say that he created a new kind of lyric poetry—a poetry dramatic
and immediate rather than musical, Shakespearean rather than
Spenserian in its use of language. He dealt with particular experience, whether with his introspective relationship to himself
or with his relationship to other people, or to God. Yet though
his experience was centred in himself—Jack Donne who lived
exuberantly in nerves, senses and body—there was always the
alter ego that sought, strenuously if unsuccessfully, for forgetfulness of self in union with God. And Dr. Donne, Dean of St
Pauls, the great divine, speaks to us with peculiar urgency precisely because we have all been nurtured on his legacy of spiritual turmoil. Greater religious poets of earlier generations
inevitably seem to us in some sense alien. John Donne, for better
or worse, both as humanist and as divine, is part of our consciousness—and perhaps of our conscience.

The famous *Hymn to God the Father* that Donne wrote at the
end of his rich but tormented life expresses this dualism with
extraordinary force:

> Wilt thou forgive that sinne where I begunne,
>   Which is my sin, though it were done before?
> Wilt thou forgive those sinnes, through which I runne,
>   And do run still: though still I do deplore?
> When thou hast done, thou hast not done,
>   For, I have more.

[1] Schott & Co., Voice and Keyboard Series, No. 6. Edited by M. Tippett
and W. Bergmann.

Wilt thou forgive that sinne by which I'have wonne
   Others to sinne? and, made my sinne their doore?
Wilt thou forgive that sinne which I did shunne
   A yeare, or two: but wallowed in, a score?
When thou hast done, thou hast not done,
      For I have more.

I have a sinne of feare, that when I have spunne
   My last thred, I shall perish on the shore:
Sweare by thy selfe, that at my death thy sonne
   Shall shine as he shines now, and heretofore;
And, having done that, Thou haste done,
      I feare no more.

The first line establishes an intimately dramatic, non-liturgical note. This is a particular human being, at a specific time and place, talking to his God: since the Fall, all men are sinners and I, as a sinner, am merely a representative of the human race; yet this doesn't alter the fact that for each act of sin I am personally responsible. The sense of individual responsibility is emphasized in the next two lines: the rhyme on 'runne', and the repetition of the word which carries the movement forward, gives the verse an urgency, almost an agitation, that was not present in the first two lines. Then comes the break in rhythm and the clinching conclusion, which epitomizes the state of division in a pun—and an egocentric pun, moreover, on the poet's name. The lines hint either Your act of forgiveness will be useless: or You will always be deceived in thinking I belong to You, because there is no end to the flow of my sins.

The second stanza follows the same pattern, only here Donne looks beyond himself to the effect his sin has on others; there's almost a suggestion of pride in the thought that he can influence other people's destiny, even for evil. The rhyme words 'wonne' and 'shunne'—the metrical rhythm conflicting with the spoken inflexion—have immense energy; and there is a certain indulgence, perhaps, in the extravagance of 'wallowed' and in the hypnotic repetition of the rhyme scheme throughout the three stanzas.

In the third and last stanza the paradox inherent in the poem is fully admitted to: for it has two contradictory, if complementary, meanings, depending on another pun. His 'sinne of feare'—

that he will perish on the shore—is more dreadful than all his sins of pride: indeed pride becomes a virtue. For he spins his *own* thread (the rhyme on 'spunne' again gives the verse muscular power); his thread is not spun for him by fate. His fear is lest, having controlled his own destiny, it should be to no apparent end: lest he should be left on the desolate shore, without heaven or hell. So he fiercely bullies God to swear that at his death 'thy sonne Shall shine as he shines now, and heretofore'. Spelling son with an o could mean that if God will swear that he really became a man, like myself, and died for my salvation, that this was historically true and will be true eternally: then I, John Donne, belong to You and have cast out fear. If, however, you spell sun with a u the meaning is that though my own little life may be snuffed out, none the less the sun, the source of creative energy, will go on shining as it has always shone: so although You have taken my life away, that is all you can do, and in the sight of eternity it is not much. One way ends in triumph, when the humanist submits to God's will. This other way ends in defiance, which is also a kind of triumph, because the humanist says he is prepared to accept his lonely self-sufficiency. As in Raleigh's poem *What is our life?*—and in much Jacobean literature—the sun is regarded at once with reverence and with horror, since it is both creative and destructive, breeder of seed and of the maggots in carrion. On this interpretation the pun on 'done' probably disappears from the last stanza. It simply means You've done all you can—even You're done for; and we end with the humanist's affirmation: I fear no more. Of course the two contradictory interpretations are not mutually exclusive. They are both present simultaneously, at least to our subconscious minds: which accounts for the powerfully disturbing effect the poem makes.

Thus although this is a religious poem, it is also a dramatic dialogue between the Self and the Alter Ego, with God as silent listener: so it is not surprising that a composer of a later generation than Donne's should set it operatically. For although Pelham Humphrey treats the poem strophically, he also sets it in lyrical arioso. Each stanza follows the same pattern; but none is identical. The arioso line follows the speech-accent, as though it were a particular voice speaking at a particular moment; and the music reflects the growing, half-conscious conflict in the speaker's mind.

It is not altogether fanciful to think of the song as an episode in a play. We see and hear Donne-Humphrey praying to his God, as the King in *Hamlet* struggles to pray, on the stage, for forgiveness.

The repeated notes with which the vocal line opens have a suggestion both of liturgical intonation and of operatic recitative. The liturgical flavour disappears, however, when the line descends through a diminished fourth, to land on F sharp on the word 'sinne'. The harmonic tension within the melody here makes us feel, almost physically, the weight of sin's degradation. The next clause emphasizes the word 'my' since the phrase rises in crochets, instead of quavers, modulating to the relative major as my personal sin is related to the sins of mankind. Perhaps the modulation even gives a hint of prideful satisfaction. The repetition of the words 'Wilt thou forgive' repeats the original musical phrase, but a fifth higher. The increased urgency communicates itself to the rhythm: for the accent on the first 'runne' and the melisma on the second drive the music forward. This is a marvellous equation between speech accent and lyricism: we live through the process whereby the human voice, speaking in passion, grows spontaneously into song. The process is further developed in the punning refrain. The verbal stress on 'not' turns musically into a Lombard syncopation, dropping through a diminished fourth, creating almost literally a sob. Then the music explodes in an arabesque, on the crucial word 'for', to express the uncontrollable flood of his sins. The rest before the words 'I have more' is a stammer, a break in the voice; suggested, perhaps, by Donne's comma; he can hardly bring himself to utter the words.

The refrain has brought us back to the tonic, after the heightened urgency of the middle phrase had carried us sharpwards to the dominant. In the second stanza, when the poet turns to the effect of his sins in the external world, tonal movement is more rapid and more varied. We begin with the same phrase, but a fifth higher: so when it stabs through its sinful diminished fourth it carries us flatwards to the subdominant, C minor. But on the verbally stressed rhyme word 'wonne' the minor triad unexpectedly changes to major, and turns into a modulation to the subdominant of C (F major). There is a sense of positive energy in our assertion of power over others. In the next clause we hover between D minor (relative of F major, dominant of G minor) and the tonic. As in the first stanza the cross accents between harmonic and melodic rhythm are subtle: consider the stress on 'their' created by the high D in the phrase 'their doore'; or the weight given to the rhyme word 'shunne', approached by a descending tritone; or the modulating cadence in D minor for the wallowing, with the voice in its lowest register. The refrain repeats that to the first stanza exactly, suggesting, perhaps, the hopelessness of repentence. Whatever I or You do, my sins can never be curbed.

The crucial last stanza begins, for the first time, with the major, not minor, triad. It is, however, almost immediately contradicted by the minor chord on the word 'feare'. The major third returns on the word 'spunne', but this time turns out to be part of a dominant seventh chord that modulates flatwards to C minor. The setting of the words 'I shall perish on the shore' does not deflate the lyrical exuberance with which the stanza had opened; on the contrary, it repeats the stepwise ascent in modulating to the relative major. Then the voice descends to its lowest register in order to approach the final consummation. From this point speech-inflected arioso grows with remorseless power into aria; and the triumph of song is not a return to the old quasi-liturgical modality, but a triumph of operatic exhibitionism. The 'swearing' seems to return to C minor, though it proves to be major, with the sonorous major third on the word 'self'. As the vocal line rises up the scale, first in quavers, then broadening to crochets, we modulate sharpwards from C to G minor with a chilling break in the movement on the word 'death': then to the relative B flat major, then sharpwards again to the dominant of the relative; then back, in a noble consummatory cadence (with trill) to B flat, on the word 'heretofore'. While these stepwise phrases are an extension of the recitative-like phrases of the previous stanzas they have now become lyrical and (in the strict sense) superb. And this time the final clause abandons the recitando style. The grandly falling arpeggio on the words 'And, having done': the abrupt descent through a diminished seventh to the word 'that': the stress on the second 'done', with its acute dissonant suspension in the bass —these are operatic projection. We sense the defiant toss of the head, almost the clenched fist, on that final 'that' and on the second 'done'; and the last statement of the refrain-line 'I feare no more' is set to the same descending diminished fourth that, in the first line of the song, disturbs the ostensibly liturgical intonation with the burden of sin. The music of the last stanza perhaps fits the defiant better than the simply triumphant interpretation of the poem: as one might expect, since Humphrey is further removed than Donne from Christian mysticism. But the Christian meaning is by no means obliterated; and the music's tragic grandeur is inseparable from its wide range of emotional reference.

12

FROM ARIOSO TO ARIA

Henry Purcell: *The Blessed Virgin's Expostulation[1]*
Music for a while[2]

By Pelham Humphrey's time, we have said, the main creative impulse had ceased to be religious and had become dramatic. The theatre—or the opera house—took the place of the church; and the styles and conventions of music were all basically operatic. Dowland's ayres are chamber music that does not need an audience. Almost all Purcell's solo songs were written as incidental music for the stage; and his more ambitious works for solo voices with continuo are miniature operatic scenas which at least imply imaginary stage action.

Consider, for instance, his song—or cantata or scena—for solo soprano and continuo, *The Blessed Virgin's Expostulation*. One can call this a religious piece only in the sense that Nahum Tate's words are based on an episode from biblical history: the episode, recounted in the Gospel of St. Luke, when Christ, at twelve years of age, withdrew himself to the Temple. Significantly, Nahum Tate and Purcell are not concerned with Christ's action in itself, nor even with its potential implications; they are concerned with its effect upon Mary, his mother, who behaves as any other human mother would do in such alarming circumstances. So Purcell's Blessed Virgin is not for one moment a mystical abstraction; she is a specific young woman, in a specific situation, 'expostulating' directly to you and me. At the typically abrupt opening the repetitions of the words help to form a musical phrase; but they are also realistic, for the young woman is stuttering breathlessly in her agitation. The falling sixth in the snapped 'Lombard' rhythm on the word 'pitying' is again (as in Humph-

---

[1] Schott & Co., Voice and Keyboard Series, No. 1. Edited by M. Tippett and W. Bergmann.
[2] ibid. No. 2.

rey) literally a sob; while the chromatic rise on the repetition of the word 'Where?' implies not merely the *idea* of searching but also a physical straining up of the limbs. The arabesque on the word 'sweet', followed by the cadence on the dominant major, suggests the relaxation of strain; remembering her child, she melts in tenderness, with perhaps a lulling or rocking motion in the rhythm. But the major third is immediately obliterated by the harsh reality of the minor third as she realizes that he isn't with her but, more probably, with a Tyger or with Herod, which is worse. The repetitions of the word 'cruel' build a musical climax: yet again grow naturalistically from her horrorstruck indignation, as do the snapped syncopation, the whirling arabesque, the biting tritone that between them create a snarl. On the other hand, the melisma in dotted rhythm on the word 'ah' hovers over one major triad, as opposed to the rapidly shifting chords in the setting of the word 'cruel'. This passage in the relative major dreamfully soothes; and so leads into the immediate vision of the child's 'little footsteps' stumbling in Lombard rhythms that are now as tender as a caress, through the wastes.

The long arabesque on the word 'through' is the physical movement of pressing onwards: she sees her child so vividly that she becomes identified with him and runs (as it were) across the stage—which is also the wilderness. We move forwards, sharpwards, in tonality too—to the dominant of the relative. This thrusting major is transmogrified to a sighing minor in the passage about the mild savages. Here the melting appoggiaturas suggest their relative gentleness, compared with Herod, whose 'tyrant's court' carries us, in violent fioritura, back to the tonic minor. The building up of harmonic tension on the repeated 'Why?'—a progression from major triad to augmented fifth to dominant seventh—leads into the waking dream that foretells the child's 'wondrous birth'. The wonder is expressed in an arabesque that relaxes the anguish in major triad harmony, in the relative major: it is as though she unfolds her arms to embrace the vision. But she is not sure whether it is a vision or a cheat. As she calls on the angel Gabriel to come and tell her, the music becomes dramatic action. She turns to seek him as she cries out. She waits. He doesn't come. She gives up hope in drooping chromaticism, as though she were sinking to the ground. Seated, limp, worn out by emotion, she sings a little retrospective aria—

in the tonic major and in regular dance rhythm—describing how she was once happy. The dotted triple rhythm is a conventional musical image of communal rejoicing; but the illustrative arabesques on 'once caressed' and 'most blessed' are here ornamental rather than physically descriptive, for she is not telling us of what is actually happening, but singing to herself of a happiness that is past.

The effect of Purcell's arioso depends on the fact that it is sung, if not in strict time, at least with an implicit metre that governs the relationship between melodic line and harmonic tension. This is why he can change from declamation to air and back so convincingly. There is now—on the words 'Fatal change'—an abrupt switch back to the reality of arioso and minor tonality: with a procession of Lombard sobs for the distressed mothers. Purcell's notation indicates that at the cadence the voice should literally break. This leads into another aria, in the tonic minor this time, in which she asks herself how she can deal with the situation. The first aria had been a dream. This aria, though a kind of agitated meditation on the experience which the arioso has lived through, faces up to the present; and deals with the necessity to control grief if we are not to go mad. The restraint exercised by dance rhythm and by ordered tonality relates her personal experience to that of Society; and the arabesques that portray the motions and labouring of her soul are now half stylized, half physically descriptive (for although the movements of her soul are metaphorical, the labouring distress she's going through is not).

The piece does not, however, end with aria. It passionately returns to arioso and actuality. On the last page the woman is living her life, or playing her part: pleading before us in falling fifths and sevenths, dissonantly harmonized, and in the longest melismatic passage in the work. This is the composition's climax. She knows, she says, that her son is God and in that fact she should have trust; but none the less, as a human mother, she can't help fearing for her child. The conflict of emotion is wonderfully conveyed in the winging yet drooping melisma on the exclamation 'oh'. Even the final cadential ornamentation (there *must* be a trill here, if not a brief improvised cadenza) is physical action—a shiver.

Some years back a distinguished English soprano used to sing this song, with organ accompaniment, in a justly celebrated imitation of English cathedral treble. Nothing could be less appropriate. The singer should persuade us that it is being sung by a flesh and blood young woman and mother, who is going through the experience she is singing about. The piece implies the woman's physical presence—on an operatic stage; and for its expressive interpretation calls for operatic virtuosity. Campion's songs are intimate in character and intended for amateur performance. Even Dowland's greatest songs, though they demand strength, sensitivity and subtlety from the performer, are not virtuosic: *In darkness let me dwell* was sung by Dowland himself to his own lute accompaniment and almost, one might say, to himself as listener. But *The Blessed Virgin's Expostulation* not merely addresses an audience, like the songs of Lawes; it involves an audience in drama. And this is true even when Purcell writes a song that is prevailingly reflective. Though aria appears in *The Blessed Virgin's Expostulation* the piece is conceived as arioso: the evolving here-and-now of experience. Consider, however, an air like *Music for a while*, which is a lyrical song occurring within a spoken drama.

For this song Purcell uses the convention of the ground bass, a technique much favoured in the seventeenth century, for reasons which we shall have occasion to discuss in Part II of this book. Now the ground bass technique is of its nature static; theoretically, at least, it is independent of time and can go on for ever. In the context of the play, *Oedipus*, Purcell introduces the song as a moment of lyrical reflection, the point of which is to contrast the tempestuous passions of the drama with the divine serenity induced by music. As we shall see in Part II, he is using music here in much the same way as it is employed by Shakespeare. None the less for Purcell music is inevitably dramatic action; so even this song, which is ostensibly concerned with the cessation of action, involves a kind of dramatic projection. He cannot conceive of a purely passive serenity; the quietude here is relative, because instinctively aware of the violent passions the play deals in.

Thus Purcell allows the melody, over the regular, periodic bass, considerable freedom; and in so doing gives the bass a changing harmonic significance. The bass line itself involves an increase and diminution of tension in that its rising fifths change into augmented fifths and back again; and Purcell even alters the notes of the bass, though not its fundamental pattern, in order to attain a modulatory climax in the middle. When the bass starts again at the original pitch it is half a bar out with the melody; it does not adjust itself until the final return of the first phrase in a kind of da capo. So Purcell has given to a technique which is static and reflective a beginning, a middle, and an end —implying an increase and relaxation of tension.

The structure of the song is not, however, what first catches one's attention; it is rather the vocal line and the way in which Purcell, even in a lyrical song, approaches his text. In a lyrical song of Dowland, such as the famous *Flow my tears*, the contour of the melody grows out of the natural rhythm of the words, and the setting is almost entirely syllabic. In his late work, such as *In darkness let me dwell*, Dowland approaches—by a discreet use of arabesques and repeated words and phrases—a more evolutionary, and in that sense dramatic, conception; but the drama is all introspective, within the composer-singer's mind, absorbed into lyricism. Purcell's phrases are still irregular compared with the formalities of the eighteenth century; yet his musical structure depends much more than Dowland's on an architectural balance of clauses—as one would expect in a song built over a harmonic ground. It is interesting, however, that when, seeking this architectural balance, Purcell repeats a phrase, it is always associated with words that are poetically significant. For instance, his setting of the word 'all' in the phrase 'shall all your cares beguile' is an exaggerated musical stylization of the rhetorical, perhaps slightly ironic stress an actor might give to the word in declaiming. Music can beguile us, after all, only 'for a while'; and can we really believe that it will assuage *all* our cares? Similarly, the three-fold setting of the word 'eas'd', in the phrase 'wond'ring how your pains were eas'd', is like a physical gesture. The easing actually happens in the resolution of the dissonant appoggiaturas: one can feel as much as hear it. Similarly again, the snakes that drop from Alecto's head become physically descriptive: one can hear them plopping on the ground. Purcell uses this falling figure not merely because it is a neat musical symbol, but also because by means of it a scene comes to actuality.

Again, when Purcell writes melismatically, even in this lyrical song, the purpose of the 'decorative' notes is to act, not merely to illustrate, the sense. The cooing setting of the word 'beguile' is a simple example; while the sequential treatment of the descending scale on the word 'wond'ring' suggests a shake of the head. Even in the conventional arabesques on the words 'eternal bands' the protracted twiddles convey not only the idea of eternity, but also the physical sense of constriction. The flattened As make one feel tied up in the coils of the semitones; and the relief, when the wriggling stops and the snakes fall with a blessed silence in between each plop, is the more welcome. Throughout *Music for a while*, which is essentially a lyrical and reflective song, the music acts the words so completely that it suggests the bodily gestures of an actor-singer. It is theatre music, even if divorced from the stage.

Of course, it should not be so divorced. In this chapter we have discussed Purcell's word-setting in comparison with that of the madrigalists and the composers of ayres; and in so doing we have discovered that the change in musical style is also a radical change in intention and in convention. To understand this we shall have to examine, in Part II of this book, the evolving relationship between music and theatre between Dowland's day and Purcell's.

Part 2

FROM MASQUE
TO MUSICAL COMEDY

MUSIC IN THE SHAKESPEAREAN THEATRE[1]

In Part I of this book we have traced the process whereby the relationship between music and words changed, during the course of the seventeenth century, from the liturgical to the operatic. In Part II we shall start from a consideration of the function music fulfilled in the Elizabethan theatre; and trace the process whereby drama gradually absorbed music to create the simultaneously musical and theatrical conventions of heroic opera.

Now poetic drama, in so far as it is drama—an imitation of human action—deals with human experience here and now. But in so far as it is poetic it tends to see human experience in relation to the suprahuman, or at any rate in a wider context than naturalistic drama. Greek drama, for instance, mated action, poetry, music and dancing on more or less equal terms, being at once drama and religious ritual. On the whole, the human drama went into the poetry and action, the divinity into the music, for Pythagorean science related the laws of the cosmos to the vibration ratios that govern musical intervals. Yet it is hardly possible, in Greek drama, to draw a dividing line between poetic-dramatic and musical technique: the declaiming of the verse itself becomes music. Similarly, one cannot make sharp distinctions between heavenly and earthly elements, between gods and humans. Such a separation comes, perhaps, only with Christian Europe: with the medieval dichotomy between spirit and flesh.

The ceremony of the medieval Mass is, like Greek tragedy, a ritual drama. But the human element is now 'sublimated' into music and movement. Even the language is hieratic: a different speech from that of ordinary life. The values of medieval music,

[1] Several points in this chapter show a striking, and to me gratifying, resemblance to points made by Mr W. H. Auden in an essay on the same subject originally published in *Encounter*: so I should perhaps add that my chapter was first given in lecture form more than ten years ago.

like those of Greek music, are non-personal, its order being related to the mathematical laws of the cosmos and to astronomy. Plainsong begins as an intoning of words; but these words, unlike those of Greek drama, are generalized rather than specific. The purpose of the music is not to particularize experience but to induce in the listener a state of receptivity to God. Even when a medieval composer writes polyphonically he organizes his music in linear, mathematical, even doctrinal terms, inducing a timeless, generalizing abstraction—as we noted in our comments on Dunstable's *Veni Sancte Spiritus*. Moreover he remains indifferent to the *particular* meanings of the texts he sets, disguising them by elaborate rhythmic figurations derived from number symbolism, by distorted note values, or merely by having several different texts, sometimes in different languages, sung simultaneously. In Dunstable's motet, as we saw, the three texts are doctrinally related and thus of significance to the composer-worshipper; but they cannot possibly be audible, let alone fully apprehensible, in performance.

With the growth of Renaissance humanism music developed, as we have seen, its own human drama, based on harmonic tension organized by metrical rhythm. The development of harmonic as opposed to linear textures complements an increasing—or at least an increasingly overt—interest in the flesh at the expense of the spirit. Yet the effect of this was not at first evident within drama itself; on the contrary, the theatre tended to identify music with its old, divine connotations. Not only in the medieval morality play, but also in early Tudor drama there is, of course, music associated with human junketings—feasting, dancing and so on. But all this is earthly experience in a social, 'functional' sense, without reference to the drama of the personal life; and the music would be identical with that played for a functional purpose in real life. All the serious music in these plays is related to supra-human elements: to experience outside Time. Both angels and men conversing with angels would sing monodically, in a style more or less the same as plainsong, the doctrinal idiom of the Church. The human drama would be contained in the poetry and action; the music would remind the audience of the spiritual values which, in early Renaissance as in medieval theory, gave the human drama significance.

One reason why men of the Renaissance were obsessed with

the classical world was precisely because flesh and spirit were not then separated. None the less, even when poetic drama matured into its Shakespearean form, music continued to fulfil its traditional function: only now it did so with negatively dramatic significance—with what one might call irony, so long as one does not assume that irony is necessarily funny. This repeatedly comes out in Shakespeare's treatment of love as a fusing of flesh and spirit. When Cleopatra is trying to while away the great gap of time her Anthony is away, she says 'Give me some music: music, moody food Of us that trade in love'. [Act II, 5.] Everyone calls for 'The music, ho!' At which point 'Enter Mardian the Eunuch'; and Cleopatra says 'Let it alone; let's to billiards'. In Anthony's absence she calls for music to soothe her spirit, not to appease her desire. It comes with Mardian the eunuch, who is a negation of the flesh; and seeing him, Cleopatra realizes that she doesn't want music after all, that it wouldn't really help. So she sends him, and it, away with a bawdy joke. The whole passage, of course, is two-edged. She doesn't want music because she cannot *as yet* comprehend spiritual values (her metaphor from *trade* is revealing). But the connecting of music with Mardian, who is a maimed creature, carries its own irony: against which Cleopatra's bawdiness stands for life. The implication is that life has to be lived here and now, in the flesh: but that it won't be lived fully if we remain insensible of the divinity within us. Cleopatra learns this during the course of the play; and in one form or another it is probably a dominant theme in all Shakespearean drama—not merely Shakespeare's. The poetic dramatist is inevitably concerned with man's experience in the flesh: indeed, it is precisely because he is so alive that he is so conscious of the flesh's mortality. Yet, nurtured on a medieval heritage, he still sees man's experience in relation to the divine; and the perennial question for him is whether, and in what sense, man can be sufficient unto himself. In Marlowe, in Shakespeare, this conflict between spiritual forces and temporal-material forces is acted through, experienced in, the poetry. Music is important in Elizabethan drama, but is not in itself dramatic. On the contrary a dramatic point is made of its non-dramatic nature.

In Shakespeare's day people were highly conscious—as we have seen in Part I—of 'jarring discord' as a threat to music's cosmic order. Discord, indeed, was directly related to the corruption within human nature since the Fall: so that it was pos sible for music itself, symbol of the divine, to become an agent of the devil. Fortunately, however, 'bad' music was easy to recog nize because it was always dance music, associated with regularly periodic time, and was usually new and usually discordant (like 'modern' music at any period). Significantly, there is not much 'bad' music in Shakespeare. The witches' music in *Macbeth* is an obvious example, and that is hardly music at all. On Shakes peare's basic assumptions, witches are incapable of song; they should croak and grunt to a kind of rhythmic racket. One reason for thinking the Hecate scenes may be spurious is that they tend to be more song-like, though this may be a low, music-hall par ody of music's natural (or rather divine) function. In this case the witches are projections of Macbeth's inflated ego; they sing because he wants to be a horrid, perverted god.

There is certainly a connection between 'bad' music and the excesses of Renaissance egoism. Edmund, in *King Lear*, deflating the cosmic order so that he can inflate the Self ('I am that I am'), ends by equating the destruction of the natural order with dis cord in music. Gloucester, he says, pretends that these 'late eclip ses of the Sun and Moon' are superhuman events: 'an admirable evasion of whore-master man, to lay his goatish disposition on the charge of a star'. [I. 2.] And when Edgar appears, putting on an act, taking as his cue 'villanous melancholy, with a sigh like Tom O'Bedlam', he croaks cynically 'O these eclipses do por tend these divisions. Fa, Sol, La, Me.'—the old terminology for the tritonal tetrachord.

But for the Elizabethans, music was still normally equated with the vision of social and planetary order that Edmund thinks he has demolished. Shakespeare usually employs music to re present the lyrical and reflective state—the state of Being, as opposed to the Becoming which is the play. He thus uses music to remove us from particular, personal experience; and in so doing to cast a new light upon it. 'Good' music may be either social or planetary. The simplest kind is the instrumental dance music, which represents the public life: social values as opposed to personal relationships. The dances postulate certain assump tions about living together, disregarding the fact that any con course of human beings is a complex of individualities. Some times this public life is a simple positive: the Good Life for those who are not too complicated to accept it (for instance, the rustic dances in the pastoral scene of *The Winter's Tale*, and to a lesser degree the 'rural music' in *A Midsummer Night's Dream*). This kind of positive social music would be very close to folk dance: a symmetrical tune with the most rudimentary harmonic accompaniment or perhaps only with metrical percussion, for no inner tension between social and personal relationships is involved.

More interesting is the ceremonial, courtly dance music. This would be grand and stately, with the melodic element no less important than the rhythmic, and with 'old-fashioned' counterpoint in the inner parts. The dance element represents human togetherness, the songfulness a fundamental religious creativity, and the counterpoint a unity that is both social and religious. This 'good' music may be used positively, though Shakespeare often makes an ironically dramatic point of the contrast between the music's assumption of order, grace and gallantry and the realities of experience. There is a subtle instance of this in *Macbeth*. [I, 6.] The 'music of Hoboyes' that introduces the 'temple-haunting martlet' scene should, of course, be courtly, ceremonial, regal; probably a pavane, certainly with an old-fashioned polyphonic texture, since Duncan is representative both of social order and of divine grace. A 'music of Hoboyes' is heard again at the beginning of the next scene, when the procession of servers brings in Macbeth's banquet. To this music Macbeth enters to hiss his soliloquy 'If it were done, when 'tis done, then 'twere well it were done quickly'. Abruptly we are switched from the vision of social order and spiritual grace (which in the old King's time had presumably been a reality) to the dark turmoil in Macbeth's mind. If the music is the same as for the previous scene, its effect is now ironic. If it is different, it should be more 'modern', more dance-like and martial: still ironic in so far as its festive glamour is contrasted with the chaos within Macbeth, but related to that chaos in so far as it is brash, harsh, insensitive. This ironic use of ceremonial music possibly appears in the later banqueting scene when Macbeth sees Banquo's ghost. [III, 4.] The divine grace of Duncan is not involved here, so instead of a solemn pavane one might have a galliard: conventionally ceremonial, but homophonic, with little independent part-writing or inner harmonic tension—neither 'bad' nor 'good', just empty. Music is not here mentioned *specifically*, however, and a silent banquet is perhaps dramatically more effective, for the ceremonial muse is stifled.

Dance music similar to Macbeth's, but richer and more splendid, should be heard when 'hoboyes' play 'Loud Music' in the second scene of *Timon of Athens*. Here the material riches are a positive value, not just a pretence as in *Macbeth*. Yet the point of the play lies in the limits to Timon's generosity, and even in this scene Apemantus pricks the bubble of merely material wealth. Timon himself says that friends would be 'sweet instruments' hung up in cases if their love was never expressed in action. He bids music make his guests welcome, and witnesses a masque-dance of Ladies, introduced by Cupid, god of love. He fails to see, however, that the essence of love is of the spirit: and that if it is based on material values alone it will inevitably degenerate into self-interest. Apemantus, who appears to be Timon's polar opposite, sees this from the start, both in his Grace and in his comments on the masque ('I should fear those that dance before me now Would one day stamp upon me'). When the masque is over, after 'much adoring of Timon', the Rich Man bids the Beggar-outcast not to 'rail on Society', but to 'come again with *better* music'. But Apemantus says 'I'll lock thy heaven from thee': for he knows that while Timon wants to hear the 'good' music (which is ultimately divine) he cannot, because he has only material, not spiritual generosity. At the end, when Timon is alone with Apemantus, and then with himself, he hears the wind and the sea: the unknowable mystery that surrounds our waking lives. But he hears no music; and we realize that he was the predestined companion of Apemantus who is tone-deaf, oblivious of music, whether human or divine. Timon sees the sun, moon, earth and stars as *thieves* because he can think only in terms of possession; and Apemantus can 'love' Timon, after his fashion, when Timon has learned to feel, see and hear nothing. Perhaps even Timon's hate of Apemantus becomes inseparable from love, as he sees in him his mirror-image.

The music that Timon fails to hear is the music of social Good: but still more the planetary kind, which was old-fashioned in style, vocal and polyphonic in conception, though usually played upon instruments because it was thereby released from the human contagion of words. This planetary music, in the style of the instrumental fancy, was the ultimate good to be sought, though one's chance of hearing it, in the conditions of temporal mortality, was slight. There was even a suggestion that the divine music must of its nature be unheard, except in moments of mystical illumination reserved for purgatorial sufferers or saints or —assuming you are going to heaven—at death. This theory— which is common to eastern civilizations for whom music is ritualistic or magical—is discussed in Lorenzo's well-known speech about music in *The Merchant of Venice*. [V, 1.] 'Such harmony is in immortal souls, But while this muddy vesture of decay Doth grossly close it in, we cannot hear it.' This is why Jessica is 'never merry' when she hears sweet music; none the less the fact that she is so moved by music is evidence of her spiritual nature. A man who is not so moved is not to be trusted because, like Apemantus, he is unaware of man's potential relationship with the divine.

When, in Shakespeare's plays, doctors prescribe music for their patients the idea is that the divine order of music may heal the divisions of the sinful mind. Thus whereas the social-ceremonial dance music tends to be contemporary, and sometimes popular, in style, the purgative music is usually archaic. In Lear's 'restoration' scene music is called for to cure the 'great breach in his abused nature': to 'wind up the untuned and jarring senses'. [IV, 6.] This music would certainly be a fancy for viols, in the old, contrapuntal, vocally-founded tradition, without metrical time sense, resolving the Many in the One in its polyphony. But its part-writing would be poignantly dissonant too, because the scene is within the action—a climax to it. We have to be immediately aware of Lear's suffering: while at the same time his dissonant pain is assuaged in the flow of the lines, in the supra-personal unity of the counterpoint. So the music would be serene and positive: but with a valedictory dying fall. We may recall what the seventeenth century theorist Thomas Mace said of the string fancy:

> We had for our grave music fancies of three, four, five and six parts interposed now and then with some Pavanes, Allmaines, solemn and sweet-delightful ayres, all which were, as it were, so many patheticall Stories, rhetorical and Sublime Discourses, subtle and acute Argumentations, so suitable and agreeing to the inward and secret and intellectual faculties of the soul and mind that to set

them forth according to their true praise there are no words sufficient in language; yet what I can best speak of them shall only be to say that they have been to myself and many others as Divine Raptures, powerfully captivating our unruly Faculties and Affections for the time, and disposing us to Solidity, Gravity and a good Temper, making us capable of Heavenly and Divine influences.

Similar music is called for in the 'rebirth' scenes in *The Winter's Tale* and *Pericles*: except that in these cases the style might be more old-fashioned, less dissonant because, though we have come through the wheel of fire, we are now far removed from it; years have elapsed, in which the purgatorial process has worked its way. In *Pericles* Marina restores her father to life by singing to him, but we are not told what she sings. [V, 1.] This is a case in which the healing power of music derives from its relation to cosmic order; the words don't matter, only the celestial serenity of her song, which should be simple and incantatory: a snatch of a folk-song, perhaps, unaccompanied. When instrumental music appears in this scene it is indeed the music of the spheres. No one hears it except Pericles in his moment of mystical rebirth —and, of course, the audience, who are in a privileged position. This 'unheard music' would also be a fancy, but probably for recorders, the traditional instrument of divinity as compared with the more humanly expressive (and therefore purgatorial) strings. Similar music should be used for the 'solemn music' in *Cymbeline*, especially that before Arvigarus enters carrying Imogen 'dead' in his arms. [IV, 2.] The music tells us what we wouldn't know without it: that her presumed death is the prologue to a richer life. In all these cases the fact that music is played while the characters are speaking tends to de-personalize them: to make them agents of the divine as well as suffering and joying mortals.

Occasionally Shakespeare uses supernatural instrumental music for what one might call negative dramatic effects. A case in point is the 'music i'the air' that anonymous soldiers hear in *Anthony and Cleopatra*. [IV, 2.] This is not a music of viols, the human purgatorial instruments, nor a music of heavenly recorders. It is a music of 'hoboyes', which as we have seen may sometimes represent social ceremony, being public instruments, often played in the open air: but which may also represent the unknown, the mysterious. This music should certainly be quiet, contemplative, distant (they are under the stage). Yet although the texture would be contrapuntal, like a fancy, it would not have the harmonic expressiveness, the delicacy of nuance, of the fancy for strings; and the nasal tone would emphasize the strangeness of the sound, the ambiguity of its meaning. The soldiers themselves aren't agreed about it. One thinks it is 'i'the air', another under the earth. One says it 'signs well'; another 'it does not'. And both are right. For what it tells us is that 'the god Hercules, whom Anthony loves, now leaves him'. On the face of it, this seems bad, and gives us an insight into his destiny which Anthony, who doesn't hear the music and apparently triumphs in the battle, has not. In another sense, however, the music is good: for Anthony's material success is an illusion both because it is belied by later events and also because he has to lose his life in order to find it. Both he and Cleopatra live magnificently in their senses; both spiritually triumph in their physical defeat. When Cleopatra becomes 'air and fire' and gives her other elements to baser life she is flesh metamorphosed into spirit. The 'unheard music' vibrates in her words and we, as audience, don't need to be reminded of it by audible representation.

Music does not make many appearances in the history plays, apart from the obvious martial noises: for they deal with the various kinds of mundane glory and deceit. There is, however, a touching and subtle use of music in *Henry IV* part 2, when Falstaff calls for music to be played while Doll Tearsheet sits on his knee. [II, 4.] Its effect on him is far from merry, let alone aphrodisiac. It turns Doll's conversation from beds to churches, and makes Falstaff plead with her that she should not speak 'like a deathshead': 'do not bid me remember mine end'. Falstaff pathetically cries for kisses though 'I am old, I am old', and Doll professes sincerity and constancy: while as counterpoint to this the Prince and his cronies carry on a scurrilous, debunking banter. If we took all this without the music we might be tempted to regard Falstaff merely as a figure of fun in this episode. By this time in the cycle he has been exposed as a lecherous old reprobate whom Hal has to discard; and as for Doll, nobody would trust the word of a whore. But the music forces us to think of this more equivocally, even if the words don't. It tells us that although Falstaff's dream of an eternity of frivol—all being boys together—is a negative refusal to face up to reality, it might also be a positive, because it is based on love, not policy. It is right for Hal to throw Falstaff aside if that is the only way he can grow up. But his values—as we shall see in *Henry V*—are not complete in themselves; and there may be a sense in which, in losing Falstaff, he has lost a valuable part of himself. Dreams may be more real than reality. So the music—not to mention his narrated death scene—discounts the critical notion that by the end Falstaff has become an entirely evil character. In this scene the music should be dance music, because it refers to a mundane world: but dance music with a dying fall and some mildly dissonant counterpoint, because it must be full of regret for love lost and for human potentialities (both Falstaff's and Hal's) unfulfilled. Perhaps any genuine reference to love must involve a hint, however remote, of the music of the spheres; one of the simpler Dowland pavanes might be appropriate. The snatches of song that Silence utters in the orchard scene are similar in effect. [V, 2.] They refer back nostalgically to what we thought was an eternal youth when summers were warm and women all loving. It would be presumptuous indeed to claim that such dreams are false, as compared with the bedraggled remnant of an army, or even with the steely grandeur of the new king.

The world of Falstaff's dreams—apart from the libidinous ones—is not so far from the world of *A Midsummer Night's Dream*: in which, indeed, he finds himself in *The Merry Wives of Windsor*. Though there is a lot of supernatural music in the *Dream*, it is a very different matter from the celestial music in *Lear, Pericles* or even *Anthony and Cleopatra*. The difference consists in the fact that the *Dream* is not touched by tragic experience. It is about youth, and the various kinds of illusion to which youth—and innocence in general, for the low characters are not particularly young—is subject. Many of the characters are supernatural and *ipso facto* musical; yet they are not perceptibly wiser than the mortals, and indulge in the same petty jealousies and misapprehensions. The relationship of mortals to fairies parallels the relationship of Greek humans to gods. A divine hierarchy exists, only the human mind cannot conceive it as much less muddled than our own. Perhaps the only difference lies in a wish-fulfilment: the fairies can put things right by magic, we can't. So the mortals suffer for their mistakes and the fuddled fairies help them to start afresh: which is perhaps a synonym for learning by experience. But nobody believes in solutions; the humans will commit the same idiocies and perversities as before and the fairies will emulate them: then a bit more magic will be needed to start the ball rolling again.

All this means that there should not be any sharp distinction between human music and fairy music. The human dances and so on want to be full of the hopeful dreams of our youth, and in that sense potentially divine. Conversely, the fairies' spell-music, which lulls to dream, should not have the intensity of the Lear restoration music which (in the profoundest sense) wakes him up; nor should it have the sublimity of Hermione's statue music or Pericles' music of the spheres. But it should be slightly archaic in flavour, lightly contrapuntal but in dance rhythm, in the style of a Morley canzonet. Chaste recorders would be more apposite than expressive viols. Bottom's 'rurrall musick' should, of course, be different from either the fairies' music or that of the courtly lovers. It wouldn't be contrapuntal, unless the yokels sang a catch, nor, probably, would it be harmonic. It would be heavily rhythmic, accompanied by percussion only or by the most rudimentary chordal bumps, all tonic and dominant: but would differ from the 'bad' music of the witches in *Macbeth* in having a good tune, probably traditional, certainly vocal and modal.

In *The Merchant of Venice*, which contains the famous speech about the magical effect of music, we have also an example of music's practical use as an agent between the human and the divine. Portia employs it to help Bassanio choose the right casket and, with characteristic cunning, gets the best of both worlds. [III, 2.] If he makes the wrong choice, he will at least find a 'swan-like end, fading in music'; music will offer celestial consolation for what they cannot experience in real life. But if he chooses right, music will assure that their love shall have spiritual sanction, and so shall be durable and soul-satisfying as well as flesh-appeasing. The music that is played while she speaks should thus fuse vocal, fugal serenity with harmonic sensuousness; it is probably a pavane for strings, with imitative part-writing and tense false relations (for the outcome is still in balance). The song that accompanies Bassanio's choice deals with true and false love, with appearance and reality. It should be more dance-like than the instrumental music: but should have a contrapuntal refrain for the ding-dongs, which are a funeral oration on false-seeming. Truth, after all, is godly.

This brings us to the field of vocal music. Normally Shakespeare uses song to make generalized comments on particular experience. Again, the songs introduce a different dimension, are negatively dramatic, sometimes ironic, in their context. An obvious instance is the Willow Song in *Othello*. [IV, 3.] This is a naturalistic interpolation because it is sung by Desdemona herself, in the course of the action. The story it tells parallels her own story; but the fact that Shakespeare re-hashed it from a folk-ballad generalizes her experience. Instead of experiencing a private pang, we feel that her story is one instance of the sorrow inherent in being human. This makes it the more moving: yet at the same time easier to bear. The remorseless action of the drama stops; and in the stillness we feel a curious assuagement. Yet paradoxically the stillness only makes our suppressed awareness of Time and impending doom the more acute: we can hear, almost feel, Othello's step through the silent night. Though most of this is in the lyric itself, the effect would not be the same if it were spoken rather than sung. For the music at once complements and intensifies the poem's delicate equilibrium between personal and communal experience. The tune has a folk-like simplicity and is probably based, like the words, on a traditional source. Yet it isn't merely folk music: for it is Desdemona's suffering, at this particular time and place, too. Thus the poignancy depends on the harmonic aspect—the bitter-sweet equivocation between spirit and flesh that is Elizabethan false relation. The melody seems impersonal and timeless: while the harmony tells us that the sands of time are fast running out.

Ophelia's distracted ditties [IV, 4] are comparable in effect, though simpler. There is no equivocation in them, since in going mad she becomes innocent. She is thus not consciously aware of the relevance of the fragments of traditional songs that she croons. There is no sophistication of harmony for her; all her snippets are unaccompanied, and belong to the peasant community rather than specifically to her. They thus carry her outside Time, identity and the action, and only we as audience and the onlookers on the stage realize how her innocence strikes to the roots of truth. Such completely 'artless' song is usually reserved, by Shakespeare, for the mad. One finds it in Edgar as

Tom O'Bedlam, and in Lear's Fool: for Edgar in these scenes is certainly not merely a sane man pretending to be crazy, nor the Fool merely a professional man putting on an act. Both of them deliberately release themselves from Reason—to the Renaissance the essence of man's humanity—in order to find a deeper truth when 'reasonable' self-interest has turned men into monsters. In the most profound sense their broken songs are religious. The Fool's songs, in particular, should have within their innocent pathos an incantatory quality, half way between folk-song and plainchant.

Most of the fools in Shakespeare are, of course, professional musicians, and much more sophisticated than the Fool in *Lear*. Autolycus's songs in *The Winter's Tale* are sung impromptu and should remind us of folk music. But they should also be sophisticated: not only because he is in touch with the town as well as the country, but also because a song like 'When daffodils begin to peer' is linked to the deepest themes of the play. [IV, 3.] We have to be able to take it as a song about Autolycus's irresponsible life with thrushes and aunts: in which sense it is realistic. We have also to sense its relationship to the spiritual action, remembering that Autolycus is the agent through whom restoration and rebirth become possible. So the sophistication in his music should also be an enhanced subtlety and beauty, as compared with the songs of the other rustic characters; Dowland's *Fine knacks for ladies* suggests the appropriate manner.

Most of the songs sung by professionals are outside the dramatic action; they are called for by characters who usually expect the song to reflect on their own situation. Thus in *Measure for Measure* an anonymous Boy sings to Mariana at the Moated Grange the lyric 'Take, O take those lips away'. [IV, 1.] The poem—an elaboration of the take-bring opposition—epitomizes her predicament. He is to take his lips away because they have been forsworn to someone else (but 'sweetly' also refers to her own delight in his kisses). Similarly he must take his eyes away because they are lights that *mis*lead. They break the day, like a broken heart; yet the break of day is also the dawn, a beginning, a hopefulness. This thought leads to her suggestion that he must bring *her* kisses back. She pretends that this is because she wants to be returned to her original unkissed condition; they must be returned like love letters, now the affair is over. But she also wants them ('bring again, bring again') in order to enjoy their sweetness afresh; and the seals metaphor in the last line suggests that she knows the applied analogy is false. She cannot be unkissed; and seals once broken are broken for ever. This is the more true if the seal is that of her chastity also.

So the lyric embodies with subtlety her equivocal state: she wants and doesn't want, loves and hates simultaneously. The equivocation extends to the performance itself: for in listening to the song she is both indulging in her grief and at the same time objectifying it—setting it apart from herself by having it sung by someone else, professionally. The song is thus artful in every sense. The melody has not the folk-like simplicity of the Willow song. The asymmetrical phrases, with their yearning octave leaps and suspended dissonances, suggest personal suffering; yet the feeling is not dramatically immediate but retrospective. This equivocation between harmonic indulgence and an impersonal lyric lament parallels the equivocation between self-dramatization and an objective, 'universal' sorrow in the poem. Mariana seems to recognize that this music is only partially 'good'. The Duke enters and points out that music may flatter self-deception—may 'make bad, good', but also 'good provoke to harm'. He offers her 'other comfort' and more practical advice: whereupon she abruptly dismisses the boy-singer.

A still more complicated case is 'O Mistress Mine', from *Twelfth Night*. [II, 3.] This harks back to the opening speech of the play in which music is described as the food of love, the one value which can defeat Time, or seem to defeat it. When the music stops, however, being 'not so sweet now as it was before', we are told that Time inevitably corrupts the values that render life meaningful: so that it becomes impossible to distinguish love from 'fancy'. This is a very pessimistic speech to open a comedy, though its pessimism is modified by the fact that the Duke doesn't really mean it, for his love-melancholy is a self-indulgent game. The background music, with its 'dying fall', should be Dowland-like, though not, of course, with the spiritual fervour of the Lear restoration scene. A pavane—at once 'solemn and sweet-delightful', as Thomas Mace put it—would be appropriate: suavely singing, but bitter-sweet in the harmonies of the inner parts.

The song 'O Mistress Mine' takes up the theme of Time destroying the only true value, Love. She must not 'roam' because he is approaching, and when they meet in togetherness, journeys *end*; time seems to stop. But of course journeys don't end, really; so the second stanza gives up the pretence about Love defeating Time and simply says that the only thing to do is to live in the present moment. The point of this shift in meaning depends on the fact that the song is sung to Sir Toby and Sir Andrew who, in choosing a love song rather than 'a song of good life' (that is, a religious piece), had admitted their indifference to things of the spirit. Sir Toby is no longer young; and though Sir Andrew may not be old, he too fritters Time away. Sir Toby knows that love means going to bed with a pretty wench, but doesn't comprehend the timeless element. Sir Andrew has, perhaps, a fuddled sense of love's spirit but wouldn't, one suspects, be very proficient in bed. So the reality of love is beyond the understanding of them both. The song complicates, and deepens, our attitude to them. We feel contempt (because they fritter), and also pity (because we know what they are missing). This is in the music, which is simple, but too sophisticated for a folk-song. The rhythmic ambiguity in the last clause is wistful.

All this is in the collocation of the two stanzas if we take them as a statement about Love and Time addressed, by the Fool, to Sir Toby and Sir Andrew. The meaning is very different, however, if we read the stanzas as a direct expression of the thoughts of these ageing fuddy-duddies. Then the second stanza means: Come and kiss me, now, quick, before I'm too old, or dead; and in this case the beauty of the tune, like that of the twenty-year-old girl, is ironic contrast. This nasty, scared, death-conscious meaning is reinforced if we consider the song in relation to the catch which the revellers croak a moment later. A catch is a 'low', parodistic form of the old religious, contrapuntal unity; and the words of this one refer to time and eternity, as well as to love and parting. 'Farewell, dear heart, for I must needs be gone'. But, says Sir Toby, 'I shall never die'; I am exempt, god-like. The choric Fool adds, 'There you lie': which is a pun too, because as Sir Toby says he will never die he topples over, *dead* drunk.

'Come away, death' offers a comparable comment on the love-time theme. [II, 4.] For all its rhythmic subtlety, it is a set-piece of love melancholy; indeed, the repetitions, the rather exaggerated rhythms, perhaps suggest an actor's gestures, his moppings and mowings. The Duke says he wants an 'antique song', but is then very condescending about it, calling it 'silly sooth' that 'dallies with the innocence of love, like the old age'. It dallies, if it does, because *he* dallies, being unable to understand either innocence or love. During the course of the play the serious characters learn something about love through experience and the comic characters learn a little about themselves. Yet the queasy note remains in the Fool's final song about the wind and the rain: which, for all its innocent, ballad-like manner, is more weary and worldly than wise. Indeed the point seems to be that anything one may learn from experience does not count for much: the wind and the rain blow on, and that's all there is to it. When we are children it doesn't matter because we live by toys and baubles—like a Fool. When we come to man's estate it still doesn't matter because we all become some kind of knave or thief, shut off from society, in the wind and the rain. When we get married we are no longer alone; but having lost our independence are reduced to uncreative swaggering. So we get drunk to forget; and being drunk in bed turns into being dead drunk, like Sir Toby, and that's the end of us. The last stanza ('A great while ago the world began') reduces our individual lives to pettiness: it's all one, we couldn't care less, as the current saying has it. Of course this is not the total effect of the song as epilogue to the play; in the context the sadness does not affect us as being bitter, but rather as a resigned shrug of the shoulders. It does not make young love seem unreal or synthetic, though it suggests that it won't last. That the verse is sung rather than spoken is important, for the lyricism mollifies the words' innate savagery. The tune to which it is usually sung, though not contemporary, is right in spirit: not lyrically sustained, but simple and haunting, like a nursery ditty. The Fool is enjoying his privileged position outside life: while admitting that to be a fool is childishly to escape responsibility.

Despite the dubious meaning of the words the Fool's song is not 'bad' music, and the total effect depends on this ambiguity. A comparable instance occurs in *Much Ado about Nothing*, which is largely a prose play. The 'solemn hymn' sung over the pseudo-tomb of Hero should be a serious parody of 'heavenly' music. [V, 2.] If the hymn really meant what it said it would not square with the play's denouement; and that it doesn't mean it is suggested by the rhetorical exaggeration in the word 'groan', in the heavily stressed refrain, in the conventionally yawning graves. Though the words and music are not satirical they must indicate that the 'solemnity' of the hymn is in inverted commas. The music would do this—in conjunction with the stylized rhetoric of the words—simply by being in the liturgical manner, but not very good. This is an example of how important it is for a theatrical composer to know when to write insignificant music. 'Sigh no more, ladies' [II, 3.] is again a song that disclaims its songfulness. It is prefaced by a long conversation in which Balthazar jokes about how bad (if professional) a singer he is, and how bad his music is going to be. Benedick rounds it off with his jest about sheeps' guts haling souls out of men's bodies: which of itself deflates music's heavenly pretentions. The song, when finally we hear it, turns out to be a cynical dance-song about man's inconstancy. Being against love, it is also against music: so though we don't know what the music was like, we may suspect that it was quick, perfunctory, rather agitated. When it is over there are more japes about the horrid noise; and since we know it was sung by a professional (the composer-singer John Wilson), the croaking must have been deliberate. The point is dramatic, not musical: for the song is heard by Benedick, hidden, as well as by the Prince and Claudio who had asked for it. While they take it at its face value, Benedick must realize that it describes exactly the attitude affected by himself and Beatrice. It is at this point, perhaps, that he becomes aware that their attitude *is* affectation: so that when he overhears the conversation that tells him of Beatrice's presumed love for him, he is already prepared to admit his love for her.

A more extravagant example of this negative, ironic use of music is Cloten's serenade to Imogen in *Cymbeline*. [II, 2.] He, being unregenerate bestiality, has no music in his soul (if he has a soul): so he employs a professional to make music—for its supposedly aphrodisiac effect. What he wanted was, of course, 'bad' music. We do not know what he in fact got from his professional, though presumably it was spring-like and lovely, an evocation of what Imogen stands for: the dramatic point being the contrast between the Imogen-concept and the real purpose for which the serenade was sung. But since the singer was professional, paid by Cloten and informed by him of the purpose of the musical exercise, it is possible that an undercurrent of nastiness should be audible in the music, belying the words. Shakespeare often presents professional musicians as malcontents, aware of the gulf between their heavenly potentialities and their material motives. They sing to live: whereas man's destiny ought to be—in the deepest theoretical, even theological, sense—to live to sing.

In this connection it is worth noting that the wonderful dirge for the 'dead' Fidele is spoken, not sung. [IV, 2.] This has often been considered odd, and various practical explanations have been proffered, such as a shortage of competent actor-singers in the company. Such a shortage may or may not have existed; in either case the speaking of the dirge is profoundly appropriate for it deals, not in any metaphysical redemption, but simply with the fact of physical cessation. That which was living—susceptible to the sun's heat and the winter's rage—is now nothingness, dust, a kneaded clod: impervious to sensation. The ritual incantation at the end forbids all super-natural intrusion ('no witchcraft charm thee'); oblivion is enough. Dramatically and poetically the point lies in the fact that Imogen and the bestially headless Cloten are buried side by side. She mistakes Cloten, in the clothes of Posthumas, for her lost husband; and is reborn in finding that which was lost and—posthumously—presumed dead. Music comes with the process of rebirth.

In some early plays Shakespeare completely inverts the normal function of music in his plays: which is to represent the timeless values beyond the distraction of Becoming. The world of *Love's Labour Lost*, for instance, is a conscious contrivance of the sophisticated mind; and here the songs serve to prick the bubble of pretence. Thus the songs 'When daisies pied' and 'When icicles hang by the wall' serve as epilogue. [V, 2.] This is what life is really like, they say, beneath all this highfalutin behaviour and quibbling over points of etiquette. Love in spring is delightful, but the cuckoo mocks in betrayal. In winter we warm ourselves at the fire, but the 'staring owl' reminds us of mortality —a most dubiously 'merry note'. The pastoral dream is replaced by reality: Joan is greasy, Marion's nose is red and raw. This is true, but not the whole truth: so the effect of these songs is simpler than that of the equivocal songs in *Twelfth Night* or

Much Ado. Again, we do not know what the original music for the songs was like. It ought to have been rather self-consciously rustic, perhaps: heavy, time-dominated in rhythm, yet a bit sophisticated too, for the implication is that although Marian's nose may be red and raw yours and mine, in our charmed circle, are not; or at least we can agree to play the game of pretending that they aren't.

The songs sung to Jacques in *As You Like It* [II, 5.] are half-way between this early, critical use of music and the more normal Shakespearean attitude. Since he is a malcontent, full of jars and discords, one would not expect him to be musical. But what he criticizes is the illusory nature of social institutions: he has no taste for the jocund music of social ceremony because he longs to hear the divine music of the spheres. You won't find that, he says, where people are engaged in the policies of the world; you may hear it, if you listen, in rural hermitage. So he stays, still listening, when the others return to the world; and at the end it is suggested that he embraces the religious life, casts humanity aside to become purely musical. Again we do not know what the music to the songs was like, but it should certainly hint remotely at the music of the spheres. Very remotely, perhaps: for Shakespeare did not believe that Jacques's misanthropy, his horrified escape from the world, was the best way to achieve knowledge of God. Nobody in this play attains the union of flesh and spirit that Shakespeare's tragic characters—such as Lear, Marina, Hermione, Cleopatra, even Anthony—seek and find. Jacques's religious retreat is a negative withdrawal; and the people who return to court celebrate worldly love in a solemn homophonic dance. They pay homage to Hymen for the very practical reason that she 'peoples every town'; and this worldly fulfilment becomes a substitute for heavenly salvation:

> Then there is mirth in heaven
> When earthly things made even
> Atone together.

So the human drama concludes in the humanist ritual of a masque: in which music ceases to represent the divine order in becoming, in association with the dance, a symbol of solidarity in this world.

While Shakespeare was writing his plays men such as Peri,

Caccini and the great Monteverdi were, in Italy, creating opera; and the essence of these first operas was that they were plays in music. The creators imagined they were reviving the dramatic techniques of classical antiquity; and however much the recitative style may have been an inevitable development out of madrigalian drama, it was intended to be of dramatic rather than of musical significance. Basically, recitative is almost a play spoken: which is why the operas have no musical structure apart from the structure of the drama. If we cannot understand the words these early operas are meaningless and tedious, except in so far as, when the voices speak in passion, the recitative is liable to be heightened to lyrical intensity—to become arioso. This happens rarely in Peri, frequently in Monteverdi who—for all his Shakespearean concern with the interplay of human passions—was pre-eminently a musical genius. In Monteverdi's early operas (as in his madrigals) music begins to become dramatic, and drama to approach the condition of music. It is not an accident that *Orfeo* should deal, mythologically, with the power of music to help man to face suffering and the fact of death.

Yet the theory behind Monteverdi's early operas is still that the play is the thing, embodied in the musically heightened speech of recitative, as Shakespeare's play is embodied in his poetically intensified dialogue. And counterpoised against the recited play is the instrumental and occasionally choral dance music, which is a direct transference of the social ritual of the masque. The sung speech is the drama of the personal life; the dance music is the communal values of the public life. Opera, as we know it, was the gradual interpenetration of these two forces: which happened from both directions. In Monteverdi's first opera the drama of sung speech became inherently musical. Complementarily, the ritual of the masque showed an increasing awareness of the realities of passion. It is this process that we have to examine in the next few chapters.

2

THE GENESIS OF MASQUE

Thomas Campion: *Masque in Honour of Lord Hayes*
William Browne: *Inner Temple Masque*
John Milton: *Comus*

Whether in folk-song or in plainchant, monody—as the term implies—is a Oneness: a religious act that expresses man's relationship to God. Man sings from his spirit, without harmonic conflict, without division, in lines that move by step or by smooth vocal intervals. Even though folk-song may be pagan rather than Christian it is still unconcerned with personal identity, seeing man's individual experience in 'elemental' terms.

In Renaissance polyphony each line—we have seen—starts from the same premises; but together the lines interact to make harmony. So polyphony is at once a religious and a social act: for the individual parts must be integrated by man's conscious volition. In homophonic dance music this equilibrium between the growth of melody and harmonic order is less evident. The imposed order of metre restricts the freedom of melodic line; the parts must move symmetrically in step, creating harmonic order, marshalled by the domination of Time. The interests of the individual are sacrificed to the whole; and in this sense dance music, at least in western Europe, tends to be a social and communal, rather than religious, activity.

Neither harmonic assertion nor a regularly periodic time-sense occur in the music of eastern civilizations, which have experienced nothing comparable with Europe's Renaissance. Though elaborate metrical patterns are, in Indian music, counterpointed against the growth of the melody, they are related to a science or magic of numbers rather than to the tread of human feet. Even in Europe, in the Middle Ages, dance music was largely functional, the metrical and harmonic pattern being repeated until the dancers got tired. Dance metres occurred in 'serious' ecclesiastical polyphony: but not in association with tonality, as a constructive principle. Again, they are related to the medieval science of numbers rather than to the passage of time. During the Renaissance, however, dance rhythm became a basic constructional principle in serious music; and the technical change was, as usual, at bottom philosophical.

In Part I we have noted that there are, in the Jacobean madrigal, two basic elements: a desire 'humanistically' to interpret a poetic text, largely through the expressive power of dissonance; and a supplementary desire to curb the turbulence of harmonic passion by means of dance rhythm. In so far as it came to terms with poetry and dancing simultaneously the madrigal is perhaps the most representative art-form of the Renaissance; certainly its preoccupation with dance rhythm reflects the profound significance which the dance had for Renaissance man. From this point of view we may say that the masque was an extension, in visible symbols, of what was implicit in madrigalian technique.

In 1596 Sir John Davies published a long poem, *Orchestra*,[1] which dealt in poetic terms with the Elizabethan theory of the dance. In defending dancing from its detractors he points out that the universe came into existence through a cosmic dance of which the motive force was love (or 'great creating Nature'):

> Dancing, bright lady, then began to be
> When the first seeds whereof the world did spring,
> The fire, air, earth and water did agree
> By Love's persuasion, Nature's mighty king,
> To leave their first disordered combating
> And in a dance such measure to observe
> As all the world their motion should preserve.

The sun, stars and moon dance their pavanes and galliards; even Time seems to be subjugated to Dancing as the minion of Love:

> Yes, Time itself, whose birth Jove never knew
> And which is far more ancient than the Sun,
> Had not one moment of his age outrun

[1] *Works of Sir John Davies*, edited by Grosart; Fuller's Worthies Series, 1869. Part of the poem is reprinted in the *Oxford Book of Sixteenth Century Verse*.

> When out leaped Dancing from the Heap of things,
> And lightly rode upon his nimble wings.

If it can subdue Time, dance movement can likewise redeem human institutions from chaos:

> If sense hath not yet taught you, learn of me
> A comely moderation and discreet,
> That your assemblies may well ordered be:
> When my uniting power shall make you meet
> With heavenly tunes it shall be tempered sweet,
> And be the model of the World's great frame,
> And you, earth's children, Dancing shall it name . . .

> For that true Love, which Dancing did invent,
> Is he that tuned the whole world's harmony,
> And linked all men in sweet society.

Moreover, the wickeder man became, the more cruelly destructive, the more was it necessary for him to frame 'grave and solemn measures' to preserve order and proportion:

> Since when all ceremonious mysteries,
> All sacred orgies and religious rites,
> All pomps and triumphs, and solemnities,
> All funerals, nuptials, and like public sights,
> All Parliaments of peace and warlike fights,
> All learned arts and every great affair
> A lively shape of dancing seem to bear.

Thus dancing is a victory of humanism, for it is a man-made order, telling us that the assertion of the ego need not mean submission to chaos. It is interesting that on several occasions in his poem Davies refers to dancing as 'this new art'. Of course it was not new; but it seemed so to the Elizabethans, in so far as they made of it a new social philosophy—almost a substitute for traditional religious belief.

From this point of view we may regard the masque as a social ceremony, a ritual of the state. It 'sublimates' into mythology the court dances with which the noble lords and ladies entertained themselves and, in so doing, expressed their pride in worldly power, their consciousness of their humanity. As symbol of their Golden Age they used the world of classical mythology precisely because that world was not Christian, and implied no separation of spirit from flesh. But the masque's vision of Concord—in which

> divers men and women ranked be
> And every one doth dance a severall part,
> Yet all as one in measure do agree,
> Observing perfect uniformity—

was not meant to be historical. Although the discussion in Davies's poem is supposed to take place in classical antiquity, the point lies in the fact that the poem ends with a prophecy. The ultimate realization of Love's order (dancing) will occur two thousand years hence, in the reign of Elizabeth: 'our glorious English court's divine image, As it should be in this our Golden Age'. So the masque was essentially contemporary: not quite art, but 'art at an emergent stage'. We can never really 'experience' a seventeenth century masque (as we can a seventeenth century play or opera), not only because we cannot adequately reconstruct the dances which—far more than the poetry or the plot—are the essence of it: but also because we can no longer enter into those dances as a ritual relevant to our own lives.

For the presentation in spectacular ceremony of the forces that lie 'behind' the madrigal becomes literally a ritual apotheosis of humanism. The point of the masque is the revelation of the masquers' identity at the end; and when the chief masquers are unmasked they prove to be not legendary creatures from classical mythology nor divine abstractions after all. They turn out to be the King and Nobility, who are the temporal State. Far from being unreal, the masque is based on the assumption that its apparent myth is fact. The gods are ourselves: or at least the King and his angel-minions, who are our representatives.

Campion's Masque in honour of Lord Hayes[1]—presented at Whitehall on Twelfth Night in 1607—is a beautiful example of this simple, ceremonially positive version of the masque. Being devised for a specific occasion, it was a ritual of contemporary life as much as a work of art: a marriage piece that paid homage to Hymen as symbol of human solidarity. In the first place, marriage is a triumph of humanism because it is sensual fulfilment.

[1] *Works of T. Campion*. Edited by Percival Vivian (O.U.P.)

So the nine masquers (the magic number, three times three) are disguised as Knights of Apollo, who is great creating Nature, 'father of youth and beauty'. The sumptuousness of the floral decor, the sensuous richness of the poetry, the lavishness of the musical equipment (a big orchestra of broken consorts, several choirs and solo singers) are not so much material ostentation as an expression of Nature's bounty. But marriage is not only sensual fulfilment; it is also togetherness, and thus a triumph of Concord. Moreover, since the lovers who are coming together are socially important people their marriage-concord is also a symbol of public unity.[1] In the lovely flower-song 'roses, the garden's pride', are 'flowers for Love and flowers for Kings, In courts desired and in weddings'. So the fulfilment of the flesh and the prosperity of the State are equated in the traditional rose image. And we must remember that this is a danced song. Not only the music but also the poetry—with its 'strow about' refrain and its slow final couplet, suggesting a formal grouping—seems to be conceived for physical movement. The song is performed by treble, tenor and bass who dance as they sing, accompanied by four sylvans with lutes and bandora. The music is formal and homophonic, with only a vestige of counterpoint and one false relation.[2] It is gracious rather than passionate: for its purpose is to celebrate the grace that comes of consummation and solidarity, rather than to express the human strife that is, in reality, necessary before such grace is attained.

The plot of the masque revolves around a discussion between Flora (equated with the sun and Nature's creativity) and Night (equated with Diana and the moon) about the relative merits of marriage and chastity. After the singing of the flower song Zephyrus prophecies faithfulness and fruitfulness; there is a song in dialogue, wherein the superiority of the married over the single state is established; and this leads into a general chorus in honour of Hymen. At this moment, however, a curtain is drawn back, revealing the hill of Diana and the grove of Night,

[1] Lord Hayes was a Scot, Honora, daughter of Lord Denny, an English girl. A dedicatory epistle comments on this 'high and everliving union between Scots and English'; King James is also equated with King Arthur, reborn in fulfilment of Merlin's prophecy.

[2] All the extant music is republished in *Songs and Dances for the Stuart Masque*. Edited by A. J. Sabol (Brown University Press, 1959).

with black pillars starred with gold, and with all manner of artificial clouds, bats, owls and other night-birds drifting about. Night has nine attendant Hours (again the magic number), each carrying a lighted torch. It appears that Night and Diana are annoyed with Flora for her insults to virginity; and in pique have turned Apollo's nine knights into trees, lest they might seduce Diana's nymphs. Out of respect to Apollo they are permitted to be *golden* trees; but this does not make them more mobile. This part of the masque is the Apollo and Dafne story in reverse.

At this point Hesperus—the evening star and guardian of the marriage-night—acts as liaison officer between day and night, persuading them to cease their 'needless jars'. Venus, the queen of love, brings 'into the naked world the green-leafed spring', and marriage is creative, like the sun. But there is no need for the moon to be jealous, both because there are plenty of virgins still left, and also because marriage has its own sanctity. These flowers, he says, are 'hallowed and immortal', the 'ceremonious ornament of maiden marriage', and 'this place is sacred'. So peace is made; Diana is content that her nymph should become a bride, especially since the marriage is graced by King James, the British Apollo: and sends a jewel, with a promise that the nine knights shall be restored to human shape. This introduces the transformation scene, the climax of the masque: in which, however, the 'ingenious ingins' did not work as well as they should have done, whether through the 'simplicity, negligence or conspiracy of the painter'. In the transformation the virtues of the old religious world and of the new 'humanistic' world are reconciled. Trees and flowers are metamorphosed into the nobility, so that human society becomes the ultimate expression of Nature's riches. But then they lay their green trappings at the foot of Diana's tree as an offering, and proceed in ritual splendour, glorious in carnation satin and silver lace, towards the bower of Flora, while a 'solemn motet' is sung to Chastity by six chapel voices, to the accompaniment of six cornets. This music is lost. It must presumably have been based on the old liturgical style: yet must have been more regularly periodic in rhythm, since both the singers and the cornet-players moved ceremonially, in procession. What was called for was a true marriage of earth and spirit—of dance homophony with vocal polyphony—such as we find in the big pavanes and galliards of Gibbons, Bull or Dowland, where the metrical basis of the dance dissolves into the interweaving counterpoints.

There is no evidence, in Campion's extant work, that he would have been able to produce such music. Indeed, the harmonically simple, non-contrapuntal nature of his music—as compared with Dowland's—is related to his interest in the masque: for masque music has to be superficial if it is not to deny the masque's evasion of some aspects of reality.[1] The dubiety of the masque composer's position is interestingly revealed in the next song. After the solemnity of the motet has been routed by a brisk dance of the violins, the masquers move forwards to make obeisances to the King and to dance with the ladies of the audience, since the private marriage must end with a vision of civilization if not as it was, at least as it seemed to be to the masquers. 'Shews and nightly revels, signs of joy and peace' will 'fill royal Britain's court while Cruel War far off doth rage, for ever hence exiled.' The Golden Age is not something out of a story-book; with sublime complacence we can believe that we have created it, as the masque's mythology merges into the junketings that round off a nobleman's party. One would expect the music to this song (it is by Thomas Lupo, not by Campion himself) to be the most proud and rhythmically stable piece in the masque. Instead, it is in an ambiguously modal minor, with many false relations; while the rhythmic periods are disturbingly asymmetrical. It is as though, momentarily, the music wants to hint at a reality which the masque denies. But the hint is too weak seriously to affect the party atmosphere, and the two final songs (by Thomas Giles and Thomas Lupo) return to a simple G major with dominant modulations and regular eight-bar clauses, emptily buoyant, making us feel good, while glossing over the imperfections of mortality.

To such a delirium of self-confidence are we carried (as the

[1] It is not an accident that Campion wrote lyrics that depend on physical dance movement rather than on subtleties of verbal inflexion; and that he was the author of a text-book called A new Way of making four Parts in Counterpoint, wherein he advocates the four-part harmonization of a 'tune', with bass and two middle parts, as opposed to the old contrapuntal discipline as taught by Morley. Published in 1614, Campion's book was still in use in the eighteenth century.

hour gets later and the wine flows freer) that we can even believe that in such a paradise on earth Time stops:

> Time that leads the fatal round
> Hath made his centre in our ground,
>   With swelling seas embraced;
> And there at one stay he rests
> And with the fates keeps holy feasts
>   With pomp and pastime graced.

But of course Time cannot really be immobilized in a human
ritual. Perhaps we can imagine it can be only if we have grown
too drunk to notice it; certainly there is evidence that effects of
bathos were common, the sublime ritual being dissipated in a
tipsy fit of the giggles on the part of the fine ladies, or even in
the collapse of the monarch himself, his inert trunk carried out
prone, covered with vomit. Not that so extreme a deflation of the
ritual of humanism was necessary: it was in any case obvious
that the vision of paradise on earth was vitiated by two related
paradoxes that Campion's masque preferred to ignore. The first
paradox is that though the King and nobility may look like God
and his angels in this transfigured Golden Age, they differ from
divine beings in that they grow old and die. Even if the Golden
Age is not an illusion, the belief that Love conquers Time is:
so if man wants to be sufficient unto himself he must accept the
limitations of mutability. Sir John Davies, again, makes this
point when he explicitly relates the order of the dance to the
order achieved by earthly power:

> Learn then to dance, you that are princes born,
> And lawful lords of earthly creatures all:
> Imitate them, and therefore take no scorn,
> For this new art to them is natural,
> And imitate the stars celestial;
>   For when pale Death your vital twist shall sever,
>   Your better parts must dance with them for ever.

Though the order of human society may simulate the order of
the heavens, pale Death is not deceived. His sinister *frisson* disturbs the gracious, lucid rhythms.

The second paradox is that man, by himself, is fallible, prone
to upset the orderly apple-cart: or, to modify the metaphor, ever
since the Fall there have been crab-apples in the Garden of

160

'Starry Quire' or 'Wavering Morrice'? The Masque and the Anti-masque
From Blake's illustrations to *Comus*

Eden. It was only because the passions of Renaissance man were so wildly exuberant that the controlling of them, in man-made institutions, was necessary: as Sir John Davies points out when he introduces the metaphor of masquers directly into his poem—

> Lastly where keep the winds their revelry,
> Their violent turnings and wild whirling hayes,
> But in the air's translucent gallery
> Where she herself is turned a hundred ways,
> While with those masquers wantonly she plays?
> Yet in this Misrule they such Rule embrace
> As two, at once, encumber not the place.

Order, that is, is valuable only in the light of what is ordered; and in admitting an 'anti-masque' of satyrs and buffoons—bubbling up from the dark of the unconscious—the Renaissance masque was following the precedent of the medieval Church which, at the Feast of Fools, encouraged a deliberate inversion of values, when choirboys became bishops and bishops choristers. Yet although the masque admitted the existence of unruly appetites and grotesque affronts to human dignity, the admission was made only to make the triumph of the masque's concord the more impressive. The dionysiac chaos does not constitute a serious threat to the masquer's earthly paradise, for the issue between Masque and Anti-masque is never in doubt. Indeed, the possibility of choice can hardly exist, in a society as serenely gracious as ours, or as we think ours is. This is why the anti-masque is fundamentally comic, or at least grotesque. The uncomfortable elements in fallen man's nature must be laughed away.

In Campion's Lord Hayes's Masque marriage-concord becomes equated with public concord in the State; the values of togetherness (marriage) and oneness (chastity) are reconciled in a union of flesh and spirit, earth and heaven. The division and strife possible in the state of 'twoness' are perfunctorily discussed in dialogue, only to be dismissed. There is no conflict; there is no anti-masque at all. In William Browne's Masque of the Inner Temple,[1] on the other hand, there is no doubt about the presence of the beastliness in corrupted man, for it is based on the (significantly popular) Circe story. From one point of view Circe is a leader

[1] *Works of William Browne.* Edited by Gordon Goodwin (The Muses Library, 1894).

of the anti-masque, a Lady of Misrule: she can disrupt Nature, make 'brave rivers run retrograde' and 'with the winter solstice bring all Flora's dainties'. Yet she is also a life-force, in so far as she is daughter to the Sun. The Sirens have to obey her until 'some greater power her hand can stay'. That power would presumably be not Nature, but God. He never appears.

The Sirens invite the sailors to 'Come on shore, where no joy dies till love hath gotten more': an eternity of sensual pleasures, which Time cannot stale, is the humanist's heaven. An anonymous setting of this Sirens' song is the only music that has survived from the masque.[1] It is a languidly passionate piece in C minor, with much expressive ornamentation and subtle verbal accentuation (consider the stress on the word 'no' in the phrase 'no joy dies'): and it can be musically alive precisely because it is not, like much masque music, a pretence. Such yearning for sensuous delight, such wistful regret at its inevitably no more than partial fulfilment, lies at the heart of all masques; and it is certainly no accident that in this case the heart-felt song marks the point where the myth is given a most interesting twist. Circe's love for Ulysses seems to become a positive: for she explains, in response to Ulysses' doubts, that the anti-masque of swine have been transformed into beasts not by her art but by their own choice. Love itself is not beastly; the beastliness is, or is not, in the mind of the lover. They—the other stupider, grosser, less favoured mortals—become pigs, dancing in clipt rhythms, farouche, ungainly, inhuman; she and Ulysses, on the other hand, fulfil their natures in loving, and so create paradise on earth. There is a kind of deceit even here, of course, for Circe's case depends on the assumption that the bestial and inchoate elements in man's nature can be dismissed by an act of conscious choice (anti-masque music is always empty and grotesque, never rhythmically complex or harmonically horrid). But Circe is sound enough on the positive side; Ulysses is convinced that their rhythms are so flowing, so compulsive, and at the same time so dignified that they seem god-like, as eternal as the sea. He accepts her belief that swinishness is unnecessary: so she wakes up the knights, not to become swine but to perform a ceremonial dance with her attendants. They 'imitate the sun', the source of life;

[1] Republished in *Songs and Dances for the Stuart Masque* (Brown University Press).

and as they dance 'move the earth to suffering' . . . 'for whilst you beat earth thus you love her'. Dressed in leaves, like Green Men, they are godly in their abundant creativity: human in their awareness of suffering and time, as their feet tread the earth, measuring mortality. Since Circe's girl attendants were originally called the Second Anti-masque but dance the final dance with the knights, we can say that the masque represents the triumph of human love over black magic and inchoate desires. God has nothing to do with it.

In this masque it is admitted that if human love seems to defeat Time it is only an illusion within the mind, not the less welcome, of course, for being illusory. 'If it lay in Circe's power Your bliss might so persever That those you chose but for an hour You should enjoy for ever.' At this point the masque turns into real life, and the unmasked knights dance with the ladies 'the old measures, galliards, corrantos, etc.' into the small hours, until the party is over. They dance 'the old measures' because Tradition gives a sense of stability. It's the best we can do to offset Time's threat: but it is not much; and the masque ends with an invocation to Time that dissolves all human delights.

In Campion's masque, then, marriage-concord is equated with public concord, and the values of togetherness (marriage) and oneness (chastity) are reconciled without conflict. In Browne's Inner Temple Masque the corruption within human nature is aggressively present, but is dismissed as unnecessary: the Anti-masque of Grillus is entirely comic, in a jogging rhythm sharply contrasted with the voluptuous elegance of the Circe poetry, and accompanied by such low instruments as 'treble violins, sagbut, cornamute, and a tabor and a pipe'. And corruption is unnecessary because man may be redeemed, not by God, but by human love. In Milton's *Comus* both the myth and the theme are the same; but the issues are immeasurably more complex because every aspect of the experience is so much more deeply felt. No longer can one say that the issue between masque and anti-masque—between good and evil—is not in doubt: for the doubt, whatever Milton's conscious doctrinal intentions, is in the poetry.

The central image of the Lady wandering, lost, 'in the blind mazes of this tangled wood', strikes home with a force quite alien to the conventionally ceremonial masque. We have all been there, in this *selva oscura*, facing the grisly shapes that peer from the trees; and that this Lady, apparently of pre-lapsarian innocence, should find herself there only makes the shock more acute. As for the anti-masque, we could never consider Comus, or even his myrmidons, as comic or grotesque. Being a piece of us, he is a sympathetic character, in a smaller way a tragic figure anticipating Milton's Satan, stealing the masque-poem as Satan steals *Paradise Lost*. He is, we remember, 'aw-strook' by the Lady's Echo-song as, in innocent solitude, she calls to her brothers—to human companionship. Indeed, paradoxically Comus first presents his rout as though it were not anti-masque but masque. He describes himself and his followers as 'Vow'd Priests' of Hecate, and says that they 'who are of purer fire [!] Imitate the Starry Quire, Who in their nightly watchful Sphears Lead in swift rounds the months and years. The Sounds and Seas with all their finny Drove Now to the Moon in wavering Morrice move.' Though we can take all this as heavy irony, it is not merely, as later events prove, a reversal of values. There is a valid relationship, Davies's poem told us, between the dance of Nature and the dance of the heavens. In a positive as well as a negative sense Comus is Nature, since he is son of Circe, who was daughter of the Sun. We may doubt whether the 'measure' which he and his rout dance is simply the 'barbarous dissonance' it seems to the (in some ways) blinkered Brothers. Certainly it is a double-edged irony indeed that Comus should describe his rout as a Starry Quire, while the Lady tells us that Nature put the stars in heaven and 'filled their lamps with everlasting oil to give due light To the misled and lonely Traveller'. Could Comus, perhaps, be a light to her?

Of course, the virtues of the Lady's virtue are not in question. The limitations of virtue are, however, unconsciously admitted: to be 'clad in compleat steel' can hardly be conducive to humanity, and Comus's defence of his earthly paradise is so rich in imagery and rhythm that we cannot believe the Lady's (and Milton's) statement that it is all deceit. With marvellous potency he evokes Nature's bounty; wherefore, he says,

> did Nature poure her bounties forth
> With such a full and unwithdrawing hand,
> Covering the earth with odours, fruits and flocks,

Thronging the Seas with spawn innumerable,
But all to please, and sate the curious taste?
And set to work millions of spinning worms,
That in their green shops weave the smooth-hair'd silk
To deck her Sons, and that no corner might
Be vacant of her plenty, in her own loyns
She hutcht th'all-worshipt ore, and precious gems
To store her children with; if all the world
Should in a pet of temperance feed on Pulse,
Drink the clear stream, and nothing wear but Freize,
Th'all-giver would be unthankt, would be unprais'd. . .

If Nature's riches are left to fust in us unused, the mind and
body will be blotched with cankers. Whatever Milton's conscious
intention, the anti-masque is here not merely presented as the
masque; it has become a positive in its own right, unironically.
The Lady's answer to this thrilling speech is oddly unconvincing.
She does not, after all, attempt to deny Nature's bounty; instead,
she introduces a note of social criticism, saying that Nature's
riches ought to be shared by all equally: which Comus has never
denied. She then curiously refers to the power of Chastity as
'Sun-clad': so it would seem that Milton's unconscious admission
is that Comus and the Lady need one another. Campion's Lord
Hayes's Masque also reconciled senses and spirit, but without
recognizing the perverse complexity of motives and impulses
that both 'virtue' and 'vice' conceal. In *Comus* the equivocation
suggests that the choice isn't simply between chastity and licence,
neither is it merely a matter of fulfilling one's sensuous nature
under the discipline of reason. That, perhaps, is the ideal. To
achieve it, however, is a more troublous matter than the Inner
Temple Masque implies.

This ambiguity of attitude remains when the story is over
and the masque returns to real life. Sabrina's chaste lyricism—
the glassy texture, the precise, meticulous movement of her
songs—is certainly a positive, and the chastity she protects in
such gem-like verse is a jewel of great price. But when the Lady
is restored to her parents we hear no more of Sabrina's watery
muse. The Lady is welcomed by a dance of masquers on the
lawns of Ludlow Castle; and this time the masquers are not ideal-
ized, idolized nobility in a legendary Golden Age but ordinary
folk, of the earth earthy. They 'triumph in victorious dance O'er

sensual Folly and Intemperance'. And then the Spirit epiloguizes. He says he must return to Heaven, having preserved order and justice; and the heaven he describes is sensual enough, if not intemperate. There 'eternal Summer dwells', and the hours are 'rosie-bosomed'. One sucks 'liquid air' and languishes on beds of hyacinths and roses, toying with Adonis. Cupid and Psyche go to bed on baroque clouds and from her 'unspotted side' joy and youth are born. This is a curious mingling of pagan and Christian symbolism: for although Psyche did not see her lover, she presumably felt him; she was hardly a virgin mother. Finally, the Spirit says he can reach to 'the green earths end' and 'to the corners of the Moon'. Both Comus (son of Circe, who was daughter of the Sun) and the Lady (dedicated to Diana) are here complementary. One could not attain to the Spirit's Heaven by pretending that Comus did not exist.

Though *Comus* may not achieve a complete resolution of these paradoxes at least it admits to their reality. And as soon as the masque recognizes the reality of conflict it ceases to be a vision of order as it is or might be and tends towards drama—whether it be poetic drama or the drama in music that came to be called opera. Despite its magnificent poetry, *Comus* is unsatisfactory as an 'entertainment' because it falls between the conventions of poetic drama and of opera. Although it contains a dramatic conflict, it does not become poetic drama because it does not create the illusion of actuality. For instance, it is within the masque convention, but dramatically ludicrous, that the Brothers should coolly discuss Divine Philosophy while they suspect that their sister is facing a fate worse than death. On the other hand, the musical elements in *Comus* do not raise it to the status of opera.[1] In a superficial sense, the music seems to be more operatic than the music in Campion's masques, because it is conceived as more or less continuous arioso, with vocal lines that follow speech inflexion. The effect of this arioso, however, tends—here, as in Lawes's songs—to be narrative rather than dramatic, because there is little interpenetration of speech-inflected melody with harmonic tension, controlled by a latent dance rhythm.

[1] All the surviving *Comus* music is republished in *Songs and Dances for the Stuart Masque*. Edited by A. J. Sabol (Brown University Press). Novello also published a cheap, more easily accessible edition, though the (Victorian) editing and continuo realization are unacceptable.

Indeed, there is less of this inner tension than there is in an ostensibly lyrical song like Dowland's *In darkness let me dwell*. This is not merely because Henry Lawes is a lesser composer than Dowland; it is also because of the hybrid nature of the convention in *Comus*. One may even suspect that the tendency towards an operatic manner is misplaced: for neither the Spirit's nor Sabrina's songs ought to suggest the immediate here-and-now, as does operatic arioso. Sabrina's 'rushy-fringed bank' is the most successful song because the most simply lyrical. The Spirit's invocation of Sabrina, though lovely, would have been still more moving in its context if it had been rhythmically more simple, more self-contained in its lyricism. Even the Lady's song, where the wayward, evolving experience of arioso would seem appropriate (since she is lost, searching for her brothers), is also an echo-song. She becomes, for the moment, disembodied, you and I lost, as well as herself; and her voice sounds to Comus like some heavenly bird. Again, the simplest lyrical setting would be more effective than arioso, however touching. Significantly, Lawes's arioso style comes off best in passages which are neither lyrical nor dramatic, but sensuous; the music describing 'young Adonis' on his bed of hyacinths and roses reaches the heart of the matter.

That matter is not, however, drama; and it would seem that, in the seventeenth century, compromise between musical and dramatic conventions did not work. The artist could, like Shakespeare, put all the action, the 'Becoming', into poetic drama and use music negatively to reinforce the drama; or he could, as Purcell was to do later, make the music become dramatic action, thereby creating opera. But masque is not opera, and a confusion of genres is bad for either. Certainly by far the richest use of the masque convention, though it involves much music, makes no approach to operatic techniques. On the contrary, Shakespeare's *The Tempest* is the work of a professional dramatist.

3

MASQUE INTO POETIC DRAMA

William Shakespeare: *The Tempest*

Like Campion's Lord Hayes's Masque and Browne's Inner Temple Masque, *The Tempest* deals with Man's potentialities, though the Golden Age is now within the mind rather than without; like Milton's *Comus*, it deals with Man's corruption and the possibility of redemption. The difference lies, of course, in the subtlety and humanity of Shakespeare's apprehension of the relationship between good and evil; and it was precisely because of the depth of his understanding that he transformed the masque from ritual into art. The basic themes and conventions of the masque have become dramatic poetry.

As in the real masque, the King and nobility are the masquers, the potential representatives of God on earth. But whereas the king and nobility are presented, in the masque, as symbols of human perfection, the king and nobility in *The Tempest* are fallible sinners, being guilty of usurpation. This is not, of course, a new theme in Shakespeare who, all through his career, has asked how far man can be, should be, a law unto himself; and has suggested that all human authority, simply because it is human, inevitably involves a degree of usurpation. Prospero, when he lived in the real world, had been a Duke, a ruler, a master of men. He has, however, withdrawn from temporal reality, and in so doing has relinquished his power in the State. He has done this, we are told, partly as a consequence of usurpation: but also by conscious choice, since he has been more concerned with his Art—which explores man's moral and spiritual nature—than with practical affairs. He admits that the usurpation was in part his fault, for in neglecting his worldly duties he 'awaked an evil nature' in his brother. [I, 2, 88.] Indeed, that Prospero and Antonio *are* brothers is significant; they are the light and the dark complements of Renaissance man's desire for self-sufficiency. Prospero would be god; Antonio 'is what he is', oblivious of and contemptuous of divinity: so that both are guilty of pride, deadliest of the deadly sins. But Prospero's 'fault' is not all deadly; in so far as it brings in a Christian overtone it becomes, like Adam's, a source of blessing. He goes over the sea —the unknown and unknowable that surrounds our waking lives: the unconscious from which our conscious reason springs —with his baby daughter, and the winds of the tempest 'did them but loving wrong'. They were 'blessedly holp hither'. [I, 2, 58-148.]

The island on which we find Prospero and Miranda is outside Time, a state of mind rather than a physical fact. Here Prospero has exercised his Art—Renaissance man's aspiration towards Godhead through learning, nurture and self-knowledge. He has a degree of control over nature; like Browne's Circe, he can provoke tempests, play havoc with the seasons, and prophetically disrupt the natural order in the sundry ways that post-Renaissance man has been able to explore through the agency of Science. Further, he fulfils an ideal of Renaissance man in that he has both spirit (Ariel) and flesh (Caliban) under his control. They are, or at least he thinks they are, his servants. Through his metaphysical studies he has been able to release Ariel from imprisonment by the witch Sycorax, whose name means crooked, and who derives her power from a dead planet, the moon, and a moon-god Setebos, whose name means hostile. So we may say that Sycorax is the Earth fallen, dead and corrupted; and that fallen Earth, having locked up the Spirit in a devilishly cloven pine, could not free it again. Ariel suffered 'a torment to lay upon the damned, Which Sycorax could not again undo'. Only through man's aspiration to grace can fallen men be redeemed and the spirit liberated: so Prospero says, justly, 'it was *my* art made gape the pine and let you out'. [I, 2, 286.]

This is a heroic achievement: though there is a fallacy—and a deficiency in self-knowledge—in Prospero's freeing Ariel from the pine only in order to make a slave of him. Not until the end of the play do we (and Prospero) realize this: that there is something odd about the relationship between Caliban and Prospero is evident from the beginning. Caliban, we are told explicitly, is a bastard son of Sycorax, got by the devil. He is a consequence of

169

the Fall, lapsed man in a state of nature. He is repeatedly described as a fish, a direct descendent from the sea of the unconscious and the slime of creation. [V, 1, 267.] Since both the sea and his mother were controlled by the moon, he's sometimes called a moon-calf, and Stephano, facetiously pretending to be his god, refers to himself as 'the Man i'the Moon, when time was'. There is a parallel by opposites between Caliban as Sycorax's son and Miranda as Prospero's daughter. He, the offspring of fallen Nature, is one 'on whose Nature Nurture can never stick'; so although Prospero tries to teach him Reason—for Renaissance man the gateway to self-knowledge—he fails. Caliban is only further corrupted by knowledge and experience: 'you taught me language and my profit on't is, I know how to swear'. [I, 2, 319 et seq.] Miranda, on the other hand, as the offspring of man's aspiration to natural and supernatural knowledge, learns by experience. Caliban has never seen a woman other than her and his mother (whom she excels 'as great'st does least', being man's chance of a rebirth after the Fall); she has never seen a man other than Caliban and her father. Their two kinds of innocence are thus complementary. Miranda's is the point from which true knowledge and experience starts; his is the irrational element within man's nature that cannot be—perhaps, as Prospero learns, shouldn't be—tamed and mastered.

Because they are complementary, one cannot adequately understand Prospero's relationship to Caliban apart from his relationship to his daughter. It is impossible to read, still less witness, the early exposition scene between Prospero and Miranda without feeling that Prospero, as man-god, comes off poorly; and one certainly can't explain away this impression by saying that Prospero's testy and schoolmasterish behaviour is a stage device for conveying essential information. Prospero's metaphysical studies, his aspirations to divinity, impressive though they may be, seem to have chilled his humanity: whereas Miranda, 'ignorant' though she may be of what *she* is, is all compassionate awareness of other people's suffering. She suffers with those that she saw suffer; her heart 'bleeds' for them; she says never a word about her own pain, only deplores the trouble she must have caused her father ('Alack, what trouble was I then to you'). So we may say that Miranda is the humanity Prospero has forgotten in pursuing his divine ambitions. She is indeed the descendent of Cordelia, who was the true *heart* that Lear denied, and of Perdita, the good that Leontes *lost*; and she is her father's futurity in that, through her, he must be born again.

Prospero's harsh treatment of Caliban is thus an extension of his attitude to his daughter. He beats him with briars because he is scared of him; he fears that godly ambitions would be doomed if the inchoate desires beneath the surface of his nature were allowed to come into conflict with Reason and the Will. This is the more pointed if one remembers that Caliban, like Ariel, is in one sense within Prospero's own psyche. Since Miranda is life untainted but already suffering, while Caliban is Original Sin, it is inevitable that he should attempt to ravish her; and if his violation is in fact incestuously Prospero's, we can understand why the god-man's attitude to the uninhibited libido should at times approach hysteria. Caliban is probably right when he refers to some of his Prospero-induced tormentors as agents of the devil. Man may sometimes be more devilish than the devil's earthly progeny.

Into contact with these inhabitants of the magic island—Prospero, Miranda, Caliban and Ariel—come the representatives of 'real' life. Like Prospero and Miranda before them, only guided by Prospero's volition, they travel over the unknown sea, through the tempest of suffering. In the storm that opens the play the anonymous Boatswain is a kind of yardstick of common humanity, impervious to, because ignorant of, the fury of the unknown and the unconscious. He admits that he loves none more than himself, has no criterion but self-comfort; and shouts that if anyone claims to have power over the sea's tumult, let him use it. ('What care these roarers for the name of King? Use your authority . . . If you cannot, give thanks you have lived so long.') Gonzalo, the aged counsellor, simplest and most honest of the people from the real world, sees that there is something to be said for the Boatswain's attitude, if one hopes to stay quietly happy; but neither he nor the other noblemen can accept it, if only because they're more 'conscious', or merely better educated. Their response varies between Gonzalo's appeal for 'patience' and Sebastian's cry that he is 'out of patience'. Lack of patience leaves no resource but impotent cursing ('A pox o' your throat, you bawling, blasphemous, incharitable dog'): the braggadocio of desperation ('We are less afraid to be drown'd than thou art'): and the shifting of the blame for one's misfortunes on to someone else ('We are merely cheated of our lives by drunkards').

Prospero's island, to which the seafarers are guided by Ariel's magic, has the fauna and flora of a masque decor. There is, however, an important distinction between the Golden Age of the masque and *The Tempest*'s island: for the real masque presents us with what seems to be a legendary world but turns out to be the world in which we live, or think we live; whereas the world of *The Tempest* also appears legendary but differs from the masquers' world in being outside Time. The play is about the effect —or, in the case of some of the characters, the lack of effect— of such an excursion outside Time on people who are as time-ridden and earth-bound as are most of us.

Gonzalo is good, but simple: which is a different matter from being stupid. Though he seems to some of the characters an old bore, he is also representative of the possibilities of simple moral worth in the ordinary world. It was he who saved the lives of Miranda and Prospero in the first place. It is he, as we have seen, who advocates 'patience'—a key-word in Shakespeare ever since *King Lear*—during the storm that opens the play. Though he prays that 'the wills above be done', he is not ashamed to ask for 'a dry death', an 'acre of barren ground', rather than 'a thousand furlongs' of the unknowable sea. But although he has not Prospero's divine-seeking Art, he repeatedly uses religious language, says they were saved by 'a miracle' and is, at the end, described by Prospero as 'holy Gonzalo'. His humanism carries its own sanctity, which is all that most men can reasonably expect. Because he is single-hearted, he can see the island as 'lush and hospitable' and can find divine sanction in the preservation of their clothes from the storm's fury. At the same time, his simple goodness has to learn not to tolerate but to accept the existence of evil. In the course of the play he learns to weep: and to relinquish his material vision of a Golden Age in which everyone would be free and no one sinful—the masque-paradise come true. Sebastian points out that though there would be no sovereignty in Gonzalo's ideal commonwealth, yet Gonzalo would be king of it. [II. 1. 137 et seq.]

Of course the mere existence of people like Sebastian and Antonio, alongside Gonzalo, makes evident that the Golden Age does not square with the facts of (lapsed) human nature. What hope can there be for the simple-hearted and single-minded when the affairs of the world are run by people who believe neither in man nor god: who having no motive but self-interest, explain away everything in negatives? ('I have no hope that he's un-drown'd' is their way of saying I hope he's drowned.) They are frighteningly modern types: Antonio, the smart alec, the cynic who knows all the answers without ever having asked any of the questions that matter; Sebastian, the weak man, who jeers, with Antonio, at both simple goodness and divine aspiration, not through deliberate malice, but out of the pettiness of his heart. Together, they live on derision, blaspheming against Nature *and* Nurture; and this is the more wicked because, unlike Stephano and Trinculo, they are nobly born and ought to know better. Antonio, the usurper and Prospero's dark complement, is the last of Shakespeare's egoist-villains. He believes in nothing save 'I am that I am', and has his own kind of rock-bottom courage. But even his courage is mean; he has none of Edmund's (or Comus's) satanic majesty, nor Iago's superhuman cunning.

Between the extremes of Gonzalo's humane credulity and Antonio's destructive cynicism stands Alonso, the king who has betrayed his trust: a guilty man with a conscience who believes that, for his sin, he has lost a son, his life's continuity. In fact, his 'fault' goes deeper, for he has lost a daughter also. [II, 1, 62 et seq.] The contrast is emphasized between Prospero who preserved himself in preserving Miranda out of the storm, and Alonso who was wrecked while returning from the marriage of his daughter Claribel to the king of Tunis. Whereas Prospero finds himself in finding Miranda, Alonso gives his daughter away, in a far country, to a black man she doesn't love; and Claribel's name makes the contrast between her luminosity and her husband's darkness the more telling. Gonzalo and the smart alecs, in conversation about the marriage, make great play with the identity between Tunis and the Carthage of antiquity; and re-peated harping on the Dido story emphasizes the theme of be-trayal. This time the father, not the husband, is the betrayer, and Antonio is correct—in his habitual anti-compassionate, unimaginatively reasonable way—to say 'The fault's your own'. This tells us that Antonio's 'reason' knows nothing of the heart: but also hints—at a level of which Antonio certainly wasn't conscious—at the affinity between Alonso's sin of insufficient love and Prospero's neglect of worldly duty.

The destiny of these creatures from the material world is worked out by Prospero—man with god-like potentialities—through the agency of Ariel, who is the Spirit he thinks he has tamed. Being pure spirit, Ariel is purely musical; and his music, unlike that in Shakespeare's other plays, directly influences the action. Thus the effect of the first song he sings to Ferdinand —'Come unto these yellow sands' [I, 2, 375.]—is to help him transmute his personal sorrow in the communal innocence of childhood (a round game) and in the courteous ceremony of a masque dance, through which the 'wild waves' may be stilled. But the charm would not work if the transmuting were merely an evasion; and the watch-dogs that bark 'dispersedly' are not the less potent for being a long way off. They, the hounds and satyrs of the anti-masque, are the Caliban within us; while the reference to 'strutting Chanticleer' telescopes the idea of a new dawn with that of treachery and betrayal (Peter's cock). Just as evil would seem to be necessary in the purgatorial process, so death is the necessary prelude to rebirth. When, a moment later, Ariel sings the sea-dirge 'Full fathom five' we learn that Ferdinand's father, who is not in fact dead, must *suffer* a sea-change in the waters of the unconscious; his eyes will become pearls when he learns to see. The bell-tolling burden is a death-knell that affirms life. In such songs Ariel's music must be innocent and artless, like folk-song: but also sexless and spiritually ecstatic, like plainchant. Robert Johnson's charming contemporary settings hardly achieve this; but there are few composers who could have achieved it, just as Ariel is a part that is virtually impossible to play.

Ariel's songs to Ferdinand effect a spiritual change in him which makes it possible for him to bear suffering. The suffering of the son parallels that of the father: for Prospero pretends to accuse him of treachery and usurpation, and submits him to the ordeal of the woodcarting. [III, 1.] But Ferdinand punningly says that this (material) heaviness is (spiritual) light to him; and his purgatory doesn't hurt very much, because Shakespeare didn't believe that the sins of the father are visited on the children. Moreover, Ferdinand falls in love with Miranda while carting the wood; and this is part of Prospero's plan for righting old wrong. Ferdinand suffers with and for his guilty father; Miranda suffers because, in her untainted innocence, she is essentially compassionate. This is why Ferdinand thinks her a goddess, perfect and peerless, 'created of every creature's best', as compared with the women he has known in the ordinary world; that she should think him divine is understandable enough. Because they love in suffering, their bodily passion may be equated with spiritual grace: as is marvellously epitomized in Prospero's compositely metaphorical blessing—'Heaven rain grace on that which breeds between 'em'.

Ariel's music varies considerably, of course, according to whom it is played to, and the different characters respond to it in different ways. Ferdinand hears everything that Ariel puts into the songs he sings him; but the 'solemn music' Ariel plays to the other noblemen has no consistent effect. [II, 1, 176.] It lulls the 'good Gonzalo' to sleep immediately, and the conscience-stricken Alonso (who wants to sleep but can't) after a while. Sebastian and Antonio, on the other hand, plot their treachery while the others sleep. In planning to betray the betrayer they suggest how treachery feeds endlessly on itself; and Sebastian hints that Antonio's wakeful words are in truth a sort of sleep, bringing not peace but nightmare. ('It is a sleepy language, and thou speak'st Out of thy sleep. What is it thou didst say? This is a strange repose, to be asleep With eyes wide open; standing, speaking, moving, And yet so fast asleep.') There are many echoes here of Macbeth's murder of sleep, and Antonio too says he has no such 'deity' as conscience in his bosom. Engrossed in their destructive self-interest they cannot, of course, hear the divine music at all—almost certainly a fancy for strings.

Sometimes Ariel's music is deliberately a deceit: as is the catch that literally 'catches out' Stephano and Trinculo, or the pipe and tabor that lead the anti-masque of drunkards and monster into the mire, where they belong. [III, 2, 120.] This would be 'low' music, folk-like, but tenuous and rarified. In so far as Stephano and Trinculo hear any music it is, or seems to them to be, 'bad' music in the Elizabethan sense. But Caliban, who speaks in verse, can hear Ariel's heavenly music since although he is below reason he is not, like Stephano and Trinculo, corrupted by conscious volition. For him, the isle is 'full of music'; and his tragedy is that being beyond Art, Reason or Nurture, a natural corrupted not by his own fault but by the Fall, he cannot recognize heavenly music when he hears it. Though he knows, dreamily, that the music hints at a beauty he has lost or never known for what it is, he kneels to worship the urban sots, brave gods 'that bear celestial liquor'. He calls Stephano a 'wondrous man'; and in a material sense imagines himself aspiring to his 'godly' power: 'Beat him . . . after a little time, I'll beat him too'. His 'new master' won't produce a 'new man'. The pathos in his position consists in the fact that he, a natural rebel against Prospero's reason ('Flout 'em and 'scout 'em. Thought is free'), puts himself in thrall to urban man in its lowest common denominator, and instigates yet another treachery: the rebellion of this lowest against the highest of which man is, however misguidedly, capable. Perhaps this is inevitable because the Prospero-Caliban relationship is, as we have seen, of its nature false, whereas like seeks like as Stephano and Trinculo become mingled with their moon-calf under the gaberdine, when the 'dregs of the storm' (appropriate metaphor) are not quite past. Caliban worships a false god, more corrupted than himself; but we can hardly be surprised that he fails to worship a Prospero who feared him and who was himself a usurper, depriving Caliban of the Eden of which he had been king.

Caliban's worship of Stephano suggests another relation by opposites between him and Miranda. Both, in their innocence, mistake human beings for gods; but whereas his choice is as wide of the mark as could be, hers at least makes sense, because she and Ferdinand, in loving one another, strive to fulfil their humanity: which proves to be about as far as human beings can go in the aspiration to godhead. Moreover, though Miranda's innocence can hardly bear to look on Caliban's innocence, they are complementary. As she grows up, and loves Ferdinand, she will learn to deal with Caliban with the compassion her father hasn't been able to manifest. In this sense her suffering future is part of her father's growth to self-knowledge; and there is a similarity between the relationship of Caliban to Miranda and that of Comus to the Lady. The 'Sauvage Man' is not only the chaos of bestiality; he is also the instinctive springs of animal life which man, being an animal, cannot ignore, or ignores to his peril.

On several occasions Shakespeare uses conventions directly

derived from the masque. The first is the Banquet of Life [III, 3], presented by 'Strange Shapes' in a ritual dance, to Ariel's 'Solemn and Strange Music' (perhaps a fancy for oboes or recorders). The reactions of the various characters to this show are interesting. Gonzalo says it is 'marvellous sweet music'. Alonso asks 'What harmony is this?'—with a question mark. Sebastian and Antonio do not mention the music at all, probably don't hear it, but make facetious comments on the 'shapes'. Sebastian suggests that they should make use of this show gratuitously provided by the island's entertainments committee. Alonso maintains that the food ought not to be touched: but is persuaded by Gonzalo, the man of faith, that he 'need not fear'. The banquet may be an allusion to the banquet that was among the temptations of Christ as well as to Eve's apple (Antonio compares the whole island to an apple, to put in your pocket and take home). But it seems more probable that the banquet is not an illusion; and that the point is that these erring mortals are not yet ready to celebrate. With thunder and lightning, Ariel descends like a Harpy, half woman (flesh) and half bird (spirit), and snatches the banquet away. Then he makes a speech—which Gonzalo does not hear—to the 'three men of sin'. He says they have 'drowned their proper selves'. The 'never-surfeited sea' has thrown them up on this 'most desolate isle'—desolate to them, not to Gonzalo—because they were 'unfit to live'. Only if they suffer a sea-change, being renewed in the waters they have drowned themselves in, will they find 'a clear life ensuing'. He vanishes with more thunder, and a soft, gentle music follows— a dance piece, contrapuntal in style, probably scored for recorders—to which the Shapes remove the banquet.

At this point, nemesis begins. Prospero says Ariel's harpy was a figure of 'grace'; and Alonso tells Gonzalo—who stands 'rapt, in the name of something holy'—how for him the tempest seemed to sound like music: how the thunder became a 'deep and dreadful organ pipe' that did 'bass my trespass'. As a consequence of this, he must seek his son—even though he must descend deeper 'than e'er plummet sounded'. Antonio and Sebastian merely trust to their swords ('I'll fight their legions o'er'), which Ariel has already proved impotent. In so far as they do not learn by experience, the smart-alecs turn out to be the fatheads.

The second appearance of the masque convention occurs a little later [IV, 1], when Prospero puts on a marriage-show for Ferdinand and Miranda. Like Campion's Lord Hayes's Masque and Milton's *Comus*, this accords equal rights to flesh and spirit; and Prospero prefaces the masque with a speech about the importance of pre-marital chastity and the holy significance of these 'sanctimonious ceremonies'. While this would have been much more meaningful to an early seventeenth than to a twentieth century audience, we have also to see Prospero's somewhat frenetic comments on chastity in the light of his own fear of the Caliban within him. This is probably why the masque seems, in the stylization of its rhyming couplets, deliberately removed from the real world, as the true masque was not. Prospero himself calls it a 'vanity' of his Art; and Iris's richly sensuous vision of Nature's bounty—

> Earth's increase, foison plenty,
> Barns and garners never empty,
> Vines and cluttering branches growing,
> Plants with goodly burden bowing:
> Spring come to you at the farthest
> In the very end of harvest!
> Scarcity and want shall shun you,
> Ceres' blessing so is on you—

is tempered by a reference to the Persephone story that brings in the Fall, and by touches in the ceremony that might almost be suspected of discreet parody (for instance, Juno's notorious approach). [IV, 1, 85.] It is as though Prospero were saying: 'the masque's golden age is only a dream. Both chastity and marriage may be holy—or may be vicious; to pretend otherwise is make-believe'. His own redemption begins when he turns suddenly and brusquely away from the show, which vanishes in 'a strange, hollow, and confused Noise'. Significantly, he says the masque had made him forget Caliban. He turns from it to Caliban's pathetic revolt, not because the revolt constitutes a serious threat, but because it reminds him of man's folly and mortality. But it is not Caliban he is really thinking of; it is himself—or at least the Caliban that is part of him.

So immediately he makes his speech about the cloud-capped towers: which is the beginning of his self-knowledge; an admission that though man's god-like reason and spiritual potentiality may carry him far beyond Caliban's bestiality, yet they too are limited. Our life is little, rounded with a sleep, because there are mysteries we can never penetrate. He finds self-knowledge perturbing, as we all do, and begins, perhaps, to feel obscurely guilty over Caliban: which is why it is now he who is troubled, disturbed, and the young people, Ferdinand and Miranda, who are at the threshold of life and have had as yet no thought but to live, who wish *him* peace. This is a remarkable development: Prospero, who has been liberal in bestowing blessings on, and withholding them from, other people, is himself blessed by the young who have not attained, and never will attain, a god-like detachment from human suffering. This is implicit in the restoration scene, when Prospero reveals the young lovers playing chess. [V, 1, 172.] In playing chess together they are growing up, controlling their destinies as well as they are able, working out their conflicts; not always will Ferdinand be able so blandly to deny Miranda's accusation that he plays her false. Though the masque will come true for them it is not an end, not the 'paradise' that Ferdinand says it is. Time will bring them their Winter's Tale; they may drink, and see the spider.

It is this recognition of man's ultimate limitations that prompts Prospero to 'abjure his book' [VI, 33], forgive more fallible mortals, and return to the world. He says that he (like Browne's Circe, daughter to the sun) has learned to some extent to control Nature; to 'bedim the noontide sun', 'call forth the mutinous winds', split the atom, and so on. He even blasphemously says that he has brought the dead to life—significantly his first reference to powers that would have seemed to contemporary audiences black magic rather than white. Most of this magic has been fulfilled by post-Renaissance science: hearts that had ceased have been made to beat again. Yet Prospero now sees that this magic is 'rough' because incomplete and never to be completed. For this reason he will relinquish it, after a final invocation of heavenly music to restore the erring humans to their true selves. Ariel says that, if he were human, he would show pity; and Prospero sees that 'the rarer action is in Virtue than in vengeance.' When he weeps for Gonzalo—as holy but humble Gonzalo had wept for others—he is reborn, reinheriting his daughter's compassion.

So the restoration scene is the masque-finale, when the

masquers discard their false-seeming. 'Though the seas threaten, they are merciful; I have cursed them without cause', says Ferdinand as he kneels to receive his guilty father's blessing; and the Christian concept of redemption comes in when Prospero reproves Alonso for despair. [V, 1, 139.] 'Irreparable is the loss', says Alonso, 'and patience says it is past her cure': to which Prospero retorts 'I rather think you have not sought her help, of whose soft grace for the like loss I have her sovereign aid. And rest yourself content.' Physically, Alonso is a dying man, destroyed by the 'deity' conscience that Antonio knows nothing of; but spiritually he lives, for he learns to accept death—returning to the 'mudded ooze' whence life sprang—without despair. Though he goes home to die, his sin of accidia is purged.

When Miranda says 'O brave new world that has such creatures in it' she speaks with the wisdom of innocence, for everyone is offered 'a second life'; they may be new-born in finding themselves, whereas before 'no man was his own'. Alonso finds himself and, in being forgiven, recovers the son he had lost; perhaps he finds the daughter he had given away also, for Gonzalo hints at some kind of reconciliation to the foreign marriage. Gonzalo, who had dared less, has less to save, yet he too grows wiser as well as older, as he learns to 'weep' for the evil in man's nature. He gives up the folly of pretending that the Golden Age is realizable simply through man's innate goodness, and comes to see the island as a deceit, a place to escape from ('Some heavenly power guide us Out of this fearful country').

The character who learns most through the purgatorial process is, of course, Prospero himself, who in a sense instigates retribution for his own salvation. In so far as he abrogates to himself qualities that belong to God, he is simultaneously heroic and sinful, a Faustian figure; and the point of the play is that he, far more than Alonso and Gonzalo, learns humility. He 'finds himself' in recognizing that he need no longer be afraid of Caliban; in being able at last to say 'This thing of darkness I Acknowledge mine'. [V, 1, 274.] (Observe how painfully Prospero has to strain across from his end-stressed 'I' to his acknowledgement.) And as soon as the 'monster' is freed he ceases to be monstrous, no longer needs his freedom, indeed, but says he will be 'wise hereafter, and seek for grace'. [V, 1, 294.] Man's instinctive animal nature can be redeemed, if it is accepted for what it is.

Moreover, Prospero's acknowledgement of Caliban is inseparable from his freeing of Ariel, who is also beyond the control of Reason. Prospero accepts Caliban's irrationality; and learns that the Ariel-spirit comes where it listeth, and cannot be controlled by a conscious exercise of man's will. His two discoveries are perhaps at bottom identical: for in his final song of liberty Ariel tells us that he is at home with bats and owls as he is with bees and blossom. [V, 1, 88.] Ariel and Caliban cannot exist apart from one another.

The process of redemption is not, however, universal. While Caliban admits the possibility of grace, Antonio can see nothing to him but 'a plain fish' that might 'no doubt, be marketable'. [V, 1, 264.] Miranda's 'wonder' is indeed not for him; his only notion of value is commercial. He and Sebastian remain the same negative smart-alecs at the end as they were at the beginning. During the restoration scene Sebastian allows a 'Most high miracle' (which may possibly be ironic) to escape his lips, but Antonio utters never a word. Only when the low characters— Stephano and Trinculo and the mariners—re-enter does he feel on safe ground again, and so able to resume his derisive banter, which Sebastian soon sycophantically copies. They cannot 'seek for grace' since grace is beyond their comprehension.

Stephano and Trinculo, their low complements, are also probably beyond redemption; certainly they are shown up in comparison with Caliban, when they are so easily seduced by the gaudy new clothes with which Prospero tempts them from their own usurpation. [IV, 1, 221.] The new clothes motive is here blasphemously inverted, for the clothes become, as Caliban says, 'trash', a commodity. But the trash saves them from the consequences of their sin, because they aren't, compared with Antonio, sinful at all, only irremediably trivial and sottishly irresponsible. Maybe there is even a hint of a partial redemption for them, for Stephano says, as he staggers in in his stolen apparel, 'Every man shift for all the rest, and let no man take care for himself'. He is probably saying what he thinks he means backwards, because he is drunk; even so, the subconscious may be uttering its own truth. [V, 1, 256.]

Though *The Tempest* is based on the traditional masque theme and uses masque conventions, there is a certain queasiness beneath the joy with which it ends: a wry quality that is not present in the apotheosis scenes in *The Winter's Tale* and *Pericles*. It is at once a triumph of humanism and a recognition of humanism's inadequacy. Prospero breaks his staff and *drowns* his book —returns it to the unconscious waters from which it came. When he returns to the real world he says he has now only his own strength, 'which is most weak'; and that his 'every third thought' will be his grave. This probably doesn't mean that he gives up the struggle towards an almost god-like assertion of Renaissance man's powers: only that he now admits the validity of that 'almost', and sees his endeavours in relation to what he can know of the will of God, not man. Recognizing that his life is little and the dark sea surrounding it so vast, he turns to us, the audience, and says that he cannot be the arbiter of his own, let alone any one else's, destiny, but is dependent on our prayers. He, who has shown divine-seeming mercy to others, asks for mercy from us, which alone can save him from despair and free his 'fault'. And then, with a final shift, he puts us in his place: 'as *you* from crimes would pardoned be, Let your indulgence set me free': for *in potentia* he is Everyman.

4

MASQUE INTO OPERA

Shirley-Locke-Christopher Gibbons: *Cupid and Death*[1]
John Blow: *Venus and Adonis*[2]

It is not an accident that the growth of the masque to operatic maturity coincided, in this country, with its decline as court ritual. With the triumph of the Puritan cause—and of the middle-class mind—the masque disappeared as a state-ritual, while surviving as an entertainment in the more fashionable schools and private houses. Inevitably, its golden-age grandeur was tarnished. Though the traditional themes and properties were maintained, they embraced an increasing degree of realism and even of destructive satire—the antithesis of the celebrative idea of the true masque. This is clear enough in Shirley's *Cupid and Death*, which was first produced in 1653 before the Portuguese ambassador: but simply as a 'good private entertainment' with scenes that 'needed no elegance or curiosity for the delight of the spectators.' It was revived in 1659, and the music has reached us in a score copied in Matthew Locke's own hand for this performance. Most of the music is by Locke himself, though a few numbers are ascribed unambiguously to Christoper Gibbons who possibly wrote all the music for the first performance. In any case the second performance—for which Locke was musical director—was obviously much more liberally supplied with music; and the additional numbers are the most ostensibly operatic.

The story, though based on classical mythology, has a low rather than heroic origin, being derived from one of Aesop's fables, some of which had appeared in English verse paraphrase by John Ogilby in 1651. Traditionally, the piece is about love

---

[1] Stainer and Bell. Republished in *Musica Britannica*. Edited by E. J. Dent.
[2] Editions de L'Oiseau Lyre. Edited by Anthony Lewis.

and time; but its mood is strikingly different from either the wistful lyricism of Campion's Lord Hayes Masque or the darkly sumptuous imagination of Milton's *Comus*. The setting is realistic; and Shirley's blank verse is so blank as to be almost prose. Moreover, although many survivals of the masque are mingled with the play-element, the comic aspects of the anti-masque outweigh the ceremonial aspects of the masque proper. The play itself may not probe very deep, though it goes deeper than its conscious intention. Certainly its realism is a step towards a new reality: in which sense it provides a link between Milton's *Comus* and Blow's *Venus and Adonis*.

We begin with an overture which is a miniature suite of masque dances. Though majestic, it has an earthy vigour both in its rhythms and in the acrid bite of the harmonies; the bass line of the curtain-tune, for instance, is remarkably angular, suggesting muscular energy, even tension, rather than a ceremonial swagger. The story opens, in prosy verse, outside an Inn, where the Host is telling the Chamberlain that Cupid and Death, overtaken by bad weather, are going to lodge for the night. They chatter, in mildly facetious vein, about their distinguished guests; and the first Masque Entry occurs when Cupid comes in, attended by Madness and Folly. The Entry consists of a dance overture in two parts (duple rhythmed and triple rhythmed), a song in arioso style, and an air with chorus. The singers are all outside the action; there is, as yet, no conscious involvement of the drama in music. This is why the arioso that describes Cupid, or that tells us how feeble is python-slaying Apollo compared with Love, is Lawesian in style: with physically illustrative ornamentation but no dramatic 'enactment'. Only when the chorus sing a dance-aria about love's taming of 'fiery spirits' is there a hint of emotional reality: consider the diminished fourth in the fugato theme, or the flattened F that makes the rocks 'cold'. But this is still theatrical, not dramatic, music: an interlude in a spoken play.

The second Entry, that of Death, follows immediately, and has the same structure—two-part overture, dance, arioso, air and chorus. Death's disturbing presence is allowed into the world of the masque, which had always tried to deny his existence. But he is permitted only because he can, in this relatively low context, be treated frivolously: can be laughed at, if not laughed away. Indeed, the point is going to be that, through human agency, the activities of Death and Love may be interchanged. So immediately after Death's entry, he is deflated by a comic scene: a man, personifying Despair, comes in with a halter round his neck, seeking Death; the Chamberlain gets him drunk in order to gull him into making a will in the Chamberlain's favour, but the effect of the sack makes him renounce death instead of life.

Up to this point Death's music, though more angular and jerky than, is not radically different from, that of Cupid; certainly it is grotesque rather than frightening. A change occurs, however, in Death's arioso, air and chorus, which balance those sung about Love in the previous Entry. For although the music is still outside the action, it is now more emotionally involved, since it acquires disturbing elements which are alien to the detached facetiousness of the drama. The arioso line, with its passionate descent through a diminished seventh on the word 'earth', is unexpectedly powerful; while the irregular, slightly distraught rhythmic periods of the air and chorus, the nervous oscillations between major and minor third, the melodic diminished fourth, the sharply dissonant suspensions, reveal an apprehension of 'reality' beneath the play's jaunty banter. It is interesting that Death seems here to be equated with Love in a way that is not merely a jape. 'He hath at will More quaint and subtle ways to kill; A smile, a kiss, as he will use the art, Shall have the cunning still To break a heart': one might well take this as a seventeenth century account of Cupid's activities.

This music, perhaps surviving from the original version, is by Christopher Gibbons. It ends in E minor; and Locke abruptly starts off the next entry in F major. This may be mere carelessness; or it may be meant to give us a shock in transporting us back to the world of mundane actuality, when the Chamberlain discloses, in dialogue, his trumpery plot. While Love and Death slept he has interchanged their arrows, and what fun it will be to watch the consequences! There may be a kind of idiot pride in a mortal thus playing hanky-panky with elemental forces but, as events prove, it is a singularly stupid power-complex. The music is aware of this, as the actors are not: indeed one might say that whereas in Campion's Lord Hayes's Masque or in Milton's Comus the 'social' music is unaware of the realities of the poetry, in *Cupid and Death* the music approaches the reality that the play evades; that is why it makes a step from social function towards opera. When Cupid gets up and leaves, in ignorance of his fatal powers, soprano arioso and then chorus sing of the 'pain' that he will inflict on lovers. The pathetic music, with its 'wounding' chromatics and stabbing diminished fourths, sees behind the joke of human irresponsibility an inescapable reality. Love ought, in a Golden Age, to be all a bed of roses. But roses, alas, have thorns—that 'make them bleed that should be billing'. There is a sense in which Cupid is Death: consider the seventeenth century image that identifies the ultimate consummation of the sexual act with dying. This apprehension of 'reality' is intensified and developed in the long arioso that follows. Significantly, it is not sung by an anonymous musician but by Nature, and there is even a brief part for a dying lover. So although this arioso is still narrative, in Lawes's manner, it is acquiring much greater immediacy. The ornamentation (for instance on the word 'murdering') has muscular energy; and the madrigalian device of false relation turns into a startling series of mediant transitions (from C major to E major or A major, from B flat to D major) that convey, dramatically, the disruption of the natural order. The greatest shock is reserved for the physical appearance of Death himself. Though we have grown almost accustomed to major mediant transitions, we are unprepared for the progression from an E major triad to a spine-chilling triad of G *minor*.

The perturbation of Nature has its comic (anti-masque) side too: as when Old Men and Women, shot by Death, throw away their crutches and dance an 'antic' of rural courtship, in grotesque dotted rhythm; or when warriors in armour (described by Locke as 'Hectors') drop their weapons to perform a ceremonial love-dance. But these comic elements serve to intensify the music's tragic awareness: especially when a bass arioso, vast in range, extravagant in physical illustration, epitomizes the enormities of Nature's reversal in a manner at once grotesque and heroic. This leads to an entirely serious, indeed solemn, homophonic chorus, full of pathetic false relations and stabbing tritonal descents, wherein we ask the Gods to take pity. This genuine awareness of the paradox of living (by Christopher Gibbons again) starts a process of nemesis: for in the next Entry

Death shoots the Chamberlain, who had started all the trouble by his playful presumption, and makes him fall in love with two court apes, whom he is exhibiting around the fairs. This provides occasion for a parody love scene and a farouche ape-dance: though the humour is in the situation, not the arioso (which is Lawesian and pathetic), nor even the dance. But of course the situation itself is not merely funny either: in playing tricks with Love and Death man has reduced himself to ape-like stature. So the point of *Cupid and Death* is far removed from the man-glorification of the true masque. Though it begins with an act of silly pride, its climax is man's deflation.

This is about as far as seventeenth century man dare go in self-denunciation, and perhaps the Portuguese ambassador felt it was going too far. So Mercury descends on a cloud as deus ex machina and in a long arioso—powerful but once more narrative and descriptive rather than dramatic—rebukes Love and Death for abusing Nature. This seems somewhat unfair, since it wasn't their fault but mankind's (as represented by the Chamberlain). It turns out, however, that there is a kind of social satire involved here: for Mercury says that Cupid must be punished by being banished from court and restricted to 'humble cottages'; while Death is advised to exempt from his threat 'persons in whose breast divine marks of Art or Honour shine'. The play, that is, keeps up its cynical evasion of reality and admits, mockingly, that if, wanting to be Very Important Persons, we cheat ourselves into thinking we are beyond Death, it's because we're incapable of Love too; since Love and Death are inseparable.

Cupid and Death submit to Mercury's proposals in falling parallel thirds. Nature, slowly recuperating from her exhaustion, says this is all very well but what about the lovers already slain by Cupid, and the children they might have had? Mercury says this does not matter because they are all so happy in Elysium: whereupon we hear slow soft music and see a vision of the Elysian Fields, with the slain lovers on thrones. An air (by Christopher Gibbons) paints the familiar Golden Age; the most exquisite pleasures of the senses are fulfilled in the harmonious spheres, where no flower dies and birds carol for evermore—all in the simplest tonic and dominant, with regular rhythm and virtually no dissonance. It seems to be admitted that this is only a wish-fulfilment ('If this place be not heaven, one thought can make it, and Gods by their own wonder led mistake it'). Mercury advises the blessed spirits to return to their shades lest they should fall in love with the mortals and, in being unfaithful to their former loves, should lose the 'calm' they have attained. So heavenly bliss would seem to be another kind of evasion: a liberation from experience. Those who aren't so liberated, after singing a grand chorus with the lovers, are wafted back to earth by way of some rapid modulations (A major to B minor, to F sharp minor, to E major and so to A again); hardly triumphant, if fortified by a dream.

Cupid and Death is not a coherent and convincing work of art and its failure complements that of Comus. In Comus, we have suggested, the music does not measure up to the 'realities' of the poetry; in Cupid and Death the music strives after a reality that the play denies, or tries to deny. In Blow's Venus and Adonis the realities of experience are, by the end, accepted, if not fulfilled.

Venus and Adonis was produced in 1683, after the Restoration of the monarchy. It is called 'a masque for the King's entertainment', and begins as such in the sense that the Prologue and Act I are conceived as a ritual of contemporary life rather than as a dramatic history. Being a court rather than a private or school masque, it attempts to emulate the grandeur of court ritual —especially that of Louis XIV's world. We open with an overture which is modelled on the French pattern; and this was a metamorphosis of the masque dances such as were used for the Entries in Cupid and Death. The pavane turned into the slow opening section of the overture, rendered more stilted and ceremonial by the double dotted rhythm, more personally involved and dramatic through the dissonant texture of the inner parts. The galliard turned into the quick, triple-rhythmed section which, although conventionally fugued, was harmonically conceived and in effect a round-dance—a symbol of human solidarity. All through the hey-day of heroic opera the overture and prologue were to preserve this relationship to the masque; they set the mythological story in the context of contemporary life and related it to the latest political events, while the King and nobility took part in the preludial dances.

Venus and Adonis, too, begins in contemporary life. For the Prologue, Cupid ushers in the shepherds and shepherdesses, who are the ladies and gentlemen of the court; and the precocious Cupid was himself the eight-year-old daughter of the performance's Venus, Mrs. Mary Davies—one of the King's mistresses, whose talents must have embraced more than love. As in the true masque, the Golden Age these people think they live in is the present; so Cupid sings in Lawesian declamation, baroquely decorative, illustrative (consider his arrows), but no more dramatic than the earlier arioso in *Cupid and Death*, since the passions are not seriously involved. He invites everybody to entertain the God of Love: hedonistically appeals to the senses, invoking the humanist's heaven—that eternity of sensual pleasures that Time cannot stale. They all sing a masque dance-chorus: 'Come, shepherdesses, sing and play, Be willing, lovesome, fond and gay': extremely simple in rhythm, harmony and tonality. The only possible snag is that something might go wrong with sensual enjoyment; so there is a middle section in the relative minor about sexual failure, more heart-felt, with passing dissonances. This is brushed aside, however, and everybody asks Cupid to stay 'till every bosom's full of love', in a simple masque-dance, all tonic and dominant, with no harmonic complexities, because the experience is purged of reality.

At this point it becomes apparent that the Restoration court cannot attain the grandeur it aims at: the middle-class debunking spirit that we observed in *Cupid and Death* survives, as realism—not reality—comes in with an abrupt transition to social satire. Cupid admits that this Golden Age is a sham: for there is no faith in the courtiers or constancy in the women, unless they're old and ugly. Of course, we are not meant to believe this either: it merely gives a wink to the audience, is a shrugging of the shoulders similar to that we commented on in Caroline lyrics and in Lawes's setting of them, as well as in *Cupid and Death*. In the earlier masque there is never this quibbling between the actual present and the pretence of the Golden Age. Here the text says: of course we know it isn't true, but let's pretend that beauty and pleasure are not bought, that Nature moves all women to warm desires, that every youthful swain by nature loves—all in the sweetest, unsullied pastoral G major—like Christopher Gibbons's Elysian song in *Cupid and Death*. Then Cupid brings us back to the actual world—the court—with a bump, inviting the lovers to 'retire to the close shades' and 'do what your kindest thoughts invite'. This modulates rather abruptly to A minor, with much more tortuous, less dreamy progressions in the arioso, because the love-dream is, momentarily at least, coming true. The Prologue concludes with the ominous words *Exeunt Omnes*.

If this is reality of a kind we become aware of its implications when the opera proper opens with a curtain tune for recorders that introduces an altogether deeper level of experience. The sarabande rhythm is elegant, courtly; but the languishing apoggiaturas and sobbing Lombard rhythms come from the heart, and introduce the love-arioso between Venus and Adonis. For a moment, in their sighing dissonances and portamentos, there is a hint of the realities of human experience, of the sweet pain that love is. But it is only for a moment. When Venus sings of Adonis's 'delightful youth, full of beauty and of truth', she returns—despite a certain chromatic fervour—to a Lawes-like superficiality. The 'reality' goes out of the music when she says, in masque-like vivacity, she'll be 'ever tender, ever kind'—with a tootling recorder obbligato.

At this point their comparatively uninvolved sensual dalliance is interrupted by hunters' music, tonally simple, sharply rhythmic, with aggressive Lombard syncopations. This is partly a love-chase, of course; but the hunters are the public world, Society, and thus don't approve of any extravagantly personal passion. In *Cupid and Death* the chorus tends to be ourselves—what we feel about the human implications of the situation. Here, as in most heroic operas, the chorus tends to represent public values, as the realities of passion become increasingly absorbed into the lives of the actor-singers. At this point, perhaps, the hunters have some of the characteristics of both masque and anti-masque, being at once positive and negative. Adonis says he doesn't want to go to the hunt, since he has already caught his 'noblest prey'; but Venus, still singing in Caroline narrative arioso, says he must. For she does not feel deeply, or at least does not know she feels deeply. She sends him off first because it is the done thing, socially, to go to the hunt (what will the Joneses think if you're not there?): and secondly for selfish reasons, to attain greater sexual gratification ('I would not have my lover tire'). We can't take very seriously the limp descending chromatics in the bass—any more than the Lawes-like arabesques in which she describes their potential 'pleasant days and easy nights'. In a muddled way Adonis senses that the love-experience is not as simple as Venus pretends ('Yet there is a sort of men who delight in heavy chains, Upon whom ill usage gains'). Venus pooh-poohs this, however: and wins the day when a male chorus of huntsmen appears to challenge Adonis's martial valour.

A high tenor solo sings a rhythmic song about a fierce boar that defies all their efforts to destroy it. The singer—or possibly the boar—is given heroic stature by the high tessitura and the extravagantly physical ornamentation that emulates the animal's roaring and thundering. In so far as he is a phallic boar he is the realities of sex—or at least the aspects of sex that Venus had omitted in her wanton pleasantries. The chorus, as Society, want to obliterate him. Adonis, being passionately in love, cannot ignore him: but cannot control him either, because he hasn't faced up to the facts of experience. Significantly he refers to the boar's tusk as a 'dart', thereby relating it to the darts of Cupid. So this takes up the theme of *Cupid and Death*: Adonis is killed by love, equated with death; and Venus, goddess of love, drives him to it. Meeting the huntsmen's challenge, he goes off with them to a dance that calls up the hounds in a rhythmically grotesque piece depending on cross accents between 3:4 and 3:2, with aggressive syncopations and numerous false relations and clinking parallel sevenths in the cadences. Here the huntsmen and hounds are unambiguously an anti-masque of satyrs, who drive Adonis to his death.

Apart from the first entry of Venus and Adonis—which hints at the reality of love beneath the surface—all this first act has been in the same spirit as the Prologue: there is more singing than in a mid-century masque, but the singing is of a masque-like nature. The turning-point comes in Act II. It opens in masque-like fashion with a whimsical dialogue between Venus and Cupid, non-dramatic, all in Lawes-like decorative arioso. In the episode of Cupid's Lesson we are jerked back to contemporary life again, with social satire directed against the empty-headed, heartless flibbertigibbets who, at court, call themselves lovers. 'For him that's faithless, wild and gay, Who with love's pain doth only play, Take some affected wanton she As faithless and as wild as he.' At this point there's nothing to tell us that Venus isn't one of them. She asks cynically, uninvolved, how she can keep Adonis constant: to which Cupid retorts 'Use him very ill'. The cascade of baroque mirth into which Venus breaks is frivolous but also nervous—a betrayal of feelings deeper, perhaps, than any she has been called upon to deal with. The frivolity turns into a dance of Cupids—those blithe babes of the seventeenth century who are all too obviously the fruits of a sensual paradise. They indulge in a sexy game of hide-and-seek; and in the middle of all this banter and persiflage, Venus calls on the Graces 'to keep the magazine of Beauty'.

Her invocation—a mysterious undulation between major and minor third—quivers on the edge of knowledge; and as soon as the Graces start to sing we know that the tide has turned, that we're no longer pretending that love is only a game. They sing a paean of praise to the Queen of Love; but the words admit that 'the world for that bright beauty *dies*', the tonality is minor, the rhythm disturbed by silences and by cross-accents between 3:4 and 3:2, the harmony agitated by piquant false relations between treble and bass. Though love 'begets desire and yields delight', the pain is inherent in the pleasure; again, sexual fulfilment is like dying because it reminds us of mortality. This is evident too in the Masque of Graces that follows: each dance grows less 'social' (harmonically stable, architecturally balanced), more personal (dissonant and chromatic). The dances culminate in a piece on a chromatic ground that grows progressively more intense in harmony, more agitated in figuration. The 'public' order of the repeated bass cannot subdue the cumulative passion: which, having led into Act III, has left the world of the masque far behind.

The repeated notes and rising chromatics of the Act Tune suggest a speaking intimacy. When the curtain opens and Venus is discovered alone she has become a heroic figure, calling on Adonis in rising fifths and sixths which are a noble development from her original, as it were embryonic, cry to him at the beginning of Act I. The arioso she then sings, with its upward yearning appoggiaturas on words like 'sighs' and 'grief', is now fully developed physical and psychological enactment, like that of Purcell's Blessed Virgin. She is no longer indulging in a prank, nor even induging in her emotion: nor pretending to live in a Golden Age. She is facing up to what experience is really like: to the suffering within love and to the fact of death. It is not

Apri dente Adonis interimitur.

The Anti-Masque Triumphant : Adonis slain by the Boar
From an anonymous, undated book of engravings in the Library of the
Barber Institute (Italian, 17th century)

exactly a tragic situation because it is not caused by anything they do; it is simply what life, or rather death, does to them. None the less there is a sense in which they have a tragic awareness: know that indirectly they are responsible for being so irresponsible, for taking love so frivolously. If they did not attain to this awareness they could hardly achieve so miraculous a transformation not merely in the quality but in the very nature of their music. For when Venus sings 'Alas, Death's sleep thou art too young to take' to a falling tritone, followed by a savage descent through a major seventh, and strives to rise again through chromatically straining 'groans', we know that Blow has done something which had not been attempted before in English music: which was never to be excelled except by his pupil Henry Purcell. He has made drama become music and music become drama. He has achieved operatic fulfilment.

When Adonis has died, Venus's desperate ululation—her Lombard sobs that at times become almost screams—is emotional torment that finds relief in physical gesture without ceasing to be music. Her arioso is disjointed, for she is really heart-broken —by what she'd intended to be a jape. Her mental state is superbly reflected in the string postlude, with its weeping syncopations and hesitant, limping rhythm, like a bird with a broken wing. She pulls herself together sufficiently to invoke mourning Cupids to bear her Adonis 'through the yielding air' and translate him to the heavens; while she remains below to weep (in fragmentary arioso) until she falls into 'as cold a sleep'. This is an acceptance of reality at a deeper level than anything in *Cupid and Death*, because it is felt as the experience of a fully 'realized', sentient human being. She cannot in fact believe that he is in the heavens if his sleep is so cold; and if she were in truth a goddess she could join him at will. What has happened is that she has grown up—from a goddess to a human woman. So the final chorus of mourning, sung in the forsaken grove, is acutely expressive, full of double suspensions. We weep for the Golden Age: though now we have grown up we know that it never existed. Only in Purcell's *Dido and Aeneas* is the theme of human passion and disillusion more deeply explored; only in Handel's *Acis and Galatea* is regret for lost Eden more poignantly expressed.

5

PURCELL'S CEREMONIAL ELEGY

Four-part Fancy No. 4 in C minor
Hear My Prayer
Welcome to all the Pleasures

By the sixteen-eighties, one might almost say, England had to produce an operatic composer of genius if her artistic life was to be fulfilled. She produced Henry Purcell; and it is not an accident that his earliest music should be at once an elegy on the past and incipiently operatic. When he was a young man the traditions of English polyphony were still vigorous in ecclesiastical vocal music, and still more in the domestic fancy for strings. Purcell began by composing, ostensibly, in the old manner; yet he created new music. His teacher Blow had metamorphosed masque into opera almost by accident; Purcell's first works reveal how the creation of opera involved not merely a new vocal technique, but a radical rethinking of traditional approaches to harmony and form.

On the surface, Purcell's string fancies, written in his twenty-first year, look like exercises in an obsolete style: contrapuntal studies in the tradition of Gibbons, William Lawes and Jenkins. The fourth four-part fancy in C minor,[1] for instance, is a double fugue exploiting every conceivable contrapuntal ingenuity. Yet far more than in the six-part madrigals of Wilbye or Ward, or in any earlier string composer, the counterpoint now exists within, indeed creates, the harmonic context: which is by implication dramatic, even 'theatrical'. Thus, though the theme enunciated by the bass moves by step, in vocal style, it also creates harmonic tension: for having risen through a minor third it descends from E flat through a diminished fourth to B natural, the sharpened seventh. The complementary theme played simultaneously by the tenor is not itself harmonically

[1] Miniature score published by Boosey and Hawkes. Edited by André Mangeot.

tense. It contains, however, the expansive leap of the minor seventh; and the high F on which it lands creates a dissonant ninth with the E flat of the other theme. Together the two themes—one beginning with a rising third, the other with a drooping third—effect a precarious equilibrium; and when the other two voices enter, the harmonic texture grows increasingly clotted and almost savagely dissonant. The sharpened seventh in the 'bass' theme repeatedly creates anguished augmented fifth chords and an astonishing sequence of false relations, These are, to begin with, usually a diminished octave apart—F natural in the first viol clashing with F sharp in the lower octave. But as the section grows, they become semitonal grindings and, at the end of the section, a clash between B flat in the highest part and B natural in the lowest part, two octaves below. Despite the noble, vocal nature of the themes, this texture is essentially instrumental. So acute a succession of dissonances would be extremely difficult—and comparatively ineffective—if sung.

Moreover, the organization of this section is as much tonal as contrapuntal. The fugal exposition covers a cycle of fifths. The first three entries establish C minor; the fourth entry modulates sharpwards to G minor, but then flatwards back to C minor, and then again flatwards to F minor. This also introduces the fiercer, semitonal false relation of A natural and A flat. From this point there is a momentary relaxation of dissonance as the music modulates from F minor to its relative, A flat major. Then we move sharpwards to E flat major, in more song-like expansiveness. E flat changes to its relative, C minor; and we move in a sharpwards-tending cycle of fifths from C minor to G minor to D minor to A minor. Then a strained leap of a minor ninth in the bass reverses the process: we move flatwards by fifths to D minor and to G minor, ending with a major third which proves to be not a consummatory tierce de picardie, but a dominant in C minor.

This 'sharpening' of the music's emotional energy has been accompanied by an increase in *physical* energy; the leaps in the parts grow progressively larger as well as harmonically more intense. In the opening clause there had been leaps of minor seventh, octave and major ninth; now there are also leaps of the tritone and of minor ninth. Moreover, the parts enter in ever closer stretto, often at the interval of the minor second—with the suspended lower part resolving (or failing to resolve) on to another dissonance. So this cumulative urgency leads into the fancy's second section: the instrumental counterpart to what would, in a vocal motet, be the setting of the second clause of the text. This section is in one sense a climax to the first section's screwed-up tension, because it moves faster, in quavers. In another sense, however, it is a resolution, or an attempted resolution, for its harmony is less dissonant, its tonality clear, modulating from C minor to F minor, and then to E flat back to C. Though false relations still occur in this section they are no longer points of rhetorical pathos; they are 'passing' notes in the modern enharmonic minor scale, and their momentary acridity serves to reinforce the music's physical animation.

For although the texture of this section looks, and is, as elaborately contrapuntal as the first section, we do not listen to it as 'vocal' polyphony: what we hear is the bouncy dance rhythm, organized in clearly defined tonality. The savage harmonic pathos of the first section has carried us from the mystical world of the Church to the humanistic world of the Stage: and so to the human manifestation of physical action. The counterpoint has become a disciplined togetherness: a masque dance or a round in which individual human beings try to forget their differences for the good of the whole. But operatic individuality comes back in the next section which begins as a kind of recitative-dialogue between first violin and the other three instruments in homophonic consort. The rhythm is broken, separated by rests; and out of the silence emerges an extended, chromaticized version of the first theme, with tied notes lingering painfully on their suspensions, resolving in oscillating chromatic thirds. This droops to a cadence; but the drooping intensifies the pain, since the tenor leaps an octave to bump, in major and then minor seconds, with the chromatic resolution of the first violin.

This introduces the coda section, which returns to the close contrapuntal texture. The theme now, however, embraces elements both of recitative (the 'speaking' repeated notes) and of the dance (quaver movement in firm parallel sixths). Moreover, this time the theme itself is harmonically tense, for its most striking feature is the leap of the diminished fourth (sometimes stretched to a tritone): the interval which, in the original theme, had appeared as part of a stepwise melody. This coda is thus in a profound sense a summation of the previous sections. The piece starts from a religious inheritance; but in its first section harmonic drama becomes more important than contrapuntal control. Harmonic drama leads, in the second section, to the human—as opposed to divine—discipline of the dance, associated with diatonic tonality. In the third section the passion of the individual stands apart from social order in operatic recitative: while the last section seeks a synthesis between this personal passion, the social ceremony of the dance, and the old-style fugal discipline. The fancy ends with a backward glance at an outmoded view of the universe. The passion is too fierce to be resolved in a tierce de picardie; yet the minor triad would seem inappropriate in a work so polyphonically conceived. The compromise of the bare fifth sounds oddly desolate in this rich harmonic context: the more so since it follows the harsh anticipation of cadential resolution (B natural against C) in the penultimate bar.

The final chord looks back, beyond the seventeenth century, to an age of faith. The music is powerfully self-assertive, passionately humanistic, and in that sense 'modern'. Yet it is also elegiac, in that it entails consciousness that the values of the old world are gone: the final metamorphosis of the original theme consistently droops, the complementary rising phrase being omitted. This Janus-like quality—looking forwards and backwards simultaneously—has practical consequences also. The range of the instrumental parts makes it clear that the music is intended for viols, not the more emotional violins which were in habitual use in Purcell's time. The 'spiritual' tone of the viols—the 'divine rapture' they induce—gives a subtler poignancy to the music's extravagant passion. The dissonance stabs a little less fiercely than it would on violins; but we realize what we have lost with sharper nostalgia.

The early anthem *Hear my Prayer*[1] shows a comparable modification of traditional techniques, this time in vocal terms. As in the fancy, the counterpoint is of masterly ingenuity. The harmonic nature of the music is, however, suggested by the thick sonority of the eight-part writing, and by the relative regularity of the rhythm. Both of these features would be emphasized by the fact that this music was sung not *a capella*, but with the

[1] Novello, Anthems 1001. Edited by John E. West.

voice parts doubled by organ and supported by a string bass. The theme itself has two clauses. The first—to the words 'Hear my prayer, O Lord'—derives directly from liturgical declamation: three repeated Cs followed by a rise up a minor third and a fall back to the tonic, more or less identical with a priest's pentatonic intoning. The counterphrase to the words 'And let my crying come unto Thee' takes us, however, into the world of operatic lament, the sharp sixth emphasizing the egocentric *my*, while the crying yearns upwards through a chromatic oscillation from flat to sharp seventh. It is hardly excessive to say that the whole anthem grows from this tension created by chromatic fluctuation, sometimes upwards, sometimes languishing downwards in inversion: for each time the phrase occurs it creates a suspension or chromatically altered dissonance with the basic harmony. The climax comes with an elaborated, extended version of the oscillation, followed by an abrupt descent through a diminished fourth. The final cadence is as firm as a rock: yet also stark, in that the anticipation of the tonic C in the penultimate chord clashes—as it does in the fancy—with the dominant's sharp seventh.

This music has, in a more extravagant form, the quality of paradox which we noted in Gibbons's *What is our life?* Here too —and more obviously than in Gibbons's piece—the clear diatonic tonality and the regular metrical rhythm are the new positives: for all the incidental chromatics, there is only one real modulation, and that is the simplest possible transition from tonic to dominant—after sixteen symmetrical bars. These new positives represent a 'humanistic' order that is related to the social ceremony of the masque. The counterpoint—which used to be a symbol of the old 'monistic' and religious order—here serves to *dislocate* the harmony; hinting at other and more complex worlds of feeling it creates, through its chromatic ambiguities, tension with the simple positives of harmony and key. While the 'ceremonial' positives discipline the chromatic passion, it is also true that the counterpoint is a recurrent menace to stability. Thus the music is magnificent, for its pomp is an imaginative vision, not a façade, and its positive grandeur was to lead to the sublime satisfaction of the Handelian peroration. But the music is at the same time frightening, for it suggests that Purcell knew —as Racine and perhaps Lully knew in France, but as Purcell's contemporaries in Restoration England did not know—how narrow is the borderline between civilization and chaos. There were realms of experience which the buoyant, smug, middle-class Restoration court was prepared to forgo. Purcell was not so prepared, and in that sense was a greater man than his age warranted. One might almost say that his greatness is summed up in the fact that, even when he had evolved his mature, contemporary operatic style, he still preserved this elegiac consciousness of what had been lost. The strain of religious mysticism which is entwined in the humanism of his string fancies was not completely, or for long, banished from his art; and his most resplendently 'modern' ceremonial works preserved an awareness of the abyss over which his civilization was built.

We can see this in an early, comparatively unpretentious ceremonial piece, *Welcome to all the Pleasures*.[1] Because this is an ode for St. Cecilia's Day, scored for solo voices, concerted voices, chorus and strings, it bears some relation to the techniques of ecclesiastical polyphony. But it is not, even superficially, old-style counterpoint like that of the string fancies. Its convention is that of the verse anthem, which is basically theatrical; and this is hardly surprising, since it is designed to celebrate the humanist's paradise—those endless sensual pleasures that pretend to be oblivious of Time.

Given this theme, the opening is a little unexpected. It is, conventionally enough, a masque or opera overture, with a slow ceremonial section in four time, followed by a quicker section in triple rhythmed fugato. Yet one has only to compare this overture with Blow's overture to *Venus and Adonis* to see that Purcell, at the age of twenty-four, has introduced into the ceremonial manner a depth of passion that Blow attained only at the end of his opera: and that beyond the worldly passion there is another quality that is not present in Blow at all. The extraordinarily rich harmonic texture of Purcell's slow section, though more powerful than, is comparable with, the texture of Blow's music. It expresses the humanist's heaven of sensuality: but tells us that, as human nature since the Fall is no longer innocent, nor indeed 'natural', pain is inevitably involved with pleasure. This is why sexual consummation, being subject to Time, is a 'dying' that hurts as it is desired: why Purcell's ripe harmonic texture is

[1] Novello, Selected Works of Purcell, No. 4. Edited by Gerald M. Cooper.

pierced with dissonance: why he had an almost obsessional pre-occupation with false relation, which stresses the element of illusion within the joys of the flesh.

One might almost say that Purcell's music fulfils sensuality and, in so doing, seeks to liberate us from the temporal and material. The very richness of his harmony in a passage such as this prelude depends on the fact that each line desires lyrical independence. Suspended seventh, ninth or eleventh chords occur because inner parts are always seeking melodic character; multiple false relations appear because apparently decorative figurations achieve singing contours that conflict with the harmonic progression. It is significant that this overture should remind us forcibly of a much greater, more sustained piece in the same key —the opening chorus of Bach's *St. Matthew Passion*. In the Bach too each line is a singing voice that carries tense harmonic potentiality; as a result the concourse of voices has tremendous interior energy—a quality of ecstatic lyrical affirmation is combined with, flows out of, harmonic richness and anguish. Of course Bach is a man of faith as Purcell is not, so his music, though very chromatic, does not often involve Purcell's harmonic ambiguities and false relations. None the less Purcell and Bach, in moments like this, have profound affinities. Both start from a potent and immediate apprehension of the life of the senses, recognizing that sensual consummation is subject to Time and inextricably linked with pain: hence the richness and the dissonance of their harmony. Both tell us (through the singing lines of their harmonic polyphony) that out of the flesh's joy and suffering may flow a lyrical affirmation of the spirit. Purcell's visionary glimpses come, perhaps, rarely, compared with Bach's: which may be why his music has an elegiac melancholy beneath its ceremonial manner. But the visionary gleams are there; and Purcell's harmonic-melodic texture is closer to Bach than it is to Handel. This is why potentially—though not in actual achievement—Purcell may be a greater composer than Handel.

The overture to *Welcome to all the Pleasures* contains the essence of Purcell; the rest of the piece follows from, but simplifies, its mystical humanism. When the voices enter they welcome 'all the pleasures that delight Of every sense the grateful appetite'—in grand triad formations that don't, however, avoid some grinding dissonant suspensions. Then a counter-tenor solo invokes 'the god of music and of love', in an aria over a ground bass. Human love is to combine with 'divine' music (in the old, Shakespearean sense) to absolve the pain that is inherent in loving. The liquid cantilena of the voice is exquisitely sensuous, with some pathetic drooping tritones; but the passion that had been contained in the overture is lulled by the cooing vocal melody, by the regularity of the ground-bass pattern which, because it goes on unchangingly, seems illusorily to be outside Time.

This is really an explicit statement of what is implicit in the overture: music expresses sensuality and at the same time provides an escape from it. A bass solo then invites us to use our voices, 'those *organs of nature*', because singing will 'charm the troubl'd and amorous creature'. The chorus that follows is a round dance in triple rhythm, simple in texture compared with the overture, but very chromatic. Our troubled amorousness is melancholy, but delicious; there is little tension between the declining chromaticism of the harmony and the independent movement of the lines, and the final false relation on 'soft charms' is a swoon. Melancholy gains ascendancy over deliciousness; and the tenor solo sings a most beautiful dance-air in which he invites love-become-music to be an 'innocent fire' that will 'temper the heat of desire'. This air, in two twelve-bar periods, with a modulation from E minor to the relative G major, is of the utmost simplicity. It tames the passions: yet with a heart-rending wistfulness (consider the dissonant melodic note on the word 'innocent' itself, or the upward-yearning appoggiatura on the word 'lute')—as though in saying farewell to the senses we were losing all that we know of reality. This is borne out by the final chorus in which we all celebrate 'holy' St. Cecilia in a round dance—and in old-fashioned fugato. From this music, most of the chromaticism and all the false relations have disappeared. It is harmonized for the most part in simple diatonic concords, in the major. The key of E major is, indeed, somewhat unusual in seventeenth century music; and this perhaps reinforces the sense of unreality which the simplicity of this final chorus gives us, when compared with the complex 'reality' of the overture, or even with the wistful regret of the tenor's air. So this 'major' chorus does not, after all, end in sonorous splendour; the rejoicing gradually dies away, one part after another fading out, as insubstantial as a dream, until only the bass is left. In a sense, the chorus is another of

Purcell's references to a world beyond the humanist's here-and-now; but the chorus also says that if you take this world of music out of the context of human living and dying, it's no more than a dream, a fairy tale. This is one of the first of many instances wherein Purcell associates the major key[1] with illusion, the minor (which has more varied possibilities of harmonic tension) with reality.

[1] In the Heroic Age E major was often associated with Paradise, perhaps because it was the sharpest, and therefore the 'highest', key in fairly general use: we shall comment on another (most sublime) instance in Handel's *Semele*. The link between E major and heaven survived, indeed, long after sharper keys had become commonly accepted. Schubert, for instance, makes E major his Eden-key; and it crops up, with similarly nostalgic import, in the 'O past, O happy life' epilogue to Delius's *Sea Drift*. Schubert sometimes employed still sharper keys in similar contexts; and Bruckner follows him in transporting us to heaven in B, F sharp and even C sharp major, as well as E. Even in the mid-twentieth century Messiaen has used these extreme sharp keys in moments of celestial ecstasy.

6

THE TRAGIC HEROINE AND THE UN-HERO

Henry Purcell: *Dido and Aeneas*[1]

In the last chapter we have discussed how Purcell forged an operatic style even from the traditions of ecclesiastical polyphony and, in our account of *Welcome to all the Pleasures*, have touched on the essential Purcellian theme. We have now to consider his attempt to integrate technique and theme in an operatic convention; and to consider the implications of the fact that he only once succeeded in creating a real opera on the traditional heroic myth, and that opera was a miniature affair intended not for the court, but for a girls' school.

In Louis XIV's France, heroic opera was closely associated with heroic tragedy; in England our failure to produce the one was consequent on our failure to produce the other. In his two tragedies Ben Jonson had attempted the heroic, early in the seventeenth century, seeking an art 'high and aloof', involving 'truth of argument, dignity of persons, gravity and height of elocution, fulness and frequency of sentence'. But *Sejanus* and *Catiline* had had little success and no successors; and theatrical enterprise was disrupted by the Civil War and during the Protectorate. After the Restoration, as we have seen, values had changed. The new society was middle-class and mercantile; and though it had grandiose ambitions, it had no grandeur of spirit. Both the moral core and the sense of stylization were lacking, and when dramatists attempted the heroic, it was from disillusioned wishful-thinking, rather than from conviction. If we are not in truth heroic, we can put up a show of heroism: so the Tragic Hero will evoke admiration, not compassion. Even the conflict between Love and Duty was less important than the display of simulated emotion it could give rise to. From this point of view Restoration tragedy was essentially a public art, meaningless apart from its

[1] Oxford University Press. Vocal Score edited by E. J. Dent.

audience: a vastly inflated form of a tendency we observed as early as the Cavalier lyric. The dramatic and literary stylizations —the multiplicity of 'crises', the heightened diction, the paradoxes, antitheses, rhetorical questions and other devices—existed to exaggerate the display, not (as in Racine) to control the intensity of feeling in the interests of civilization. Restoration comedy is also nothing if not a public act in so far as it is not, like Molière's comedy (which the English dramatists emulated), a comedy of manners and morals, but of manners only, and mostly bad manners at that. We are invited to admire Millament and Mirabelle for the face they present to the world. Indeed, they illustrate 'the way of the world' because they function effectively in it—without being taken in *by* it. A comedy of simulated feeling may be tolerable because there is inevitably an element of disillusion in the comic approach; a tragedy of simulation is, however, a contradiction in terms.

The book of *Dido and Aeneas* was a rewriting, for music, of a full-scale heroic tragedy by Nahum Tate, called *Brutus of Alba*. The idea of translating it into an opera book was probably prompted by Blow's *Venus and Adonis*; but whereas Blow's work was conceived as a court masque and turned into an opera almost fortuitously, *Dido* was conceived as a drama which, in being transformed into an opera, became more, not less, dramatic. In part the improvement was technical. Since Restoration tragedy is an art of inflation, almost any example of the genre would be improved by having the words reduced by two-thirds, as was necessary if the piece was to be sung—especially at the end of term school concert. (We can afford to sacrifice the kind of language in which Brutus-Aeneas decides to leave the Queen:

> Give notice to the Fleet we sail to Night.
> Said I to Night! Forsake the Queen to Night!
> Forsake! oh Fate! the Queen! to Night forsake her!)

None the less, there was more involved than a technical improvement; for although the opera still accepts the traditional heroic theme, it subtly modifies it in the light of contemporary English experience. The masque opposition of love-destruction, order-disorder, is still present in Tate's libretto; but private and public order no longer become synonymous in an act of homage to Hymen. Although there is a conflict between love and duty, the two forces are no longer equally weighted. In Tate's middle-classical world, public duty becomes the destructive force; and the only reality is now personal experience—Dido's love for Aeneas. From this point of view Tate makes a significant modification to the classical myth. In Virgil's story Aeneas is called back to duty by the gods. In Tate's libretto he is called away by a witch *masquerading* as a god. This is indeed the ultimate inversion: for the anti-masque witches now 'stand for' the values of the masque. Thus it is dramatically important that Aeneas should appear a poor thing. The point is that he prefers to accept a sham (conventional) duty rather than reality (or love).[1]

This duality is already present in the overture. The slow opening section takes us immediately into the world of Dido's suffering: the stabbing dissonant suspensions, the lamenting chromatics, anticipate her arioso though they are ennobled, depersonalized, by the sustained lyricism, the grave movement, the pedal notes. The quick section, in sprightly quavers, is dance music, as we would expect. But it is not the conventional, triple-rhythmed round: and is curiously unimposing if it is supposed to

[1] Some commentators take the view that Aeneas is given a 'poor' part, with no arias, for practical reasons: he would have to be played by a man, smuggled into a girls' school! It might more convincingly be argued that Tate and Purcell and Josias Priest, having taken the trouble to smuggle him, would have made as much use of him as possible; in any case Purcell, like all great creative intelligences, was adept at turning practical necessity to artistic purpose.

What he could not deal with was the artistic convention that no longer had human significance. Tate's libretto included a prologue in the manner of the pastoral masque, celebrating Phoebus and Venus ('Her charms bless the Night, as his Beams bless the Day . . . She gives our Flocks their feeding, He makes 'em fit for Breeding'): a conventional tribute to the Golden Age we live in, though the tone is low. Purcell wouldn't have objected to the tone; but it seems probable that he did object to the content, since the celebrative masque was extraneous to a work that is, in a philosophical not technical sense, an *anti*-masque. In any case, no music for this prologue survives. Some authorities think Purcell wrote it, because the opera is so short without it. But the addition of the masque would hardly make the piece into an evening's entertainment; and a one-hour piece seems adequate if, as was probable, it was combined with other school activities. No explanation has been proffered as to why the masque music should have been lost while the opera survives. Another, more recent, theory is that Daniel Purcell wrote the masque music for a revival. See the essay by Eric Walter White in the volume of studies edited by Imogen Holst in honour of Purcell (O.U.P.).

represent public glory. Indeed, it sounds suspiciously like the witches' music: and prepares us for the identification of opposites that is to come later.

The action opens with Belinda and the chorus, both representing public or social values, trying to cheer Dido up. Belinda sings in dance movement, of course; in the jaunty Restoration dotted rhythm that was a cruder version of the *notes inégales* in French ceremonial music. 'Shake the clouds from off your brow', she says. After all, Empire's growing, pleasures are flowing, fortune smiles and so should you; we can enjoy the best of every world, with public glory and personal satisfaction working together. The minor key, the slightly dissonant texture of the choral parts, the physical action in Belinda's ornamentation intimate, perhaps, that life isn't as easy as all that. Anyway, when the chorus is interrupted by the lamenting Dido we know at once that hers is a deeper and richer reality. She creates herself before our eyes and ears—like Blow's Venus in Act III, or Purcell's Blessed Virgin. Her arioso line, broken in rhythm by her sighs, tense with Lombard sobs, weeping appoggiaturas and languishing chromatics, creates within us the 'torment that cannot be confest' so that we enter, momentarily, into her being. At the same time, her emotional arioso is poised over a ground bass, so that it remotely presages her final lament. When she takes over the ground theme and sings it in canon with the bass, to the words 'Peace and I are strangers grown', she is at once a suffering woman and a queen. The 'ceremonial' chaconne succours personal distress; we already know that Dido is the true tragic heroine, because she will suffer all, sacrifice all, for the integrity of her love.

Belinda, still belonging to the practical world, then suggests that Dido is getting worked up gratuitously. Why shouldn't she tell her love? Why shouldn't she and Aeneas marry and live happily ever after? Private love need not necessarily be in conflict with public duty; on the contrary, monarchs *uniting* ought to create order and peace. This is taken up by the chorus in rigid, rather insensitive dance homophony. Dido cuts them short, however, and breaks into still more impassioned arioso. She vividly invokes Aeneas both in his public, war-like valour (trumpet figurations) and in potential amatory bliss (softly caressing suspensions). This time her passion finds no resolution in aria: we begin to suspect that she is so upset because the realities of love are so disturbing (her shooting scales on the words 'What storms' significantly anticipate the storm which the witches will unleash). She knows, like any classical heroine, that you cannot have both Honour and Love at the same time: but not so much because (like a classical heroine) she believes in Honour as because she doubts whether Aeneas's love is as honest as hers. Belinda is so moved that she turns from the social world and, sympathizing with Dido, sings her mistress's kind of arioso.

But Belinda perhaps regards this as weakness: for she turns abruptly back to her social role and, in duet with an anonymous Woman, representative of Society, sings the jaunty 'Fear no danger to ensue'. Don't worry, they say with the infuriating helpfulness of the unimaginative, it may never happen; we're *sure* the hero loves as well as you do. We return, of course, to bouncy, self-confident dance metre, reinforced by the syncopated rhythm and the perpetual parallel thirds. The deliberate unreality of this is suggested by the first appearance of the major key and perhaps by the perky rhythm which makes hay of the verbal accents. In arioso Purcell's accentuation is always meticulous, growing inevitably from the way in which the character would speak in passion. Here, if the false accents are not deliberate, they are the kind of accident that happens only to genius. They make the 'ev*er* gentle ev*er* smiling' hero seem slightly fatuous. There is the briefest hint of minor tonality when the chorus invites Cupids to strew the lovers' path with flowers. This is a most delicate piece of irony: for when Cupids do in fact strew flowers at the end they do so on Dido's dead body, in an elegy on the care-free careless paradise that Belinda, the Woman, and the Chorus sing of in this dance-song.

Ironically too, Aeneas appears immediately on the conclusion of the fatuous ditty. Belinda—a public figure—describes him as god-like. But his first arioso, though serious enough, contains a hint of melodrama, of rhetorical self-dramatization, especially in the descending diminished seventh on the words 'no fate but you'. (The interval is common in Handel, of course, but sufficiently rare in the music of Purcell's time to call attention to itself.) There may also be a suggestion of self-indulgence in the tritonal arabesque he sings on the word 'feeble'.

The love match is symbolized, as Cupid 'throws the dart that's

207

dreadful', in a bit of traditional counterpoint—a canon two in one (!) that creates, within its unity and its regular dance metre, a rather painfully dissonant texture. Aeneas's famous remark 'If not for mine, for Empire's sake, Some pity on your lover take' puts the situation pretty accurately so far as he is concerned. The material benefits of the match, he hints, are not to be sniffed at; how would it look to the World if she were to turn down a Hero! So it is appropriate that Belinda should follow with a deliberately conventional pursuit aria that deflates the love-experience of the truth Dido has put into it. Belinda's song is in the major, of course: a love-chase with virtually no dissonance, and with 'echoes' between voice and bass, to suggest illusion. The echoes, here, are a part of the game; but when the chorus rounds off the scene with a ceremonial dance-chorus in triple rhythm, with lilting dotted movement, the echoes (on the significant words 'cool shady fountains') bring in a sudden, disturbing modulation to the minor of the dominant, followed by a false relation. So here they hint at illusion in another and deeper sense, highly characteristic of seventeenth century echoes: at the *other* reality, the world beyond this ostensible material triumph. Perhaps this is why the final triumph dance, though still in the major, has become a little uneasy, with sharply accented dissonant passing notes that hint that all may not, after all, be for the best in the best of all possible worlds.

In any case we move from the Triumph directly to scene 2[1]—and the Witches' Cave. The sorceress was Nahum Tate's invention, and is a fundamentally serious creation. Her music—in the subdominant minor, the traditional key for *chants lugubres*—contains excruciating suspended minor seconds, angular leaps and chromaticisms; yet it is spacious and noble, in the same style as the opening of the overture, and is directly comparable with Dido's arioso in both intensity and span. On no account should the Sorceress be treated grotesquely. She must have a Circe-like

[1] Tate's libretto concludes Act I with the Triumph Dance, making the Sorceress scene the beginning of Act II. This would seem to be the proper place for the act division and perhaps only practical problems of stage mechanics prompted a modification. On the other hand it might be argued that the shock-effect of the contrast between public triumph and the horror within would be weakened if there were a break before the Sorceress's appearance: and that the unreality of the hunting-idyll is stressed if it is, as it were, self-enclosed.

'Great minds against themselves conspire':
The Death of Dido (Guercino)

grandeur, because the destructive force is a reality, like love. Both, indeed, are within Dido: which is why she is a tragic character. Few people are capable of 'real' experience, true love. Rather than face up to the creative *and* destructive principles within us, we prefer to substitute something easier: such as Aeneas's 'Empire'.

Whereas Belinda had justly pointed out that the fulfilment of private love might lead to public prosperity, the Sorceress announces—in an exact inversion of heroic convention—that she intends to destroy Dido as an individual and at the same time bring ruin to the State through the anarchy of War. Moreover, she will do this by means of an assertion of public duty! From the standpoint of convention, her attitude will be absolutely 'correct'. This is why her rout of witches sing music that is identical in style with the ceremonial dance choruses except that it is quicker, more perfunctory. The anti-masque is now on the side of order, because order is presented as destructive of human integrity. The relationship of the witches to the Sorceress is similar to the relationship of his rout to Comus. Unlike the Sorceress they are funny: their quick music is based on the kind of music Lully composed for his *comic* operas and ballets. None the less they are also horrid, because incapable of apprehending the realities of passion. In a way they are naturalistic and contemporary: not so much supernatural as a gang of middle-class female gossips and harridans whose mentality is neatly characterized in their notorious couplet: 'Our plot has took, the Queen's forsook'. Their ha-ha-has are horrifying only because they are grossly inane.

The witches do not always depart so radically from heroic convention. Sometimes they sing straight ceremonial music, like a masque chorus, the irony being in the situation, not the music. Two witches invoke the storm in a canon two in one, there being a kind of blasphemy in this destructive use of 'doctrinal' counterpoint. There is certainly a blasphemy in the echo chorus 'In our deep vaulted cell': the blasphemy being inherent in the singing of such nobly ceremonial masque-music by such low types. The echoes split up the words, literally destroy meaning: so this time the seventeenth century echoes are illusion in a discreditable sense. The masque chorus is followed by another echo piece, a dance of furies, in which the texture is riddled with *false* relations and the echoes are a deceit. This illusory quality is the more pointed because the Sorceress's dark F minor has changed to a pastoral F major. Moreover, the echo-ritual and dance of furies are most cunningly placed. They immediately precede the idyll wherein Dido and Aeneas consummate their love: and so hint at the element of illusion within the idyll itself

Act II, the hunting scene, takes place away from the public world. As Belinda says, it is only 'thanks to these lonesome vales' that Dido and Aeneas can be brought together. Belinda sings with a chorus of attendants in D minor, a key that is related to the pastoral dream of F major, but 'real' because their love, or at least Dido's love, is real. The chorus sings a 'pursuit' canon; but in gentle valedictory lyricism, with a number of sighing dissonances. An anoymous woman sings an aria on a ground bass which, recounting the Actaeon myth, offers an objective commentary on the human situation, suggesting how Dido's experience parallels the Actaeon story, since she is harried to death by the force of her own passion, as he was killed by his own hounds. Despite the level, impersonal movement of the bass, the aria grows more impassioned in melodic contour, rising to its climax on a high F sharp and G. Then the vocal line stops and the instrumental ritornello takes over, once more distancing the emotion as the attendants perform a graceful, ritualized dance This extra-personal aria on a ground bass occurs halfway through the opera; it looks backwards to her first words, forwards to her last—both of which are arias over a ground.

This moment outside Time is interrupted by the storm, which the lovers regard as a perturbation of Nature: and so it is. But we know it is within their love, and an instrument of fate. The pastoral idyll, 'the open field', is indeed 'no shelter from this storm'. Belinda and the chorus switch us brusquely back to the everyday world with the rising arpeggios of 'Haste, haste to town.'¹ Significantly they go back to town, not to the heroic world of the court. Though the music is superficially agitated, it is jaunty, without interior dissonance: as unthinking and unfeeling as Belinda's earlier 'pursuit' aria which, indeed, it reverses.

¹ In Tate's libretto these words are most inappropriately given to Dido who is a tragic figure precisely because she is incapable of running away from any storm. Perhaps this was merely a typographical error, which composer and librettist corrected when the text was musicked.

When they have gone cosily 'out of the storm' the Sorceress appears, disguised as the god Mercury, and delivers the fateful message to Aeneas. His slithering 'ahs' on hearing this are very different in effect from Dido's heartrent ululations. The first thing he thinks of is 'what language can I try My injured Queen to pacify'. A deflated hero indeed, he not only gives in to a God, which is what a real Hero ought to do, after a struggle: but he gives in to a god that is a fake; and the first emotion he feels is fear of what Dido may think, feel, maybe do. Yet there is an element of pathos in his position as unheroic hero. This comes out in his final pushing of the blame on to someone else ('Yours' —high E—'be the blame, O gods'): in his submission (chord of the augmented fifth): and in his expressed preference for death, which he significantly thinks might be *easier* than facing Dido (declining phrases, broken by silences, but without much dissonance). We are meant to find this moving (Aeneas isn't the only weak man among us!) yet at the same time, as an end to the act, bathetic. And it isn't Aeneas who dies, but Dido.[1]

The last act opens with a different kind of reference to the World. This time it is Low, not High Life: perhaps because the witches have revealed to us that the values of high life are really low, or not values at all. Though we begin with a triple-hythmed dance, in rudimentary fugato, it is not ceremonial, but a sailors' dance, brisk, popular in idiom. The song the sailor sings is again an ironic commentary on the sublime. All the sailors, he says, will be taking a 'boozy short leave of their nymphs on the shore'; and the classical allusion to nymphs is a euphuism if ever there was one. Of course, all the sailors will give 'vows of returning to silence their mourning' (mock chromatics descend through the dance lilt) but they know, and the nymphs know, they'll not be intending to visit them more. They couldn't, as we say today, care less: and when you come down to brass tacks

[1] Most commentators find the conclusion of this act unsatisfactory, because it ends in a different key from the opening (A minor instead of D minor) and with recitative instead of a dance-chorus. Tate in fact provided six lines of gloating for the witches which Purcell probably set (in D minor) as an ironically triumphant gloss on Aeneas's self-pity. It is just possible—though not probable—that Purcell omitted the words on purpose; certainly the opera doesn't seriously suffer from the omission, for the end of this act must appear to some degree bathetic if the story is to make sense.

their situation is just the same as that of Dido and Aeneas; so why all the pother?

The witches rejoice at this triumph of unfeeling triviality, and the Sorceress foretells the destruction of Carthage in an aria in ceremonial dotted rhythm! Then they all sing a rigid, fierce dance-song, 'Destruction's our delight'. Played maestoso, this would be imposing in its massive homophony, for rhythm, harmony and modulatory scheme are clear and simple. Played and hissed as fast as possible it becomes the more sinister for being a positive inverted. The witches and sailors significantly dance *together*: for the evil is that the World cannot comprehend the realities of passion.

Then follows the final interview between Dido and 'lost Aeneas', which returns to the here-and-now of arioso. Dido begins by saying that no human agency can help her, so she must appeal to 'earth and heaven' (high G). But she immediately rounds on herself and says, in effect, that heaven doesn't exist: all she can do is to accept what fate has in store for her. Aeneas enters to make his broken confession of 'the gods' decree' (which is really the devil's, of course). His arioso, with its sharpened third in the ascent, flattened third in the descent, is genuinely pathetic; and we are probably meant to feel sorry for him when, after his voice has literally broken before the words 'we must part', Dido turns on him in fury. She calls him a 'deceitful crocodile', the worse because he isn't man enough to be honest but makes 'heaven and gods' (which she knows don't exist) an excuse for his own defection. This is a very English, anti-traditional version of heroism, for she is implying that the only real heroism lies in truth to one's own feelings. It's no use his breaking in to exclaim 'By all that's good' because all that's good he has forsworn. It's enough that he should have had the *thought* of deserting her; the unfaith has been committed in his mind, and what's done cannot be undone, certainly not by protestations in perfunctory arpeggios which she parodies in mocking imitations. You have lost love, she says, irrevocably; so you may as well take yourself off to your promised 'Empire'. Her descending arpeggios to the word 'Away' are brusquely ferocious, guillotining Aeneas's rising arpeggios in which he says he'll 'stay and love obey'. But when she turns to herself and says that she will fly to death, Aeneas abruptly takes himself off. Perhaps he realizes that she, unlike himself, means it; and he is afraid of death because he is afraid of love. There is a kind of savage farce about the scene; but as soon as Aeneas has stumped off, Dido recovers tragic stature. Alone, she says that he had to go (because he betrayed love): and that now he has gone, Death must take her. She 'cannot live without him'; and the cliché is strictly true in the sense that her realization that his love is not the same as hers kills her. Practically speaking, she could—even if she were not willing, as in real heroic opera, to give him up for Duty—have waited for him to save the State and return to her. But she doesn't want to wait for him: because she has discovered that in her sense he is no hero at all, but a sham. It is literally true that Dido is too heroic to live.

So when the chorus sings in solemn ceremonial homophony that 'Great minds against themselves conspire' we say, yes, that is so, and is what the opera is about. But when they add 'and shun the cure they most desire' we know this is not true, for Aeneas would be no cure for Dido's suffering nor, perhaps, would any mortal man. Aeneas is the traditional man-god gone seedy, as he certainly had in Restoration England; Dido's heroism consists in her being a woman who can still be, emotionally and imaginatively, a queen. The conditions of temporal mortality would seem to be such that private passion can never be completely fulfilled: so the only 'cure' for Dido is death. The darkness closes around her as her arioso slowly droops through sobbing Neapolitan chromaticisms; and she welcomes death, her only true lover, in her final aria on a ground bass. Here the bass descends chromatically in the ceremonial rhythm of the chaconne which, in the court masque, was a marriage dance. The apparently eternal repetition of the balanced cadences lifts her sorrow beyond the personal. Though her vocal line is as anguished in its sobbing tritones and yearning chromatics as her most fiery passages of arioso, she grows fully to the tragic queen who was presaged in her first song. Her melody describes a grand, slowly arching contour, rising chromatically, falling in relaxed diatonicism; but when she invites us to 'remember' her, her melody stays still on repeated Ds, and then on high Gs. It is significant that she asks us to remember her—as a woman—but to 'forget her fate'. Unlike Aeneas, she has no self-pity; and she blames no one for the wrongs she suffers. What we have to remember is the reality of human passion: perhaps the ultimate reality. We certainly don't forget it as, after she has stabbed herself or died of a broken heart, a dissolving chromatic descent spreads through the whole orchestra.

What happens then is interesting: for it suggests that, against our expectation after Dido's lament, the 'ultimate' reality may not be human passion after all. In a sense Purcell takes us back, in the final chorus, to the point he started from in his early string fancies. It is as though, in the orchestral ritornello that concludes the lament, sensuous chromatic passion—the essence of Dido herself—melts away, to be succeeded by strict vocal polyphony, a four-part canon, moving diatonically, mainly by step, sung by a chorus of Cupids. They are, of course, gods of love and also the plump fruits of love that a paradise of sensuality was liable to leave around; and they scatter the sexual rose upon Dido, as Belinda had said they would in her 'Fear no danger' song. But Dido is dead and Aeneas is absent; so the Cupids become also baroque cherubs on a tomb: who sing like Christian angels of the old world. This is quite different from anything in Blow's elegiacs; again Purcell ends with a nostalgic reference to a world outside the present. Human passion, and in the most literal sense sexual love, is the point we start from; but we end with the admission that the craving of the heart and senses is inappeasable. So we wish we were innocent angels, before the Fall; and on the words 'never part' the regular dance rhythm (the only survival in this chorus of the humanist ritual of the masque) breaks into sighs and silence.

7

PURCELL AND THE RESTORATION THEATRE

The Fairy Queen
The Tempest

Nahum Tate was not a poet who could offer Purcell all he needed and deserved. None the less, Purcell can always make up for the deficiencies of the poetry, and as a dramatic action *Dido and Aeneas* is a good libretto, with an important theme both closely and deeply in touch with contemporary experience. Certainly Tate's book was the best Purcell ever had: for after this small-scale attempt at a modification of the Heroic, Restoration opera expired.

Yet the English failure to achieve the Heroic meant that a man of Purcell's exceptional genius was able to reveal, in his *Dido*, a deeper and richer human reality; and even the subsequent degeneration of Restoration opera to the level of a variety show carries, in Purcell's hands, the most unexpectedly rewarding compensations. From this point of view *The Fairy Queen*[1] is especially fascinating. The Restoration habit of rehashing old plays as 'musicals' is interesting in itself, for in so doing the hack writers destroyed the values of the originals while substituting no new values in their place. Evelyn was speaking of *Hamlet* when he remarked that 'the old plays begin to Disgust this Refined Age'; and it was this Refined Age that tagged *Hamlet* in rhyming couplets and provided *King Lear* with a happy ending, marrying off Cordelia to her fairy prince. In the light of this, it is hardly surprising that Restoration writers were fond of refurbishing Shakespearean plays that could be construed simply as fairy tales, as escape art—if you were prepared to ignore, or to rewrite, Shakespeare's poetry. *The Fairy Queen* is based on *A Midsummer Night's Dream*; and its relation to Shakespeare is about the same as the relationship of the twentieth

---

[1] Novello. Vocal Score edited by J. S. Shellock.

century filmed musical to 'the book of the movie'. It is a series of elaborate and expensive masques introduced without any attempt at dramatic coherence into a spoken drama. Yet the term masque is too dignified, for the song-and-dance episodes have lost all ritualistic, as well as dramatic, significance. They are 'shows': entertainment in the modern sense, something distinct from both art and ritual. Interestingly enough, the shows were not presented privately at court for the delectation of the Lords and Ladies of the earth. They were put on in the public theatre, so that Tom, Dick and Harry could indulge in their splendours vicariously, while at the same time lining the pockets of the sponsors. It is true that *The Fairy Queen* was not a successful example of commercial enterprise. Despite the show's great popularity, the sponsors lost heavily because the 'ingenious Engins' were even more expensive than they had bargained for. Financial loss was not, however, the intention; *The Fairy Queen* is an early instance of show-business which failed because production techniques were not yet geared to full efficiency.

It is easy to say that this gallimaufry of unco-ordinated sensations represents the failure in England of heroic opera: that not until Handel's oratorios and English operas did we produce a modification of *opera seria* appropriate to our circumstances and equal to, perhaps superior to, continental achievement. Yet musically *The Fairy Queen* is longer, richer, more mature than *Dido*; only in arioso is it inferior to the earlier piece, and this is inevitable since the 'here-and-now' of physical and psychological action is irrelevant to a work conceived as a series of shows. As a whole, perhaps, it is no longer performable in the theatre; yet the lack of a central purpose becomes, allied to the fecundity of Purcell's genius, almost a virtue. At least, if we are to create a musical-theatrical convention as appropriate to democracy as *opera seria* was to aristocratic autocracy we shall have to take account of Purcell's flexibility. *The Fairy Queen* combines elements that look back to the masque and to heroic opera: elements that develop features of Lully's comic operas and ballets in more 'popular' style: and even elements that suggest English ballad opera and the Victorian pantomime and music-hall.

What is remarkable is that Purcell can achieve such extravagant variety without sacrificing consistency of style. We have already seen that in the final scene of *Dido and Aeneas* he can pass from something like savage farce to the heights and depths of tragedy in a matter of minutes: and that this ability is attributable partly to his genius but also to the conditioning element of the spiritually and culturally amorphous world he lived in. Similarly, in *The Fairy Queen* Purcell can pass from the solemn and mysterious to the frivolous and tawdry: and make the apparent contradictions a totality of experience. The Overtures, and such instrumental movements as the Chaconne and the 'Symphony while the Swans come forward', belong to the old heroic world, though they are vitalized, rendered more earthy, by Purcell's characteristically tough harmonic texture. *The Plaint* is an aria on a chromatic ground bass, rivalling Dido's lament in the manner in which the repetitions of the ground (and in this case the echoing song of the obbligato instrument) objectifies personal suffering. But whereas Dido's aria is the climax of a drama in music and can make its full effect only in its theatrical context, *The Plaint* is a self-contained 'number' in a show. For this reason it is musically more developed than the lament. It has a middle section in the relative major, when the chromatic ground gives way to a diatonic ground: a da capo of the original ground and aria, and an extended consummatory coda. A still more developed piece in opera seria style is 'Ye gentle spirits of the air', a big da capo aria which both in structure and in expressive ornamentation is more sustained than anything in *Dido*. This piece indicates how in *The Fairy Queen* the reflective arias incorporate much of the dramatic immediacy that, in *Dido*, went into arioso. We shall discuss the significance of this development—which Purcell did not live to fulfil—when we consider Handel's English permutation of fully-fledged heroic opera.

Although all the numbers we have mentioned so far are direct survivals from the masque, it is interesting that Purcell tends to make his masque scenes dramatic rather than ritualistic. There is even drama in the conventional notion of the masque of the Seasons, in the way in which the Praise chorus, with D major trumpets, returns after the astonishing chromatic declensions of Winter's bass aria. Similarly, the beautiful Night scene, scored for high strings in regular step-wise movement, is a traditional Lullian *scène de sommeil*; yet there is a dramatic intimacy beneath the elegant surface, especially in the characterization of Secrecy. He is not merely a personification but also a human

217

being whose counter-tenor ornamentation, reinforced by limpid recorders, coos seductively in our ears: 'One charming night Gives more delight Than a hundred happy days'. Sleep's lullaby and the hushing chorus further intensify the masque to drama; we can hear the silence as the chorus plead that no noise should disturb her sweet repose. The empty beats seem alive with expectancy; the appeal to sleep is the more touching because we have sensed the nameless terrors of the night. Here Purcell's theatrical instinct is equated with his musical genius.

A still subtler case is the Epithalamium, naturally a ceremonial piece that begins with a curious chugging rhythm that suggests a procession. Juno begins to sing 'Thrice happy lovers'; but on the words 'may you be forever free From that tormenting devil Jealousy' breaks into arioso arabesques that, at once agitated and ecstatic, destroy the processional rhythm. The lovers are no longer two important people about to fulfil a social contract; they have become individual human beings, about to face the joy and anguish that adult life has in store for them. The ceremonial, 'public' rhythm tries to establish itself again; but is again sundered by arioso arabesques on the words 'forever free', with no reference to jealousy this time. It is as though the chugging had implied that marriage as a social institution might be a prison: so we are relieved that the obsessive rhythm is defeated and the arioso leads into a dance aria in six-eight, beginning with an imitation between voice and bass that controls the passion, but flowering into virtuoso roulades on the words 'ever constant, ever chaste'. The effect is sensuously exciting, as a marriage should be: and also, perhaps, slightly desperate, as though the whirling coloratura were scared lest that chugging might return.

The dances provide links between the various worlds of feeling. Some of them—the Dance for the Followers of Night, which is a strict canon four in 2—belong to heroic convention. Others (the lovely B flat rondeau, the Dance for the Green Men, and the final dance chorus) are halfway between the aristocratic and the popular. Others, again, are frankly low and either rustic (the Haymakers' Dance) or urban (the Monkeys' Dance, with its cheeky rhythmic surprises). Among the comic turns the scene of the Three Drunkards gives a low, more middleclassical twist to the comic manner of Lully. Again, it is a move in the direction of realism, for the fairies that 'pinch 'em' behave, and sing, more like Restoration urchins than like supernatural beings. The end of this vaudeville turn is, however, interesting. The urchin-fairies stop singing 'Drive 'em away' in a prancing six-four; the music changes to common time, and a vocal fugato, with old fashioned flat seventh creating a bitter-sweet false relation, invites them to 'sleep till break of day'. Once more, disparate worlds of feeling interpenetrate. For all Purcell's 'modern' vivacity the reference back to older and deeper values recurrently introduces a note of nostalgia.

The music-hall manner appears again in the pastoral duet between Corydon and Mopsa, in which the girl was sung by a counter-tenor. This is not just a sophisticated titter at the country bumpkin, for the popular flavour of the dance-song is authentic. The piece is, of course, very funny: but positively so, not merely deflatory. A subtler instance is provided by the Chinese Men in the last act. The introduction of such exotics was a commonplace of classical French ballet, the point being to contrast the savage state of Nature with the hyper-sophisticated world of the court. The satire is usually double-edged: the natives are awfully quaint; on the other hand they may have an honesty and integrity that we have lost. Purcell uses this ambivalence in the Second Chinese Man's song, which is a genuine and touching appeal for kindness and understanding, yet also a parody of the ceremonial aria in dotted rhythm; in the precise, angular movement there is perhaps a hint of the stage Chink—a low note that would not occur in Lully. The First Chinese Man's song is similarly equivocal, though the effect is much deeper. It begins as an aria of Glory with trumpet obbligato, describing how the world first came to light. Then there is a middle section in the relative minor, from which all the extrovert bounce has vanished. This describes the state of Eden, 'innocence secure', when there was 'no room for empty fame, no cause for pride'. Here the phrases are broken, separated by recurrent orchestral cadences, while the ceremonial dotted rhythm becomes, in these simple but faltering phrases, tentative, groping. The effect is comic, yet at the same time pathetic and disturbing. It is as though proud man has seen through his pretences: so when he sings the Glory aria da capo the stiltedness rather than the power of the music is emphasized.

This imaginatively critical attitude to Restoration Glory is

219

evident throughout Purcell's ceremonial music. *King Arthur*,[1] for instance, was devised by Dryden as a pageant celebrating his country's might; yet Purcell's music imbues the Pastoral Scene with so dreamy a seductiveness that public valour is forgotten; we delightedly follow the Daughters of the Aged Stream who call Arthur from his Duty, entangling him and us in the tendrils of their coloratura. The climax of the work is a solemn passacaglia in G *minor*, with pathetic dissonant suspensions and passing notes. The words speak of the lover's happiness, while advising us to 'use the short blessing that flies in possessing'; and we are more conscious of the melancholy of mutability than of the joy of fulfilment. The melancholy remains dignified and noble: but is saved from frenzy only, perhaps, by the rigid discipline of the passacaglia rhythm.

The Fairy Queen and *King Arthur* are sufficiently 'musical' in conception for Purcell's genius to carry all before it. His last theatre work was, however, the music he wrote for the Dryden-Davenant version of Shakespeare's *Tempest;*[2] and this reveals that Purcell's apprehension of reality was hardly less remote than Shakespeare's from the conventional attitudes of the Restoration. In the sixteen-seventies, Dryden and Davenant had rehashed Shakespeare's original as a 'modern' play with incidental music; Shadwell had then rehashed the rehash, providing additional opportunities for music, and concluding with a self-contained Masque of Neptune which is not in Shakespeare at all. The music for this version was by several composers: whose efforts were discarded when Purcell wrote new music for a revival of the Shadwell production in 1695. The Restoration dramatists could hardly have missed the point of Shakespeare's play more comprehensively; Purcell's music—especially the Masque of Neptune —discovers, if not Shakespeare's point, at least a range of experience that is comparable in significance.

We saw that the essence of Shakespeare's romance lay in the fact that it was a *poetic* drama: the poetry being a heightened apprehension of the physical and metaphysical world in which we live. Superficially, the Dryden-Davenant version moves towards realism: but proves, in destroying Shakespeare's poetry, how

[1] Novello or any vocal score.
[2] Novello: edited by E. J. Dent.

unreal realism is. This is obvious enough in the opening storm scene, for which the stage-direction of Shadwell's adaptation reads:

> The front of the stage is opened, and the band of 24 Violins, with the harpsicals, and theorbos which accompany the voyces, are played between the pit and the stage. While the overture is playing, the curtain rises and discovers a new frontispiece, joined to the great pilasters, on each side of the stage. . . Behind this is the scene, which represents a thick, cloudy sky, a very rocky coast, and a tempestuous sea in perpetual agitation. The tempest, (supposed to be raised by magic) has many dreadful objects in it, as several spirits in horrid shapes flying down amongst the sailors, then rising and crossing in the air. And when the ship is sinking, the whole house is darkened and a shower of fire falls on them. This is accompanied by lightning and several Claps of Thunder, to the end of the storm.

What Shakespeare does with poetry—which relates the physical storm to the spiritual—Dryden and Davenant leave to the stage mechanics. The storm exists for its own sake, as a show; is extended through eighty lines that read like jottings from a nautical text-book; and involves a plethora of additional sea-faring characters. Given the resources of Hollywood, the dramatists would undoubtedly have called on 'a cast of thousands'; it is not surprising that the Storm from the Restoration *Tempest*, in which the guns break loose from their train tackle and roll about the tilting decks, was the play's main box-office attraction: one anonymous poem, published in 1679, exclaims:

> Such noise, such stink, such smoke there was, you'd swear
> *The Tempest* surely had been acted there.
> The cryes of star-board, Lard-board, Cheerly boys,
> Is but as demy rattles to this Noise.

If the naturalistic elements are played up in the Dryden-Davenant *Tempest*, the magical elements are played down, or rather deflated. Shakespeare's Prospero, though humanly fallible, is Renaissance man aiming at the control of Nature and the passions. The Dryden-Davenant Prospero is a seedy seaside-pier magician, chiefly distinguished for his ineffectuality. The masques of devils etc, that charm the visitors occur quite independently of Prospero's control; and far from attaining any self-knowledge or wisdom, he can think of no better advice to give his daughters than to warn them, salaciously, of the dangers latent in young men. ('Do they run wild about the woods?' 'No, they are wild within doors, in chambers and closets. No woman can come near them but she feels the pain a full nine months.') Neither the girls nor any one else take any notice of the disenchanted magician who, when crossed, is liable to turn from a dotard into a bloody tyrant, a Machiavel:

> To execute Heaven's Laws
> Here I am placed by Heav'n, here I am Prince,
> Though you have dispossessed me of my Millain.
> Blood calls for blood; your Ferdinand shall die;
> And I in bitterness have sent for you
> To have the sudden joy of seeing him alive,
> And then the greater grief to see him die.

The ultimate deflation of the man-god Prospero occurs in the episode of the Stephano-Trinculo plot, for the clownish Stephano exerts more control over his 'subjects' in this scene than Prospero exerts throughout the play. Moreover, the plot that Trinculo now foments with Caliban is not against Prospero but against Stephano, the real lord of the island; not only is Prospero's rule not recognized, his name is barely mentioned.

There is allegorical appropriateness in the fact that Stephano should have deposed Prospero in the Restoration world; and not only is there no man-god left, there are no 'good' characters either. Gonzalo has become merely what Shakespeare's Antonio thinks he is—a tedious old fool; Miranda has become a pretty chit hardly distinguishable from her (Davenant-invented) nymphomaniac sister, Dorinda; Ferdinand is a pimply adolescent comparable with the (Davenant-invented) Hippolito, a youth who has never seen a woman, a situation conducive to the uproariously sexy jape. If there are no good characters, it is because there are also no bad characters, for evil is not apprehended as such; it is not an accident that Ariel no longer disturbingly rides on 'the bat's back', but straddles a prettily poetic swallow. Chaos is indeed come again, and 'harsh discord reigns upon this fatal isle'. But there is little evidence to support Ariel's continuation: 'at which good Angels mourn, ill spirits smile', for the only evident response to this discord is a cynical shrug of the shoulders. The happy ending exists only at the most rudimentary sexual level. Everyone is provided with a mate, even Caliban and Ariel, but at this level copulation is merely a cult of sensation, analogous to the initial storm, and thus an evasion of responsibility. The odd thing is that Dryden and Davenant genuinely believed not only that they were making Shakespeare more palatable to contemporary audiences, but also that they were improving him by removing vulgarities (!) and making the action more probable. Shakespeare's play makes us see that miracles may be true in that through them we may be reborn. Dryden and Davenant titter at miracles and imagine that their play is more 'real' because it accepts the cynicism and hedonism of Restoration society. Appropriately and ironically, Ariel summarizes their efforts when he remarks to Ferdinand:

> 'Twas happy we had this little tryal,
> But how we all mistook so much, I know not.

What makes the Restoration *Tempest* peculiarly revolting is that so much of Shakespeare's poetry is preserved within the rehash; and the original and restored elements cannot be miscible. Nor can the addition of Purcell's music make the elements fuse in the theatre: though we can appreciate that it was Shakespeare's presence that inspired Purcell to create some of his most heart-assuaging music. Certainly Purcell's music is closer to Shakespeare than it is to Dryden; it differs from Shakespeare, however, both because—in so far as it looks back to Shakespeare—it is inevitably elegiac, and also because it looks forward, positively, to the eighteenth century. The retrospective element manifests that fusion of mysticism with humanism which we commented on in early works of Purcell, such as the string fancies and *Welcome to all the Pleasures*; and this synthesis is typical of Shakespeare's *Tempest* also. The 'progressive' element approaches an inner tranquillity of mind which is more rational than mystical: as though Purcell realized intuitively what the positive values of the new world were to be, when the cynicism of Restoration society was spent. So we can relate Purcell's *Tempest* backwards to Shakespeare and forwards to Handel; but it has little if any affinity with Dryden and Davenant.

Superficially, of course, it has something to do with Shadwell, since the additional masque was designed as an opportunity for music. Purcell probably felt relieved that the masque did not even pretend to have anything to do with Prospero's seedy activities, but was put on by the sea-gods themselves. Neptune, Amphitrite, Oceanus and Thetys appear in a chariot drawn by sea-horses, on each side of which are tritons and nereids. Amphitrite pleads for a calm voyage for the mortals, Neptune orders Oceanus to put on his most serene looks, and advises Aeolus to muzzle his roaring boys. Aeolus descends singing: 'Come, ye blusterers, swell no more.' Flying from the four corners of heaven, the winds are driven into the bowels of the earth, while the chorus chants 'send a calm'. Towards the end Ariel flies out of the Rising Sun, sings his (batless) version of 'Where the bee sucks', and bids farewell to Prospero: when the revels are over.

Since the Shadwell masque has no connexion with the play Purcell can treat it as a self-contained appeal for peace at sea—and within the mind. What we have called the retrospective elements in the music are exemplified notably in Ariel's songs, in which the rhythmic flexibility and modal ambiguity are reminiscent of the Jacobean ayre, though the false-relations and chromaticisms tinge their innocence with nostalgia. Still more do we find this elegiac note in the lovely final chorus, where the falling thirds and dissonant passing notes that tell us that 'no stars again shall hurt us' are consolatory, but wistful. The Shakespearean quality in this music derives both from the serenity that the quietly unfolding polyphony achieves, and also from the bitter-sweet poignancy of the harmony, which is Purcell's awareness of the pain—the 'hurt'—inherent in living. Nothing, except Shakespeare himself, could be further removed from the tawdry painlessness of Dryden's and Davenant's malformation.

The forward-looking elements in the *Tempest* masque are related to Purcell's growing use of Italianate conventions, especially the da capo aria. Aeolus's songs demonstrate this, for the brilliant bluster of the coloratura is not vehemently chaotic but lucidly ordered by the architectural proportions and by the resonance of the texture. Most wonderful, however, is the song 'Halcyon days', which is a new kind of music in Purcell's career. Passion is assuaged in limpid cantilena, frenzy is dissipated in extreme clarity and simplicity of harmony and tonality; and these technical features are a musical synonym for the mind's ability to control the turbulence of the passions through the exercise of Reason. Purcell is moving towards the Handelian conception of Augustan order:[1] the happiness that comes not from denying the passions; but from submitting them to the laws of both Nature and Society. 'Halcyon days' strikingly anticipates Handel's adaptation of the Italian aria da capo in some of his English works, notably *Acis and Galatea* and *L'Allegro ed Il Pensieroso*. Both Purcell's and Handel's melodies preserve, here, an English 'open-air' quality, with even a hint of folk-song in the prevalence of falling fourths and fifths. But the infinite stillness which the music attains is a product of rational reflection, which disciplines both the expansiveness of line and the sensuousness of harmony into sequential symmetry and textural lucidity. The Golden Age is admitted to be, not a physical fact, but a state of mind: a contentment which man may attain if he will allow Reason to follow Nature's dictates. The subjective nature of Augustan order was not, perhaps, consciously recognized until those English works of Handel which dealt not so much with Man in Society as with Man in the natural world. Perhaps we may say, however, that Handel's English fulfilment was implicit even in his early Italian works, in so far as the theory behind heroic opera was based on a deceit. Before we discuss Handel's English consummation we must consider briefly the nature of fully-fledged heroic opera, and its exemplification in an Italian cantata of Handel's youth.

[1] Largely for this reason, an attempt has recently been made to discredit Purcell's authorship of the *Tempest* music. (See the *Proceedings of the Royal Musical Association*, 1963-4). Admittedly, the factual evidence is not absolutely conclusive; but I can see no reason to doubt it apart from a wilful desire to prove a theory. I'd say that the elegiac and archaistic features of the *Tempest* music are quintessentially typical of Purcell and of no other composer of his period, while the 'progressive' features are just what we would expect to find in the work of a composer of supreme genius, about to enter into his years of maturity. How odd it would have been if a man of Purcell's acute sensitivity hadn't responded to the implications of Italianate aria style, which was in the air, whether or no Purcell himself ever heard any Italian opera. Scholarly research may sometimes miss the wood for the trees; if one can believe that 'Halcyon Days' was written by an obscure hack whose music is otherwise undistinguished one can believe anything.

8

HANDEL AND THE HEROIC

Apollo e Dafne

The nature of classical heroic opera depended on the fact that, the more man practised self-reliance, the more he tended to equate material power with divinity. The autocratic king could not become god in spiritual terms because he was subject to mortality. But he could attempt to become god in material terms; and in so doing he could justify himself only by considering the public or communal aspects of his role as more important than his private experience. If he did not serve an Absolute up in the sky, at least he served a concept here on earth that was larger than himself. This is why, in classical heroic opera,—which was a ritual of humanism no less than the earlier masque—the recitative and drama became gradually less significant and the dance-dominated aria more significant. Monteverdi's *Orfeo*, at the beginning of the seventeenth century, is basically a play in sung recitative, with dance interludes, the recitative being private experience, the dances the communal life. Between the private and the public elements there is little interpenetration. In Purcell's *Dido*, at the end of the century, the centre is still in the human drama but to a much greater degree the play has become music. The public rhythm of the dance begins to affect the speech rhythm of the personal life: for the norm is now arioso—physical and psychological Becoming—rather than recitative. The fusion of arioso and dance—of the private and the public experience—is the consummation the opera seeks, though the consummation is achieved only in death, so that the opera ends elegiacally.

A baroque opera represents a third stage. The recitative, the play-element, is now comparatively unimportant; it exists to tell us, narratively, what happens. What matters is the arias, which are a lyrical reflection on what has occurred in the drama. These arias are symmetrically disposed in harmonic and tonal periods, with a middle section that serves as architectural balance, not dramatic contrast, and with a da capo of the first section which is a literal repeat except for the intensification of improvised ornamentation. All the arias are contemplative, even when quick or furious, in the sense that they deal with absolutes of experience, after the event, rather than, like Purcell's arioso, with experience as it is created before our eyes and ears. These arias of love, or rage, or pity, or terror tended to be non-developing and non-evolutionary because they were not concerned with growth within the mind. What conditioned the architectural periods was a set dance-rhythm, with which arias representing the various 'Affections' were conventionally associated; and this is a literal musical equation for man's desire to submit the lyrical exuberance and harmonic violence of his passions to the discipline of public order. It is significant that the stock heroic opera contains virtually no ensemble numbers, since it is not concerned with the interaction of characters, only with their attempt to codify and canalize their experience: and that arioso is admitted only when the characters are actually mad or so 'beside themselves' with passion as to be irresponsible. Only when lunatic do we break through the conscious control of Reason and through our public identities to enter the here-and-now of physical and psychological action—in which Monteverdi and Purcell had habitually lived.

Though this was the norm, the significant achievements of heroic opera are the exceptions to the theory: those which are most ready to admit to the paradox inherent in the convention and in the central theme. At a superficial level an element of deceit is evident in the use of artificial male sopranos and altos for the heroic characters. The theory was that the artificial voice would emphasize the 'superhuman' quality of the men-gods, while natural male voices were reserved for doddering old men or low characters. Yet the man-god was essentially a super-*man*; and it was a cheat to pretend that half a man was better than a whole one. The deceit comes out more damagingly in the central theme which is still, as in Monteverdi's and Purcell's operas, the contrast between man's desire for divinity and the fallible perversity of his nature. The difference lies in the fact that whereas Monteverdi and Purcell accepted this paradox as tragic, classical heroic opera merely abandoned the conflict without resolving it.

227

The pagan, not Christian, deus ex machina descends from the heavens to put right the mess created by blundering mortals. Though everything seems to indicate that man is not in control of his destiny, civilization depends on our acting as though he were. We live for the Perfectability of Man, and if that is not in fact yet achieved, we must pretend that it is only just around the corner. The wish-fulfilment of the deus ex machina occurs in most of Handel's Italian operas; but it is indicative of the imaginative integrity of this great humanist that he abandons the deus ex machina, or uses it in a subtly modified form, in his most representative English works. Nor can it be an accident that there is no deus ex machina in the short cantata Apollo e Dafne[1] that Handel wrote, as a boy of twenty, during his Italian apprenticeship. This piece is perhaps the most brilliant and searching achievement of the first phase of his cosmopolitan career; and it deals, more economically than Handel was ever to do in his full-scale Italian operas, with the basic myth of the heroic age.

It is not surprising that the Dafne story was immensely popular with baroque opera composers, for it is a parable about the paradox of the Man-God. We have seen that men of the post-Renaissance world admired the Greek humanist precisely because his gods were humanity writ large: if man's heroic attributes were exaggerated, so were his foibles and pettinesses. Indeed, the only difference between men and gods was that the gods were not subject to Time. This is why, in the Dafne legend, the relationship of god to man is that of love-hate. Apollo, as sun-god or great creating Nature, wants to ravish humanity: but in so doing has to submit to human passion, to the pangs as well as the pleasures of love; he wants the pleasures but cannot stomach the surrender of his god-like superiority to mortal concerns. Dafne, as humanity, wants to love the sun-god but is scared to fulfil herself. She subjugates her flesh, dedicates herself to chastity, as an escape from experience, because she doubts whether she is strong enough to love; here the pagan myth gets mixed up with Christian abnegation. The eighteenth century solution of this deadlock—whereby Apollo is the Word trying to become Flesh and Dafne is the Flesh trying to become Word, both acting in apparent opposition to their natures—was that

[1] J. & W. Chester, edited by Anthony Lewis.

'an honest heart by Reason should a blameless calm restore'. That was the theory. In practice, however, it does not work out like that at all: for the paradox can be resolved only by transubstantiation. She becomes a *tree*—animate nature, growing, living, stretching upwards to heaven: rooted to the earth, but without human passions and turmoils: subject to time, without being conscious of it.

The piece opens with narration; but the recitative is so lyrically declamatory as to become almost arioso. Apollo, representative of man's god-like potentialities, tells us how he has freed humanity by destroying the Python, or the worm of corruption. His assertive upward arpeggios, his surging scales, the enormous range of his vocal line (with a descent of a twelfth to portray the Python's collapse), all help to establish him as a god-like figure; and this becomes manifest in his aria, when he tells us that all the world and all creation depend on his awful conquering arm. This is an Aria of Power, in B flat, for Handel conventionally a key of strength. The tune is dominated by trumpet-like rising arpeggios, and there is virtually no dissonance in the inner parts. In the middle section, in which (so he says) all earthly creatures shout a paean of thanksgiving to him, energy is conveyed by giant-like leaps of sixth, seventh and ninth in syncopated rhythm. He is a god because he is larger than life, a source of creation; but he is obstreperously physical, not metaphysical.

He then, in recitative, boasts of his superiority to love, the agent between the human and the divine. If he is humanity writ large he is, or would be, humanity freed from doubt, perplexity, and error. He makes this point in another power-aria, this time in D major, with trumpet arpeggios (played, in this chamber work, on oboes). The purpose of this is both to vaunt his own more-than-human potency and also to make Cupid (whose arrows are fit only for killing sparrows) look silly. As in the previous power aria, the rigidity of the da capo form emphasizes his unchanging, superhuman attributes. We do not necessarily take this as he expects us to. We see the grandeur, of course; but because we are human we may find in the grandeur a quality at worst monstrous, at best faintly comic.

Abruptly we switch to Dafne, who sings a sensuously seraphic pastoral in G major (the *subdominant* of Apollo's D) and in a lilting 12:8. The long, sinuous oboe melody, magically accompanied by pizzicato strings, creates a dream of happiness which, Dafne tells us, can be realized only when the soul is fancy free, dedicated to Diana, living apart from the world. In the middle section, in the relative minor, she says that as soon as a girl surrenders her heart she loses all peace of mind, becomes a prey to torments. So the music is exquisitely tranquil, and again the da capo form most appropriately suggests timelessness; yet at the same time the music is, with its yearning sevenths and caressing suspensions, regretfully wistful, since she is saying that she cannot hope to be happy except by denying her womanhood. Though the music's sensuousness is her feminine reality, it is, as it were, embalmed in a dream.

At this point Apollo and Dafne meet, and we become aware that Dafne's and Apollo's complementary dreams of self-sufficiency are equally illusory. In quick, dramatic recitative he says that he, a god, scornful of Cupid, is consumed with passion for her humanity. At first she recoils, and says that, being dedicated to Diana, she can have none of him. He points out, significantly, that Diana is his sister; since Nature and Spirit are allied Dafne must, in loving Diana, love him too. Dafne is not prepared to admit to the identity of Word and Flesh, and sings a curiously spiky aria in which she says that nothing shall make her relinquish her solemn vow. The angular line, the regularly moving quaver bass, the canonic chase on the obbligato instruments (oboe and violin), suggest an incipient hysteria precariously controlled; and the reason for this uneasiness comes out in the following exchange, in which Apollo, his super-human boastfulness cast aside, says that passion will excuse everything. For Dafne, having peremptorily ordered him off, immediately joins with him in a duet, in which both sing of the war that is waging in their hearts, and of their inability to bear it a moment longer. She, from her fear, admits that she wants to love him; he, from his wilful imperviousness, admits that he is driven to despair. So they are both in the same (tempest-tossed) boat, and the ecstacy of their whirling jig—with broken, panting phrases interchanged on the words 'ardo', 'gello', 'peno'—is not far from frenzy.

At this moment, significantly, the god Apollo, become slave to human love, realizes the difference between gods and mortals: the fact that all Nature's creations, as distinct from Nature herself, are subject to Time. He sings a most beautiful aria in which he compares the beloved to the rose upon the briar, which is fair today, but tomorrow fled. Unlike the rose in the Garden of Eden ('And without thorn, the Rose', as Milton puts it), Apollo's rose does not deny the inescapable briar, the pain within the pleasure. The wide span of the melody, built this time on a *falling* arpeggio, preserves the music's heroic stature, while suggesting a noble resignation; the dark-hued cello obbligato, sensuous but elegiac, reinforces this feeling. The music is by far the deepest that Apollo has yet sung; and it tells us that man cannot fulfil himself by overriding human imperfection. The aria is more, not less, heroic because it has lost the almost ludicrous swagger of his first two songs.

But Dafne, being merely human, does not grow to meet her lover. Instead, she points out that the paradox of god and human can never be resolved, and sings an aria expressing her determination to return to peace once more. She compares herself to a serenely shining star, high in the heavens, remote from terrestrial turmoil—in a slowish tune in a 4:4 dotted rhythm. Simultaneously, however, the orchestra plays a 12:8 dance rhythm, with semiquaver scales reminiscent of their love-duet. After a while her vocal line becomes absorbed in the quaver triplets of passion (traditionally equated with the sea); but her frail will prefers to hitch itself to her remote star, and as Apollo grows more human, she grows less. It is in the middle section of this aria that she says that an honest heart ought to be able to restore a blameless calm through the power of Reason. Clearly this is no more than wishful thinking; her prissy joke to Apollo ('tu non sei Dio!') strikes a truth she will not recognize, and from this point the music, and the humanity, are all his.

For when he begins to woo her in a sarabande rhythm, sensuous but with noble falling sevenths, she counters him with a return to the rigid quaver movement and the frightened semiquavers of her 'ardi adori' aria. 'Più tosto morire', she says; though the perfunctory scurrying of the empty, G major music certainly does not sound sweeter than Apollo's appeal. She runs away from him—and from herself, from the maturing of her humanity—and he chases her in an aria built over clattering semiquavers, with sharp dissonances on the strong beats. Her incomprehension perhaps prompts in him a return to his callous assertiveness—and to the power key of B flat; the ominous repeated notes in his vocal line express his cumulating desire. He catches her after a long instrumental ritornello, only to find that she disappears in her human shape. The semiquaver pursuit breaks off abruptly, and the dramatic climax is embodied in the immediacy of arioso, punctuated by shooting scales, 'horrid' diminished sevenths and savage repeated notes. This unexpected development ('qual novità!') demonstrates the impotence of Reason; so the music, and Apollo, become temporarily mad. Yet when once he realizes that she has turned into a laurel tree he uses arioso as a transition back to aria and—if not to sanity—at least to acceptance. His final Transubstantiation aria, in which he depersonalizes his grief and says that for all time Heroes will wear laurel, is a sarabande in G minor—relative of B flat, the power key in which he had opened. This music is the heroism of power, grown to maturity, to awareness of humanity. The theme, though broken in its distress, has a proud grandeur, especially in the hemiola rhythm at the cadences; the harmony has intensity, which is none the less assuaged in the superb sweep of the line. The personal pathos is disciplined by the ceremonial sarabande rhythm, by the antiphonal scoring for woodwind and strings. Dafne is sublimated into a tree; Apollo becomes truly godlike in accepting, and transcending, human suffering. The paradox lies in the fact that whereas Dafne, who is human, voluntarily surrenders consciousness, Apollo, who being a god ought to be beyond Time, grows from the bluster of his first aria to the tragic heroism of his last. And the tragic note is final. Though the concluding sarabande exists in the present and is not retrospective, like the end of Purcell's Dido, it admits to the insolubility of the man-god paradox; there is no deus ex machina.

When Handel settled in England some years later one of his first works was a re-creation of another classical myth—that of Acis and Galatea. He wrote this for the Duke of Chandos at Cannons, conceiving it for very modest resources. Partly for this reason, he adapted the conventions of fully-fledged opera seria in a manner that has points of similarity with Purcellian opera and masque. Perhaps he remembered, subconsciously, his youthful Apollo e Dafne—a work which he justly esteemed and borrowed from on numerous occasions. Certainly his English Acis also dispenses with the deus ex machina and ends elegiacally. The tone, however, is different from that of the cantata, which we have studied as a quintessential example of the Italianate concept of the Heroic. The manner of *Acis and Galatea*, as compared with that of *Apollo e Dafne*, is intimate; and this intimacy has something to do not merely with material conditions at Cannons, but also with Handel's failure to sell heroic opera to prosperous, if not spiritually aristocratic English bidders. The limitations his new society imposed on him were to be the means whereby he discovered the heights and depths of his talent.

9

HANDEL AND THE ENGLISH PASTORAL

Acis and Galatea

Superficially, Handel's *Acis and Galatea*,[1] with its sequence of strict da capo arias and its libretto based on the traditional cliché of the Golden Age, would seem to be a conventional heroic piece telling us, once more, that civilization depends on our capacity for self-deception. Yet though Gay and Handel do not modify this theme as radically as do Tate and Purcell, there is none the less a difference between *Acis* and a true heroic opera. For Gay's book does not attempt to hoodwink us into belief in the Perfectability of Man; it tells us that the Golden Age is only a dream, *and is admitted to be such*. It is not possible, Gay's poem says, for human beings to become gods; in so far as they attempt to do so they become comic, or pathetic, or both: and perhaps actively evil. Gay's admission of the comic element in the human predicament is the distinctively English feature of his adaptation of heroic convention: which could have occurred only because the English failed to attain a valid concept of the heroic in the seventeenth century. The Restoration relapse into cynicism, although in itself negative, had left a positive legacy in so far as the values of the Augustan age, as they crystallized out, absorbed satire. Perhaps this is inherent in the Augustan reliance on Reason as the main guide to human conduct: for however clearly its moral and social ideals may be delineated, the rational mind will always be critically aware of a disparity between the ideal and the real. Certainly the Augustan age in England was a period of defined positives; and complementarily to those positives, was our greatest age of satire.

So Gay's opera book, based on heroic convention, introduces too elements of masque and pastoral that are often satirically treated. These satirical features are present in Handel's music

[1] Novello. Vocal Score edited by J. Barnby.

also, trained though he had been in the grandeur of the classical baroque. His concern with absolutes is beginning to be modified by a 'recognition of other modes of experience that are possible', such as characterizes the sonata style of Haydn and Mozart. This is why there is a deeper connexion between his Augustanism and that of Pope than we might at first appreciate. He may not be fundamentally a satirist: but he shares Pope's compassionate as well as arrogant awareness of human imperfection. His vision of the splendour that Augustan civilization *might* attain strikingly parallels Pope's magnificent vision at the end of the *Epistle to Boyle on the Use of Riches*; while his ultimate mood of acceptance and resignation complements the tragic rationality of the *Essay on Man*. In a sense, the pilgrimage that ends in the final, tragic choruses of *Semele* and *Jephtha* begins with the first of Handel's English works, *Acis and Galatea*, written for the Duke of Chandos—who was the Timon of Pope's *Epistle to Boyle*. For although this is a work about youth, it is coloured with a quality that could easily become pessimism, since human hopes certainly do not conform with the realities of experience.

The piece opens, indeed, with a classical antithesis. The chorus sings of the Golden Age, 'harmless, merry, free and gay', where happy nymphs and happy swains dance and sport without a care in the world. The difference between this chorus and the ceremonial chorus of heroic opera lies in its texture, which is light and airy rather than sumptuous and pompous. The dancing polyphony has more than a hint of Purcell, while the imitative points on the words 'dance and sport' are even madrigalian. Passing dissonances, especially minor seconds, give a fleeting suggestion of instability, however: so that even in this hilarity there is already a quality of dream.

This becomes more evident in the middle section of the da capo form. Here the words tell us that the Golden Age is really an anthropomorphic apotheosis of humanism. 'For *us* the zephyr blows, For *us* distils the dew, For *us* unfolds the rose', and the seasons proceed in their ordained cycle, warming us when we're cold, chilling when we're too hot (in every sense), feeding us, refreshing us with wine. This is all very pleasant; and the music has changed from the dancing lilt to the dotted rhythm that, in heroic opera, expresses pride in being human, in being masters of our own and if possible of others' destiny. But the tonality has changed to the relative minor; and the prancing leaps of octave or sixth create dissonant suspensions much more strongly accented, and emotionally expressive, than the fluttery clashes of the first section. So there's an element of pathos in the passage's pride; and when we hear the dance chorus again, da capo, we are more conscious than we were the first time of the instability within its pastoral mirth, of the dreamy illusion within its 'antique' bagpipe drones.

Immediately following this chorus, particular human beings begin to tell us how inadequate is this Innocence to their Experience. Life, says Galatea, isn't like that at all. The glories of the field are only painted, their pleasures vain; nature's gales are 'too faint to cool my love'. 'The pretty warbling choir' of birds is far from being pretty in its effects: for it awakes her pains and 'kindles fierce desire'. The reality is in the pain, contained in the melody and the dissonant suspensions of her aria: while the magnificence of baroque ornament becomes realistic, going to the recorders which, in cooing pastoral thirds, become the birds in the trees. The birds are happy, because oblivious of human suffering; so again happiness is—so far as we humans are concerned—a sweet cheat. This is evident too when Acis sings his first aria 'Where shall I seek the charming fair'. This is heroic in that, like all the arias in *Acis*, it is a static aria da capo, dealing with a state of mind rather than (like Dido's arioso) with experience as it happens, before our eyes and ears. Yet though it is based on the conventional dotted rhythm which was one of the formulae for magnificence, it does not convey the gestures of ceremonial movement. The upward thrust of the line, the broken rhythm suggest rather a restless wandering and searching, an inward agitation. Again there is pain in anticipated pleasure: and also, perhaps, the foreknowledge of impermanence.

Galatea is an immature girl compared with Purcell's Dido; but she has the roots of Dido's 'reality' within her and Acis shares her apprehension of reality, as Purcell's Aeneas doesn't. So their tragedy, if it is such, does not come from the disparity between those capable of 'real' experience and those incapable; it is rather the fraility inherent in mortality and, in particular, in being young. To begin with, they have no hesitation in rejecting

236

Damon's advice. As choric figure, he sings a complacent, level-rhythmed, non-dissonant aria reprimanding Acis for his restless pursuit. The only way to be happy, he says, is to avoid experience, not to chase after it. 'Free from love is free from care.' Follow love (which is, after all, life) and you run 'heedless to your ruin': for jealousy and care follow in love's wake, destroying the Golden Age's anthropomorphic bliss. The melody's persistent syncopation fuses the delirium of 'pleasure' with the calamity of 'ruin'. None the less Acis and Galatea find one another and in two arias presumably consummate their love. The beautiful lyrical expansion of 'Love in her eyes sits playing' accepts the pain in loving but transforms it to pleasure; she 'sheds delicious death', which takes up the love-death, pleasure-pain motive we commented on in Purcell. Similarly Galatea's dove aria makes the bird's love-song become her own: whereas in her previous bird song the warbling choir's happiness had been separated from her own pain. Now the billing and cooing —in her lovely melody with its sensuous sixths and sevenths, in the soft semiquaver figuration—is also a panting; 'melting murmurs' can become 'lasting love'. Their personal ecstasy can, they, hope, create a real golden age for them, if not for the world at large. So they join together in a lilting jig. Happy, happy we, they cry; what more is needful if thou art all my bliss, and thou art all my joy. The chorus take up the merriment; but nothing could be further removed from the ceremonial rejoicing of heroic opera. The jig is not grand but countrified, local, 'common'; there is even a real folk-song in it. Acis and Galatea are not lords and ladies, gods and heroes. They are ordinary young people, in England, in the early eighteenth century. In them the heroic is domesticated; and the pathos in their situation is as relevant now as it was in Handel's time.

The pathos consists in the fact that their happiness is not true: or is true only while it lasts, which is not long. For Part II opens with the 'Wretched lovers' chorus which says: 'Fate has passed the sad decree; *quit your dream*'. This scholastic fugue is the first intimation of the Grand Manner of the baroque. Ordered, rigidly controlled by metre (which is Time), this represents the unalterable Law to which human love and lovers must submit. When the lovers are told to 'quit their dream', however, the rising fourth in the fugue theme changes to a diminished fourth and the suspensions become much more acute; the Law becomes humanized, as it were, when we think how it effects *us*. This makes the opening of the fugue sound almost like parody, as we recall it retrospectively. The parodistic flavour becomes unmistakable when the 'monster Polyphemus' appears in thundering semiquavers, while the fugue proceeds implacably onwards. This passage is oddly equivocal: half comic, half frightening. So is Polyphemus himself who, being the reality of experience, will prick the bubble of innocence.

In a sense Polyphemus is the Hero; at least he is the only character who assumes heroic proportions (he is *literally* a giant), and who sings arioso (if with a hint of parody) in the heroic manner. Significantly, he wants to transport Galatea to 'Empire and to Love'—the stock heroic ideals: at which point Gay's poetry has unexpected immediacy and sensuous richness, as though Polyphemus's ideal is only another, riper and more solid version of anthropomorphic humanism. But of course he is also the villain, a monster: which is what heroic ambitions tend to make of men. So when Galatea does not respond to his advances, being unimpressed by the heroic ideals of Love and Empire, he turns Tyrant, relying on brute force. There is a kind of savage pride in the aria in which he says he will disdain 'whining love'. The rigid rhythm is meant to be horrid; yet the cross accents give it a hint of frenzy too. It is not only Galatea whom we feel sorry for.

For the essential point about Polyphemus is that he fails both as hero and villain—as God and Monster; and he fails because he is human! He is in love, racked by the same soft pains as are Acis and Galatea; the 'feeble god' has stabbed him to the heart, and he feels a fool. Through pride, first of the seven deadly sins, he falls; and as fallen man he is all of us, our self-abandonment to lust, jealousy, ambition. So, like all of us, he is at once tragic (in pitting himself against god): and comic (in pretending to be what is beyond human potentiality.) This is why the thunder chorus is followed immediately by his serious, heroic arioso: and then by his aria 'O ruddier than the cherry' which, with its comic flageolet obbligato, deflates the sublime. The satirical element here is much more grotesquely emphasized than it is in the presentation of Apollo's bumptiousness in *Apollo e Dafne*, but the point is still serious enough. It is as pitiful for a god (or monster) to try to become human as it is for a human to try to become god. Or perhaps, for a rationalistic society, the implication is that the concept of a god of power is not in the long run relevant: for it is impossible for humans to envisage even a quasi-human being devoid of human imperfections.

Significantly it is Damon, standing outside experience as usual, who then reproves Polyphemus for premeditated rape, as he had earlier reproved Acis and Galatea for giving way to love. He persistently asks the stock rhetorical questions which do not expect answers because they are not involved in the Becoming which is life. The static aria da capo is unequivocally his medium from which he, unlike Acis and Galatea—and Polyphemus, let alone Handel's greater, later tragic heroes and heroines—could never dream of breaking loose. He can be impervious to experience because he is not human but only one attribute of humanity —the thinking, rationalizing mind. He is eighteenth century Reason, and his urbanity is a virtue; but we cannot believe in him, and are not meant to, because no man was ever exclusively rational. 'Would you gain the tender creature, softly, gently, kindly treat her', he patronizingly sings to Polyphemus, in a G major aria that combines exquisite sensuous charm with a kind of ironic detachment. (The 'softly', 'gently' phrases, separated by rests, sound faintly amused.) Though suffering may be the lover's part, he, at least, will have no truck with it. But Acis knows that whatever Damon may be talking about, it isn't love; and announces in a trumpet-like aria that he has no choice but to fight Polyphemus because he cannot escape his destiny, which is to love and, inevitably, to suffer. The aria sounds, in its C major bounciness, heroic yet young and a little pathetic. Damon, reasonably cautious as usual, says that's nonsense; is it worth it, anyway, considering that the pleasure is so fleeting 'that flatters our hope in pursuit of the fair'? This aria, also in C major, is in a lilting, slightly precious rhythm, with much vocal ornamentation provoked by the fleeting and the flattering. Though the music is pretty, the preciousness tells us that Damon is not real. With a part of our minds we can offer ourselves such reasonable advice, while knowing that we cannot, in fact, be so blissfully uninvolved.

It is interesting that immediately after Damon has thus condescendingly addressed Acis, Galatea and now Polyphemus, the three of them—the lovers and monster who are related in being real—join together to sing a trio which becomes the emotional climax of the work. In quasi-canon, over a regular quaver movement in the bass, Acis and Galatea sing of the certainty and eternity of their love. The repeated notes in their theme, the level movement, convey a quiet determination, though there is a hint of desperation beneath the surface, for their imitative entries create persistent suspended seconds. While they are saying that, ere they leave one another, flocks shall leave mountains, doves forsake woods and nymphs forsake fountains (taking up the themes enunciated in their original love songs), Polyphemus enters with his furious, despairing descant, in semiquaver scales related to his initial thunder music. Here we feel inevitably that the three of them are inseparable. What Polyphemus 'cannot bear' is inherent in love itself, which contains the seeds of its own destruction: as Damon had pointed out at the beginning, when he told us that the only way to preserve the Golden Age is to avoid passion altogether ('Free from love is free from care'). This, of course, is impossible: which is why there is a hypnotic, trance-like quality in the padding rhythm of the Acis and Galatea duet. This is finally destroyed by Polyphemus's pesante semiquavers which, left in stark unison, become the stone he hurls at Acis. Immediately Acis is killed; and in dying has his moment of tragic grandeur, his brief passage of heroic arioso, accompanied by chromatically dissolving strings that remind us, remotely, of Dido's end.

Certainly the Dirge, when Galatea is left alone, is a return to the world of Purcell and to the elegiac, stoic feeling of the seventeenth century, before the apotheosis of Worldly Power. Its melancholy is dominated by acute minor seconds: the very interval which had given so dream-like and illusory a quality to the Prelude's pastoral bliss. The dirge thus prepares the way for the spiritual metamorphosis. Polyphemus—Fallen God-Man—has destroyed Acis, who grows up—into tragic arioso—as he dies. With him is destroyed the Golden Age of Innocence; and this time there is no deus ex machina to put things right at the last minute. It is inescapable that the 'charming youth must die for his constancy and truth': because Fallen Man is neither constant nor true. So Acis and Galatea have to be content, not with fulfilment in this life, but with translation to another

'Love in her eyes sits playing': Galatea by Francesco Albani

realm of being. In her aria 'Must I my Acis now bemoan' she sings in sorrow, heart-breakingly tender, but much closer to heroic grandeur than she'd previously attained. Simultaneously the chorus tell her to cheer up in what must surely be an intentionally pedestrian rhythm and harmony. It's all very well saying 'Be thou immortal'; but the real point—which gives her her tenderly tragic stature—is that 'thou art not *mine*'. The chorus here is the World, as usual uttering pious platitudes; there is an unbridgeable gulf between Galatea's song and the chorus's jaunty statement that there will be pie in the sky by and by.

This critical, ironic element, existing alongside the heart-felt sorrow, has completely gone from Galatea's final aria, 'Heart, the seat of soft delight'. Acis—his 'purple blood' purged to crystal—becomes the sacrificial scapegoat, who 'murmurs' with a significance altogether different from the 'melting murmurs' of sensual fulfilment, to which Galatea had referred in her song about the dove. Here the liquid cooing of recorders in parallel thirds, the tremulous, wavering rhythm, the E flat tonality, produce an exquisite dissolution of the senses. Polyphemus is exorcized, so this love is 'gentle' indeed. But, *because* he is exorcized, the love—which in the beginning had been anything but gentle!—is as insubstantial as a dream. It is so beautiful that we want to cry, knowing that the beauty is a relinquishment. To be immortal is better than nothing: but doesn't alter the fact that they are irremediably separated. He's dead; in heaven there can be no marrying. So the fountain is a very ambiguous return to the Christian water image. Though it may be the fountain of redemption it is also, and more potently, their and our tears.

That these tears are the heart's truth is indicated by the extraordinary manner in which the voice cuts across the orchestral ritornello in the middle section, creating an immediate apprehension of Acis's metamorphosis. This gives enhanced poignancy to Galatea's three-fold murmuring in the da capo: Handel's modifications of formal convention, here as so often, become synonymous with his awareness of human impulse, and Galatea's deepened humanity communicates itself to the final (public) chorus. For although the piece advises Galatea to stop weeping, and has the regularity of a chaconne without the ceremonial grandeur, it is not dominated by an unchanging bass, while the triplet figurations create a tenderly dissonant pain. The rippling water motive murmurs of 'gentle love' until it dissolves into silence: there is no paradise on earth and 'lasting love' is possible, if at all, only outside this life. The Golden Age is thus either a dream or a metaphysical heaven, which man cannot know about while he remains physical. The question is left open.

10

HANDEL, CONGREVE, AND ENGLISH HEROIC TRAGEDY

Semele[1]

At the climax of his career, twenty or more years later, Handel composed another work based on the heroic theme of the paradox of the man-god. Whereas *Acis* was variously described as an opera, a masque and a serenata, *Semele* is a full-scale heroic opera (though conditions were against its being staged as such),[2] and the only one created in England, if we discount Purcell's *Dido* because of its brevity. The difference between *Acis* and *Semele* lies in the fact that whereas *Acis* is concerned with youth, *Semele* is concerned with maturity. The opera is more aware of the realities of experience; and the consequence of this is not merely that it is bigger but also that it departs more radically from heroic convention. *Acis* adheres pretty closely to the da capo aria: *Semele* complements its da capo arias with a higher proportion of accompanied arioso than any other work of Handel.

After his failure to sell Italian opera to the British middle-class public, Handel, like Purcell before him, had wrung triumph from frustration; in adapting the conventions and techniques of heroic opera to biblical subjects he had explored the basic themes with a profundity and universality of which no composer of aristocratic autocracy had been capable. His Saul is the leader, the god-man; and the oratorio asks what happens when the leader, who is not in fact a god, however godly his powers, is subject to

---

[1] The Novello vocal score is (very) incomplete. References here are to the Händelgesellschaft. Edited by Fr. Chrysander.

[2] For an account of the history of *Semele* as a concert work and as a theatrical piece see Winton Dean's chapter in his book on *Handel's Oratorios and Masques*.

human infirmities. Jealousy may overthrow reason, he may literally go mad: and his madness brings ruin not merely to himself but also to the State for which he is responsible. This accounts for the only element in the oratorios which is distinct from opera seria: the chorus, representing the people, becomes a central dramatic protagonist. Handel's humanity was nowhere more evident than in his realization that the 'public' life was a drama no less than, and closely related to, the private life.

All Handel's oratorios turn on the disparity between the Law (which is necessary if there is to be order and civilization) and the apparently arbitary qualities of human nature. There is no appeal to mysticism or metaphysical speculation; the problem is human and must be solved, if at all, in human terms. So although the Bible had proved a liberating agent for Handel, we can appreciate how readily he must have seized on the libretto of *Semele*, which Congreve had written in 1710 for another composer: for this book deals with the essential Handelian theme within a traditionally humanist—even pagan—convention. The piece opens, indeed, with a full-scale masque ceremony: a dedication to Hymen. The overture, in Handel's tragic C minor, is grand and noble, the conventional double dotted rhythm expressing man's magnificence, while the rising triplet arpeggios waft incense to the heavens, suggesting man's aspiration to divinity. But the fugal section of the overture is not merely a ceremonial round-dance; its acute dissonances, scurrying sequential figures, and quite elaborate tonal development hint at the drama of the human situation with which the opera deals.

Immediately after the overture a priest sings a spacious accompanied arioso which, with majestic leaps and resonant arpeggios, comments on the favourable omens. The gods (who are ourselves writ large) are apparently pleased about this marriage of two Important Persons; their assent is marvellously conveyed in the final phrase, serenely beatific, yet earth-rooted. So the arioso leads into a chorus in the power key of B flat; 'lucky omens bless our rites' in regular time-dominated metre and in aggressively chattering scales and arpeggios. There is a sudden change to D major and a warmer homophony when the words ('peaceful days and fruitful nights') refer to the personal implications of the marriage ceremony: which after all concerns two specific

244

young people, as well as being a public event. But this is swept away by a return to B flat and to massive fugato: for thus far the piece is a masque and is therefore preoccupied with public order, not personal experience.

The induction over, however, we turn from the social ceremony to the private life: and discover that things are not as simple as the masque had assumed. For while it is Semele's public duty to marry her betrothed, Athamas, because her father wishes her to and the liaison would, presumably, be socially desirable, she has aspirations to divinity. Far from wanting to marry Athamas, she has fallen in love with a god, Jupiter; and he desires her too, as Apollo desired Daphne. Nor is this the end to human perversity; Semele has a sister, Ino, and she nurses a secret passion for Athamas—the man Semele is supposed to marry. The first recitative tells us, indeed, that the pomp and glory of the masque induction were something of a sham; for before the opera opens Semele has been prevaricating—inventing excuses for delaying the marriage. When her father Cadmus and her betrothed Athamas appeal to her in tenderly noble arioso to 'invent no new delay' she breaks into impassioned accompanied arioso, with abrupt changes of key and *concitato* scales and repeated notes, wherein she admits to herself and the audience (but not to the characters on the stage) the inevitability of her passion. Then, still communing with herself, she asks Jove to help her decide what to do in her dilemma ('incline me to comply or help me to refuse'). This saraband aria is sung pianissimo throughout, as though she is whispering her most secret thoughts; the strained leap of a ninth with which she opens, the chromatics, the diminished thirds and Neapolitan descents express, with almost Purcellian immediacy, her distraught condition: which is (just) controlled by the sustained lyricism, by the grave saraband rhythm. There are few more impressive instances of the relationship between the heroic dance-aria and the 'reasonable' necessity to dam the flood of passion.

Semele immediately follows her secret saraband with a full aria da capo (interpolated by Handel) in which, like Galatea, she tries to sublimate her distress by giving it to the birds. This lark song is beautiful, but rather weakens the transition from her wrapt self-involvement (in the tragic key of C minor) to Athamas's conventional invocation to Hymen (in the power key of

B flat). His aria is sturdy in rhythm, with bouncy rising arpeggios; only a certain agitation in the syncopations suggests that he has any doubt that Semele can make him happy.

But in fact it is not Semele—whose courage is, as we shall see, both her strength and her limitation—who breaks down, but Ino, the more humanly frail sister. Unable to restrain herself in the tense situation, she cries out aloud (not, like Semele, to herself) in wildly modulating recitative which is significantly sung secco, not accompanied, for her weakness is not heroic, but all too human. Everybody is stunned by her outburst; and in the silence two violins and a viola start to weave a rich polyphonic texture over a regularly padding bass in quavers. The key is E minor: the remotest possible point from the masque's power key of B flat. The customary antitheses and rhetorical questions, as well as the polyphony and the equal movement, suggest a quiet determination; at all costs Cadmus is bent on preserving order, if not decorum, in a crazy world. His line, with leaping sixths often landing on dissonant suspensions, is tense but noble, as he protests that Ino's outburst is an affront to public rejoicing. For a long time the others are silent, dazedly nursing their private perturbations. Then tentatively Semele and Athamas begin to sing, all asking Ino what's the matter, 'of whom do you complain'. As the additional voices enter the texture becomes denser, the suspensions more painful, while the bass rises with chromatic urgency. Ino sings lamentingly 'of all, of all, but all I fear in vain'. And compassion withers in these eighteenth century beings who cannot accept without embarrassment so outrageous an exhibition of the heart. At the end of the quartet Ino is left singing pathetically alone: as her father had been imposingly alone at the beginning. Nothing could better reveal the human reality of this opera, as compared with the conventional heroic opera on the same theme, than the fact that the dramatic action starts with an ensemble number: which expresses not only conflict, but deadlock and incomprehension. However splendid our pretences, this is what human beings are like; this is the rock-bottom we start from.

This human perversity wrenches the tonality down from E minor to D minor. There is a fierce thunder chorus of anger, with shooting scales and rigid metre, as the fires on the altar are extinguished. The chorus (who are the People, auralized and visualized dramatically, milling around the stage) cry to the gods to avert these omens. There seems to be some response as the priest sings in major arioso, accompanied by whirling scales that emulate the altar's flames. But although Juno accepts the sacrifice, Jupiter does not; so the flames totter into the minor. All this shilly-shallying on the part of the gods indicates once more how they are merely ourselves, pretending to be independent of Time. Human and divine contradictoriness are then explicitly equated in a presto chorus of flight, in the major but fiercely desperate; the hurly burly is at once human tumult and the divine power of Jupiter's thunder.

We return in every sense to a pedestrian level when Ino and Athamas—the two 'ordinary' human beings—sing arias commenting on their particular predicaments, first separately, then in duet. Then Cadmus tells us why Jupiter got so furious: he, a god, couldn't let Semele go to a mere human, so he has sent an eagle to snatch Semele up to the heavens. He sings of the eagle's descent (rapid falling scales) and ascent (rising figures in sensuous thirds and sixths to portray the ambrosial dew) in ceremonial accompanied arioso; and the chorus, in a rather oddly bucolic number with intermittent flat sevenths (hinting perhaps at the illusory nature of the Golden Age), tell him that he ought to be very pleased about this translation of his daughter to higher realms. Semele certainly seems to be happy enough. Reclining on baroque clouds she sings of *endless* pleasure, endless love: the humanist's heaven in which earthly delights are the same only more so, and no longer subject to Time. Significantly, she sings a courtly dance-song, a gavotte, with an earthily arpeggiated theme modulating sharpwards to the dominant. Human and divine are one as Jupiter abandons his thunderbolts to lie in her arms; and the chorus takes up the song which becomes a masque ceremony of revel, our worldly delights protracted to eternity, without pain or decay. The key is the Golden Age's traditional pastoral F major.

This takes us to Act II and the abode of the Immortals: which is just like the gavotte-earth, only bigger and better. An orchestral prelude in B flat suggests, through its rhythmic impetus and its naggingly reiterative semiquavers, both Juno's godlike power and her human jealousy. In a B flat dance-aria Iris reports that Jupiter has installed Semele in a lovely palace, where she sports in sweet retreat, 'from mortal cares retiring':[1] and therefore with a minimum of dissonance and with the most gracefully lucid rhythm. Against this simplicity we must set Juno's arioso of rage wherein, with wild modulations (even including the old, Monteverdian chromatic transition from G to E major), swooping arpeggios, horrendous diminished sevenths and sizzling scales, she demands that Semele be swept down to Acheron. The dramatic enactment in this accompanied arioso almost suggests the Mozart of *Idomeneo*. The music is heroic because she is a goddess, yet frenziedly lunatic because she is a woman; Handel marks it *allegro concitato* (the stock direction for mad scenes) *ma pomposo*! Juno's wrath is not mollified when Iris tells her that it isn't easy to drag people down from Cytherea, for the gates are guarded by dragons whose forky stings, scaly horrors and fiery eyes (the human jealousies, the torments within the mind, that shut one out from heaven) are expressed in strangely modulating string arpeggios. But although Juno is still furious, she now realizes that she has to control her fury sufficiently to take action; so she now sings not arioso, but an aria of rage, in F minor, the key of *chants lugubres*. Savage, lashing syncopations in the vocal line, obsessive repeated notes and an upward thrusting bass convey her violence, while the tonal and architectural discipline prevents her from going 'over the edge'; and makes it possible for her to decide on remedial action. She will call on Somnus, she says in a middle section that begins with deceptively lulling repeated chords, to soothe the dragons to sleep. But the frenzy of the first section soon demolishes the tranquillity, for the torment within is the reality.

What follows is both the most musically poignant and the most psychologically profound moment of the work. Handel omits Congreve's visitation from Cupid, and from Juno's F minor switches to the remoteness of E major: where we find Semele just waking from sleep in heaven. She is drowsy, rapt, sated with

[1] Handel cuts quite a lot of Congreve's powerful delineation of Juno's human, if extravagant, passion, perhaps in order to leave more scope for his music. He also cut part of the description Iris gives of Semele's gallivanting in heaven. Apparently Flora and Zephyr were commissioned to produce a Spring that should 'never know an ending', and Aurora was paid off, since dawn must henceforth be synonymous with Semele's awaking. Such a fuss over a mere mortal makes Juno's rage the more excusable.

sensual pleasure; and she sings an air of the most ineffable tenderness, accompanied only by a rocking, arpeggiated cello and harpsichord. As compared with Juno's jerky rhythms and restless modulation, the song seems all simple diatonic fulfilment (without even the necessity for a middle section); while her curling, caressing coloratura 'weaves the garlands of repose' from her sensual satisfaction. Yet the repose—as she lingers on the high notes of the arching phrases—is also infinitely sad; and when she reaches her climacteric G sharp it is as though she cannot bear to relinquish it, lest she lose her bliss for ever. And when we consider the words she sings we find, indeed, that the air is an appeal to sleep. She cries to sleep again in order that she may dream; when she wakes her lover is not there; her bliss is a sweet cheat, and she would rather have the cheat than reality. ('O sleep why dost thou leave me, Why thy visionary joys remove, O sleep *again deceive me.*') As she asks to be deceived a little chromatic quiver disturbs the luminous serenity of the voice part, and a minor sigh disturbs the continuo's gentle rocking.

In a sense this lullaby is the climax of the opera, for it marks Semele's intuitive awareness, which she still won't admit to, that her divine aspirations are illusion. Her tragedy is that her mind will not accept what her senses tell her—until it is too late. When Jupiter returns, having left her worn out after love, he sees that Semele is upset and advises her to 'lay your doubts and fears aside, and for Joys alone provide'.[1] This he does in a sturdy, swinging A major aria in triple time, with unison violins and virtually no inner tension. He pretends to be mankind made perfect: 'though this human form I wear, Think not I man's falsehood wear'. But of course he does: for his human shape is a disguise, not his true god-self, in which form he would (and does) destroy her. That she now (after her sleep song) has an uneasy apprehension of this is hinted at in the aria she now sings, an odd, unisonal piece in D *minor*, in which she says in a quavery vocal line for the most part without any harmonic support, that if fond desiring, bliss, panting, fainting is love then she as well

[1] In Congreve, but not in Handel, he addresses her as 'my fairest, latest, only Love'. How unconsciously revealing is that little word, 'latest'. The eternal feminine leads Jupiter, like Faust, onwards, and since he is immortal he can follow. His limitation, which complements Semele's, is his lack of limit; like Marlowe's Faust or Mozart's Don Juan, he is energy with and to no end.

as he is 'one with Love'. The unaccompanied line sounds frail, pathetic, even scared; and after the aria she admits, in broken recitative, that she's worried because, she being mortal, their bliss cannot last for ever. Jupiter says, apart, to himself and us, that he understands her meaning, which is 'dangerous ambition'; and breaks into a D major aria, deliberately empty and tootling, in which he says that he must 'with speed amuse her lest she too much explain'. The human-god relationship is beginning to crack—on his side as well as on hers.

Then follow a series of masque-like dance choruses of un-inhibited love, but with an almost savage rhythmic vivacity and rather exotic, 'pagan' orchestral colour. Jupiter says he will en-tertain her with an Arcadian elysium of happy nymphs, all unsullied by the human passion of jealousy, enjoying 'the sweets of love without the pain'. These shows will distract her mind from her ambition; and in order to remind her the more effectively of her humanity, he will bring to her her sister Ino, her childhood companion. While he will remind her of her humanity, however, it will be humanity freed from the conta-gion of error; he sings 'Wher'er you walk'—a noble bel canto aria in the power key of B flat, with dominant modulations and hardly any interior dissonance—to seduce her into thinking that being a human is just the same as being a god. It is true that this is what the earthly paradise would be like if human corruption had not ruined it. It is true that this vision of grace, lucidity and order can remain an ideal within the human mind; but the ideal is now distinct from the real, as Semele's dream-lullaby has al-ready told us.

This seems evident, too, in Ino's temporary translation to the heavens. Her account of her voyage through space is indeed a visionary moment, her arioso being accompanied by twining parallel sixths on violins, to enact the earth's turning. She is received by Semele in an arioso that modulates to a paradisal E major. But the cheat in this is suggested when the chorus sing of how the 'glad earth *appears* divine': for the tonality of the sequence of choral rejoicings descends earthwards in a series of falling fifths, from E, to A, to D, to G. With each section the music becomes more sturdily earthy, more metrically dominated, until the visionary lyricism, the 'appearance' of divinity, is quite dispersed.

The sleep-illusion theme becomes explicit at the opening of Act III when, in the Cave of Sleep itself, we hear a traditional *scène de sommeil* in stepwise-moving quavers, slurred in pairs, humming on strings in sensuous parallel thirds and sixths; and descending from D major to the subdominant: at which point Juno utters a terrific yell of 'Somnus awake'! with trumpet-like fanfares and an abrupt modulation to the dominant. Her cry has no effect; so the sleep music starts again, slower and more drowsily, in 6:4, and Somnus sings an aria, of the most exquisite serenity, pleading to be left in peace. But even for a god—as for Semele—sleep is only the *illusion* of peace: for Juno says that she knows how to wake Somnus up. All you need to do is to mention that girl Pasithea. Immediately he leaps into a comic gig-aria: 'with pleasure repose I'll forsake if you grant me but *her to soothe me awake*.' The wit of the lines, the almost facetious skittishness of the music, are a deflation of the sublime, but the point of this is serious enough. Once more, it is human passion that destroys tranquillity, and defeats human ambition towards the heroic. The deceit of sleep then becomes the agent whereby the human tragedy is precipitated: Juno and Somnus sing a duet in A minor, with slightly frenzied repeated notes and double dots, wherein they make a bargain that, if Juno gives him Pasithea, he will co-operate in her plot. The agitation of the double dotted rhythm is taken over into Semele's solo aria wherein she admits that, without the illusory peace of sleep, she has nothing but racking thoughts and painful nights; and at this point the machinations of deceit begin.

Juno orders Somnus to lull Jupiter to sleep with a dream of Semele, to make him mad with desire (significantly, Semele is to be in her own shape, but more beautiful, free of imperfection). Meanwhile, Juno will calm the dragons of Citherea with Somnus's wand; and will appear to Semele in the likeness of Ino. The real Ino will be put to sleep by Somnus. So Juno, a goddess disguised as Ino, an ordinary human, comes to Semele to tempt her, knowing that her temptation will be the more insidious if it seems to come from a relatively unambitious mortal. She asks Semele if she has yet been made immortal. Semele cries No, alas, alas; and at this point the theme of pride is taken up directly, in the extraordinary mirror song. Juno encourages Semele to gaze at herself (in her perfected shape) and grow dippy with rapture.

251

The mirror-echoes in the aria between voice and violin create a trance of silliness as, self-deifying, she says 'myself I shall adore if I persist in gazing'; the fantastic coloratura becomes a delirium of narcissism: which is also Semele's deflation. Then, with Semele at this climax of self-regarding imbecility, Juno-Ino proffers her advice: when Jupiter is crazy with desire (as we know he is at the moment) Semele should refuse herself to him unless he will consent to appear in his own shape, for if she mates with him as a god, she must be made immortal too. Juno sings here in grand accompanied arioso, with rich ninths to celebrate the nuptual rites, rapid modulations for the hypothetical transition to immortality, and *concitato* thunder to underline the self-destructiveness of human egoism.[1] Semele thanks the fake Ino for her advice, condescendingly adding that when she is a goddess she will make Ino as pretty as she is, in a siciliano in F sharp minor. The music is sensuously rich in texture, yet tenderly melancholy in its sighing suspensions: for it expresses not the idiocy, but the pathos of her pride, her human fallibility, which in her heart, if not her mind, she has been aware of ever since her dream-lullaby.

Into her reverie Jupiter enters, madly desiring in G minor, with obsessive pulse and dotted rhythm, majestic but uneasy. He has been dreaming of Semele, he says, but always she ran

[1] Congreve, in a passage Handel cuts, makes the point about the self-destructiveness of pride explicitly. Just before Juno-Ino tempts Semele in the mirror episode, the heroine, alone, is given a charming soliloquy:

> I love and am lov'd, yet more I desire;
> Ah, how foolish a Thing is Fruition!
> As one Passion cools, some other takes Fire,
> And I'm still in a Longing Condition.
>> Whate'er I possess
>> Soon seems an Excess,
> For something untry'd I petition;
>> Tho' daily I prove
>> The Pleasures of Love,
> I die for the joys of Ambition.

In becoming divine, that is, Semele approximates to Jupiter's state of eternal, limitless and pointless activity. It is difficult to tell how far the comic-satiric overtone in the monologue is intentional; but that it is present may have been the reason why Handel omitted the passage. Responsive though he was to the English ironic note, it would have been inimical to his purposes here.

away from him. She sings a song—a little masterpiece of psychological penetration—in which she does not lose her pathos in
returning to self-conscious deceit. In this wheedling D minor
aria, with its extravagant Neapolitan stabs and whining
repetitions, its persistent clashes of dominant with tonic resolution, she says that though she is always granting he goes on
complaining. Desperate, he says he will grant whatever she
asks.[1] She makes him swear by the Stygian lake: which he does
in elaborate, thunder-accompanied arioso. She makes her request,
that he should love her in his own shape; and he, aghast, sings
an agitated A minor aria accompanied by canonic violins in
shooting scales ('Take heed what you press'). Perhaps it is not
an accident that this should be in the same key—rare in this
opera—as the duet in which Juno and Somnus plan their opera-
tions: for the equivocal point seems to be that although only
in sleep can one have the illusion of bliss, the bliss is inevitably
destructive of reality. In this sense, Semele desires her own
destruction.

Certainly her reply to Jupiter's warning approaches hysteria.
'No, no, I'll take no less', she screams in wild coloratura: which
is rendered more, not less, frenetic by the D major tonality.
Jupiter realizes that in her pride she is now beyond hope; and
consummates the tragic predicament in a wonderful arioso in
B minor, with lamenting descending thirds, and drooping scales
in parallel thirds and sixths. The grandeur of his line is typically
Handelian; the harmonic poignancy of the polyphonic texture
has almost Bachian intensity as, communing with himself, he
accepts destiny. 'She must a victim fall'; but it was his fault,
for making such a bargain, as much as hers. She was stupid to
aspire to godhead; he was equally stupid to hope to be human;
and now 'tis past recall'. Pathetically, he says he will employ
only his tiniest thunderbolts; but he knows that, inevitably, they
must burn her up. His compassion—the second climacteric
moment of the opera—is, like the pathos of Semele's appeal to

---

[1] Though Semele's D minor aria is not exactly funny, its tone embraces
the satirical element in the text. Handel ignores, however, the unequivocal
comedy of Jupiter's response:

> Speak, speak your Desire,
> I'm all over Fire.
> Say what you require
> I'll grant it—now let us retire.

sleep, essentially a human quality. Significantly it is followed immediately by its complement and polar opposite, when Juno sings a brisk aria of revenge, pointing out in *un*compassionate dance-vivacity how the sweets of revenge make it worth while to reign, 'and heaven hereafter will be heaven indeed'. So much for human pretensions to godhead. As the words are a parody by inversion of the humanist's heaven, so the music is almost a parody of the Handelian Grand Manner.

But Semele, a misguided human, achieves true grandeur again as she dies. Her F minor arioso—again the key of *chants lugubres*—has tremendous span in the vocal line, yet perpetually droops in sighing suspensions, in fainting Neapolitan chromatics, while even the ceremonial dotted rhythm becomes the nagging of pain. The modulations—from F minor to B flat minor to C minor—convey both a physical and a spiritual disintegration, as Jupiter descends 'in a black cloud' and the thunder extinguishes her. Her last words are a whispered expiration of the breath. The palace vanishes in Jupiter's cloud-burst; and the chorus break into expressions of terror and astonishment, grand and noble, yet with a most dramatic use of silence. Then in a fugal chorus—in which the harmonic nature of the fugal unity suggests the need for communal solidarity if we are to bear the pathos of the human predicament—the moral is pointed: 'Nature to each allots his proper sphere'. Again, however, the dominant note is of compassion, not merely for Semele, but for mankind. Though it is true that 'forsaken, we like meteors err' (with augmented seconds and occasional chromatics disturbing the regular pulse): that 'thro' the Void by some Rude Shock we're broke' (sudden, massive chords separated by silences): and that 'all our boasted Fire is lost in Smoke' (descending chromatics over a pedal point, as the texture is gradually winnowed away): yet at the same time our sinful pride is not far from a virtue. At least we accept the consequences of our sin with fortitude—as the regular movement, the sustained pedal note, tell us. What we are left with is the human capacity to endure; and it is significant that this climax to Handel's secular opera is exactly comparable with the climax to his last oratorio, *Jephtha*.

This oratorio seems to turn on the traditional conflict between the Law and personal experience; but the profundity of the work lies in the fact that the Law is not in fact God's will, but Jephtha's own presumption—the wilful perversity of his vow. In the broken ejaculations and wild modulations of his arioso 'Deeper and deeper still', we live through his suffering as he realizes that in fulfilling the Law of his own egoism he must sacrifice his life-blood. The heroism of Man as Leader inevitably involves an overreaching of his *human* nature; this is why we have to see the here-and-now of Jephtha's arioso against the power-addicted monumentality of the choruses, such as 'When his loud voice in thunder spoke', wherein the harmony could hardly be simpler, and the tremendous impact depends on rhythmic impetus, spacing and climax. The arias again seek a balance between this terrifying extroversion and the suffering introversion of the arioso. In aria, pain and horror can be assuaged in lyricism; or happiness may turn into the dance-aria that is closely related to the dance-chorus: for we are conscious of our loneliness only when melancholy. Yet in *Jephtha*, as in *Semele*, the deepest evidence of Handel's humanity consists in the way in which the private and the public life become synonymous. Thus the climax of the work is an ensemble number—the quintet. Iphis starts off in G major telling us lyrically that she freely resigns herself to heaven, and Hamor, her lover, says he accepts fate's decree. Everybody joins in, wishing them 'joys triumphant' in the next world. Then follows a heart-rending unaccompanied cadenza for the lovers: which tells us that, whatever everyone else may think, they are by no means certain that the world is well lost for heaven—nor even that they are content to be sacrificed for the good of the whole. The movement ends in the minor! This is quite unlike Bach, for whom the apprehension of heaven would override material circumstance. In the great final choruses to *Jephtha* a more Bachian tension between linear independence and harmonic passion develops as the chorus ceases to represent the public life and becomes suffering humanity. In 'How dark are thy decrees, O Lord' the texture is harmonically tense, related to Jephtha's arioso, because the personal predicament is one illustration of a general truth. Yet even here, there is no hint of metaphysical consolation. God's decrees are dark indeed; so this chorus, in which Jephtha becomes identified with the blind Handel, can merge into that grave yet turbulent setting—rigid in its rhythm, tense in its arpeggiated minor ninths—of the passage from Pope's

Essay on Man. Neither in Pope nor in Handel does 'Whatever is, is Right' mean that all is for the best in the best of all possible worlds. It means that, knowing what experience is like, we remain unafraid. Its burden is identical with that of the meteor chorus in *Semele*; both choruses are, imaginatively, the ends of their respective works.

They are not in fact the end: for in the oratorio Jehovah descends as deus ex machina, while in the opera Apollo performs the same function. But the happy endings are prophecy, wish-fulfilment, not reality. In *Semele* we return to the public world for Athamas to sing a B flat major aria comparable with his first utterance, all buoyant extroversion, built on arpeggio motives, with a minimum of dissonance. He says he will marry Ino and right mortal wrongs; but he knows and we know that the most we can do is to keep cheerful in face of the tragic reality which the chorus has expressed. There will be more erring meteors; though we can, if we like, imagine a day when a phoenix shall arise from Semele's ashes—a god more mighty than love, who shall 'sighing and sorrow for ever prevent'. Apollo descends to make this prophecy, accompanied by a grand Lullian overture similar to that which opened the opera, only more resplendent, less emotionally involved. When this heaven on earth comes, happy, happy shall we be, from Care and Sorrow free: all in an ebullient D major, with trumpets and chattering thirds and prancing scales. This paradise is on earth, but a long way off. The emptiness of the music—as well as the words, which advise us to get drunk, for only when Bacchus is born is Love's troublous reign at an end—tells us that this paradise isn't true; and we have the strength to accept this because Semele had her dream of bliss: because she was burned to ashes: and because we sang the tragic chorus wherein, admitting that 'our boasted Fire is lost in Smoke', we equated her fate with ours. Even into this heroic opera Handel has admitted, we have observed, some English satirical elements. He omits, however, Congreve's cynical conclusion whereby, after we have all grown tipsy, the proceedings conclude with a 'dance of Satyrs'. Though Handel may have his doubts about the Masque, he (like Pope again) will not allow the Anti-Masque to triumph. If he relinquished public Glory it was, we shall see in our commentary on *L'Allegro ed Il Pensieroso*, to discover a new moral and spiritual basis for his art.

27. *Semele divino Iovis concubitu occiditur.*

Pie in the Sky, or Semele transported on a Cloud
From an anonymous undated book of engravings in the Library of the
Barber Institute (Italian, 17th century)

11

THE PASTORAL LEAVES THE THEATRE

Handel: *L'Allegro ed Il Pensieroso*

We have seen that in both *Semele* and *Jephtha* Handel comes near to admitting that the Golden Age can exist only within the mind. Perhaps it is not fortuitous that although both works were conceived as heroic operas they were not in fact presented in stage form, as a social manifestation. It is certainly not fortuitous that in the latter part of his English career Handel should have created one work that is not directly concerned with man as a social animal, but rather with the qualities of man's mind and senses, in relation to the external world of Nature. *L'Allegro ed Il Pensieroso*[1] goes back to the seventeenth century (to Milton) for its poetic inspiration; and looks forward to romanticism (to Gray and Collins, if not Wordsworth) in its belief in the validity of individual experience. The piece says, in the same spirit as Pope's *Windsor Forest*, that while man may be a social animal, each individual has to put his own house in order before society can be expected to function adequately. The most direct way to recover, or discover, integrity of response is to consider man in his basic relationship to the natural world. In this sense the pantheism of *L'Allegro* is the closest Handel ever came to religious experience—even closer than *Messiah*.

So the first two parts of the work are an exploration of man's essential nature, and l'Allegro (the sanguine man) and il Pensieroso (the melancholy man) are the two poles of the human spirit, both of which are a part of Handel—and of you and me. Although they are opposing forces, they are complementary, both being within the mind; thus the work is dramatic, though the drama is not projected into social ritual. This is why, though the characters of l'Allegro and il Pensieroso are personified and sing in aria and recitative, they are not particularized, but

[1] Novello. Edited by W. H. Monk.

fluctuate from soprano to tenor to bass. It is also why the technique of the work is perhaps more 'advanced' than that of any other work of Handel. The piece contains a minimum of closed arias da capo, and those usually have some characteristic peculiarity: for the music is not concerned with absolutes.

Milton's two complementary poems were rearranged by Handel's librettist Jennens in order to provide a dramatic altercation between the two characters—or rather the two aspects of the single mind. He calls the first part L'Allegro and the second Il Pensieroso; but both aspects appear in each part, and in each part the concluding chorus achieves a reconciliation. Significantly, there is no ceremonial, public overture. Part I opens *in medias res*, with accompanied arioso: the sanguine man sings madly, in distraught dotted rhythm, with chaotic modulations and shivering diminished sevenths, of the melancholy lunacy that life habitually is, and invites us to live hedonistically, for the moment. Then the melancholy man (in fact it is a woman to begin with) is equally contemptuous about such 'deluding joys', expressed in tootling music on the fiddles. It is interesting that the two characters begin by singing the other's music, as though they know, at heart, that the one is inseparable from the other.

After this arioso induction, they make their complementary statements in aria. L'Allegro's 'Come, thou Goddess fair and free' is a naive pastoral in which the short, arpeggiated vocal phrases and the symmetrical repetitions of the oboe and violin phrases in parallel sixths and thirds convey heart-easing Mirth's delight—but also its limitations. This is a simple binary song, with no da capo. Melancholy's complementary aria 'Come rather, Goddess, sage and holy' has a suggestion of a middle section but only the briefest, most elliptical hint of a da capo. This strange piece already suggests the neurotic element within the melancholic state. The nobility of the long arching phrases, with the ceremonial dotted rhythm latent beneath the surface, is a positive value; yet there is an element of indulgence in the way in which the phrases continually curl around a nodal point, conflicting with the basic dance rhythm, and there is something approaching self-hypnosis in the line's obsessive returns to the note D. L'Allegro brusquely sweeps away this introverted melancholy with a laughing song in which everybody (the chorus) infectiously joins. There is nothing ceremonial about this public utterance; it is a spontaneous outbreak of bucolic mirth in which we forget our cares in being one with one another. Such contrapuntal unity as there is, is unequivocally comic, with its stuttering repeated notes and its twiddling arabesques derived from l'Allegro's first song. The dance-song 'Come and trip it', in which l'Allegro invites the chorus to join, is less frivolous, with a Purcellian, masque-like flavour in the tripping rhythm and the C minor tonality; the unisonal passages for the 'light fantastic toe' are physical action that also involves a quality analogous to seventeenth century wit.

The element of wit serves to point a contrast with the sequence of ariosos and arias that follows; indeed it suggests how the 'recognition of other modes of experience that are possible' is necessary if the introverted sensibility is not to end in neurosis. Il Pensieroso's appeal to the 'pensive nun' contains, beneath the sober gravity of movement, an intense anguish—consider the initial, arpeggiated rise from F to E natural. In the aria that follows the arioso, the change from the lugubrious F minor to the relative major and the regular padding of the ground bass convey an obsessed quietude. The repeated bass is an attempt at control; but acutely dissonant passing notes are not banished, and after the ground bass has returned to F minor, the agony of the arioso breaks out again, in intensified form, with the arpeggiated phrase, now more sharply in C minor, stretched out so that it rises from low C to a high A flat. The still falling arpeggios that suggest the immobility of marble, as opposed to the suffering heart, again imply the conscious control of the will; and so lead to the re-establishment of the ground bass, this time in the tonic minor, and a recapitulation of the aria. Formally, this sequence is more like Purcell than Handelian heroic opera; the seventeenth century flavour is intensified when the ground bass aria is repeated by the chorus.

L'Allegro's next appearance carries the imaginative argument a stage further. In recitative he again banishes melancholy; in aria he again invokes mirth: but the invocation differs from the preceding ones in that it deals with the relationship between a state of mind and the natural world. The violin obbligato begins by being a mirth-image, dancing and prancing across the bar lines. When, however, the poem invokes dawn and the lark, it becomes the bird's song, and suggests how man's unsullied response to Nature can become a liberation of the spirit. The luminous resilience of this music has an ecstatic freshness that we find nowhere else in Handel's music. The pastoral world is no longer a myth; it is the sound, smell and feel of the English countryside: which can bring balm to the harried soul.

This balm the melancholic may experience no less, perhaps more, than the sanguine: so il Pensieroso now sings *her* bird song, which is a nightingale-nocturne, not a lark-aubade. The nightingale is, of course, personified by a flute, in the convolutions of whose line baroque decoration becomes, once more, naturalistic. The voice sheds its sorrow in dialogue with the bird; and Handel treats this as the first da capo aria in the work in order to suggest the timelessness which the identity of man and nature may induce. Even here, however, the middle section is unconventional, for it has no relation to the aria proper, but is a most beautiful invocation to the moon, in which the slow, chromatically rising arch of the vocal line over string chords moving in regular quavers, creates the moon's solemn, ageless progress through the heavens. The music liberates us from time and the self: so when we hear the nightingale-flute sounding da capo it is as though we were listening to the voice of God. This is perhaps the nearest Handel comes to a mystical act.

L'Allegro's reappearance brings us back to earth: but to solid, English earth, for the piece is a hunting scene, not in a mythological world but in the English countryside. The horn tune, as the 'hounds and horn Cheerly rouse the slumbering morn', has the lilt of a folk-song; at the end of the binary dance-song the horn fades away romantically, echoing through the woods. Though the hunt is a social activity, what Handel is concerned with is his—and our—response to the natural world. The same is true of il Pensieroso's two night-pieces which, no longer tormented, are about the blessing of quietude that night may bring. The onomatapoeic imitation of the curfew, of the chirping cricket, of the bellman's drowsy charm, are naturalistic echoings of Nature which become a release of the human spirit—for man in his romantic individuality, if not for man in his social capacity. L'Allegro's exquisite siciliano, 'Let me wander not unseen', is in the same vein of pastoral tranquillity; and again its pastoralism is at once naturalistic (like a folk-song) and romantic (in both its harmonic colouring and its almost Rousseauistic formal simplicity). This apparently artless candour, richer than but comparable with the later music of Arne, is found again in 'Straight mine eyes hath caught new pleasures': which has a middle section wherein heroic arioso becomes a sound-picture of the hills, clouds, flowing rivers and tufted trees of the English scene. The grandeur is authentic, of course: only it is that of the natural world, not of man's conscious artifice.

But the last number of Part I suggests that the natural world may be an inspiration to man's 'art': for the flowing river scales are transmogrified into a peal of bells and then into the jocund rebecks to which the youths and maids dance in the chequered shade. The chorus joins in this sunshine holiday, until daylight falls in a sudden pianissimo. Then as coda the falling scales get slower and slower as they are translated from bells and rebecks back to the winds of Nature that lull us to sleep in softly dissonant suspensions. We droop on to the Neapolitan chord of E flat, so sleepy we can hardly stir ourselves to create the resolved cadence. The chorus fades out fragmentarily; the orchestra dissolves in a haze of suspensions that recalls the elegiac end to the pastoral in Purcell's *Fairy Queen*. Most of the later arias in Part I have implied the ultimate identity of the sanguine and the melancholy state; here they are reconciled in the dream of sleep: as they had been, in less overtly 'psychological' terms, in *Semele*.

To comment in detail on Part II is hardly necessary: though one should emphasize that it is not merely a repetition of the first part, with the stress on the melancholic rather than on the sanguine mind. For Part II begins to introduce man in a social, as well as a natural context; and alongside pieces like 'But O sad virgin', a beautiful invocation to music in which the solo cello fulfils much the same function as the solo flute in the nightingale song of Part I, we have realistic pictures of the 'busy hum' of the 'populous city' (Jennens interestingly changed Milton's romantic 'towered' to the realistic 'populous'.) Similarly il Pensieroso's solitary invoking of the 'genius of the wood', a saraband aria in which grandeur has been transformed into intimate, self-communing mystery, is balanced by l'Allegro's invitation—in bouncing, slightly self-conscious march rhythm —to visit the well-trod stage, or by his appeal to Hymen as deity of social concord. It is significant, however, that though the social values are admitted, they don't have the last word. In so far as the final chorus is a fugue of metrical regularity, it pays deference to human solidarity; but the tension between the harmonic structure and the independence of the lines make the piece the most tragically melancholic music that Handel ever wrote, with the exception of the 'dark' choruses in *Jephtha*. It is also Handel's most Bach-like music: which fact itself indicates how Handel's exploration of the mind has taken him closer to 'religious' experience than was his wont.

None the less, the references to the social world in Part II are not there by chance: for as an Augustan gentleman Handel believed that the relationship between Man and Nature should provide a model for the relationship of man to man. Maybe the Golden Age could not be a physical fact; but at least if man could learn again to follow Nature he might be reborn and might achieve, if not a perfect, at least a better world. Man is a rational animal, sensible in both meanings; it is up to him to achieve what he can through respect for Nature and through a deliberate choice of the Will. So Handel's work is not complete in its Miltonic first and second parts. Jennens added a third part of his own composition which, under the title of Il Moderato, expresses the eighteenth century compromise. This section is seldom performed nowadays owing, perhaps, to a misguided feeling that Handel ought not to be inspired by Jennens as he was by Milton, disregarding the fact that he was content with Jennens's workmanship for most of his English career. If we can forget the inferiority of Jennens to Milton we shall not find Handel's music to Il Moderato inferior to most of the rest; and the climacteric duet, at least, is among Handel's most inspired—and revolutionary—utterances. Even if Part III were inferior, it would still be essential to an adequate understanding of the first two parts.

In Il Moderato there is only the one 'character'; the mind is no longer a dualism, though it assumes multiple forms. The first aria, 'Come with native lustre shine, Moderation, grace divine', is a swinging ceremonial piece for bass. The grandeur, with the traditional triple rhythm, the double dots, and the fiddled portamentos, is rendered 'natural', even domestic; and when the words tell us that the God of *Nature* gave us Moderation 'mad mortals from themselves to save', one wonders whether the old-style ceremonial features may not now be equated with the madness.

Certainly the shooting scales hint at incipient frenzy; and the middle section is interrupted by recitative, an invocation to Temperance, Health and the domestic virtues. The da capo is sung massively by every one, in chorus. Spleen can be banished by the moderate, the rational mind.

But the next two arias suggest how precarious the curb of reason is. The soprano's song, 'Come with gentle hand restrain Those who fondly court their bane' is elegant, delicate, nervously controlled in its short phrases and repeated clauses. It suggests a cat on hot bricks; the lucidity and precision are charming, but are on the verge of breakdown, as we sense in the syncopated dissonances that suggest Domenico Scarlatti or the early Haydn. When the words tell us that we must 'safely steer two rocks between And prudent keep the golden mean' the wavery chromaticism of the music proves what a ticklish business this is. After this jittery steering we throw off the final cadential phrase with a sigh of relief. The next aria 'Each action will derive new grace From order, measure, time and place Till life the goodly structure rise In due proportion to the skies' does something comparable with the building metaphor. The 6:4 tune swings grandly along until, at the reference to order, measure, time and place, it goes into cross accents of 3:2. We can feel, physically, the tension involved in holding the building up; if it were not for the human Will, it would crash to ruin.

This leads to the climax of the whole work: significantly the only ensemble number in any of the three parts. Here the mind's dualism sings, quasi-canonically, as one; through Reason and Moderation, conflict is banished. Yet the victory is not an easy one; and the music somewhat belies the words that inform us that 'as steals the morn upon the night and melts the shades away, So Truth doth Fancy's charm dissolve, The rising fumes that did the mind involve, Restoring intellectual day'. For the music of this most beautiful duet is more concerned with the fumes of night than with the light of day; and the texture of intertwining obbligato and voice parts creates a sensuously romantic haze even out of the old, ceremonial dotted rhythm. This perhaps suggests how the quality of heroism is now within the mind, indeed is the mind's apprehension of and power over the fumes of darkness. From this point of view it is significant that the air should remind us forcibly of Gluck, whose operatic 'revolution' was precisely his discovery of this new, subjective morality of heroism. It is relevant to note too that this binary structure is at least closer to sonata form than it is to an aria da capo. The piece is a growth and a resolution; and the dualism of l'Allegro and il Pensieroso is no longer necessary because it is now contained within the mind. The Gluckian freshness of the music hints at potentialities which Handel explored no further. Nowhere has he shown a more delicate and rich awareness of the complex of human passions and desires beneath the controlling surface; compared with it the grim rigidity of the final chorus has an ironic, if not bathetic, sound. 'These pleasures, Moderation, give, In them alone we truly live.' Again the music belies the words; the metrical procession of the minims, the harsh suspensions, the curiously frozen effect of the flat seventh on the word 'alone'—all these imply that though the control of the Will may be necessary, it is not always conducive to life. Again the chorus says in effect: this is the best we can do, if we are to live together in society. The mood is that of Pope's *Essay on Man* and of Johnson's *Rasselas* and *The Vanity of Human Wishes*; and although the tone of these works is elegiac, they all tell us that the alternative to the public mask is not inevitably madness. Or if it is—and we should remember that most of the great men of the Age of Reason, including Handel, Pope and Johnson, had phases of lunacy or neurosis—then madness may often be equated with the moment of vision.

From Il Moderato the seventeenth century echoes prompted by Milton and characteristic of *L'Allegro* and *Il Pensieroso* have disappeared; it was 'modern' music in its day which looked forward, operatically, to Gluck. In symphonic and oratorio terms it also looks forward to Haydn's *The Seasons* which, on the composer's own admission, was written under the influence of those works of Handel which the Austrian heard on his English visits. Thomson's poem, like Jennens's version of *L'Allegro* but more explicitly, deals with the relationship between the external drama of Nature and the internal drama of the mind and senses. Nature may serve as a model for human conduct; and this is a democratic morality, because any man may learn from Nature to the measure of his imaginative capacity. There is little in Haydn's *Seasons* that is not hinted at in Handel's *l'Allegro*, though Handel does not, of course, have any full-scale sonata movements, dealing with growth and conflict within the mind, comparable with Haydn's overtures. Haydn further domesticates and renders 'natural' the heroic aria, dispensing with the da capo, infusing more developed sonata conflict into the simple binary form; and he transforms the ceremonial chorus into the ethical-humanistic prayer, like some of Gluck's choral writing or the Masonic music of Mozart. Sometimes these prayers become sonata movements about the triumph of Light—a cross between the Handelian power-fugue and the Beethovenian hymn of liberation, both physical and spiritual. By this time, of course, the music has ceased to be theatrical even in the limited sense in which Handel's *L'Allegro* is so. It is still social music in the sense that it has a moral purpose; but it is no longer an imitation of human action. The subjective drama is now more closely related to Haydn's—and Beethoven's—instrumental work than to any theatrical tradition: for which reason it lies outside the province of this book.

12

BALLAD OPERA, ROMANTIC OPERA, AND THE DECADENCE

John Gay: *The Beggar's Opera*
Thomas Arne: *Comus*
The Cooper
The Morning
Stephen Storace: *No Song, No Supper*
Michael Balfe: *The Bohemian Girl*
Gilbert and Sullivan: *The Gondoliers*

While the Handel of *L'Allegro* had ceased to be a theatre composer, and while his true musical successor was the Haydn of *The Seasons* and *The Creation*, a tradition of theatre music in Britain does not in fact end with him. The theatre music that survives, however, is decadent in that it has ceased to be *inherently* dramatic. It is pretty music attached to a drama; it is neither dramatic in itself (as is Purcell's incidental music) nor subservient to the purpose of the play.

The phenomenal success of *The Beggar's Opera*[1]—at a time more or less contemporary with Handel's finest English work —is a neat illustration of this: and in the case of Gay's 'Newgate Pastoral' the unequivocally negative nature of the decadence has preserved its potency down to our own day. It is significant that Dr Johnson tells us, in his *Lives of the Poets*, that the idea of a Beggars' Opera was suggested to Gay by Dean Swift:[2] whose own genius was the most terrifying explosion of destructive

[1] I have used a reprint of the 1728 edition, made by Chapman and Dodd in 1923.

[2] 'There is a young ingenious Quaker in this Town who writes verses to his Mistress, not very Correct, but in a strain purely what a poetical Quaker should do, commending her look and habit etc. It gave me a hint that a set of Quaker Pastorals might succeed, if our friend Gay could fancy it, and I think it a fruitful subject; pray hear what he says. I believe further the Pastoral Ridicule is not exhausted, and that a Porter's, Footman's or Chairman's Pastoral might do well. Or what do you think of a Newgate Pastoral, among the Whores and Thieves there?'
Letter of Swift to Pope, August 30, 1716.

negation, undermining any complacency in the Augustan positives. Rationality, says Swift, is a pretence; the rational being is a thinking horse, no better than a machine. Beyond, all is darkness. So, if opera seria has tried to persuade us that man might be a god, let us invert so lunatic a proposal. Take the mythology of the pastoral, the legend of the Golden Age: but identify its innocence with the corruption of the outlaw, the prostitute, the pimp, for in this world the only innocents are those who, abandoning pretence, live for self-interest.

We can imagine the scarifying Newgate Pastoral that Swift might have produced, had he developed this theme himself: it would hardly, however, have lent itself to music. Gay's satire, though hard-hitting, is more genial; yet it fulfils Swift's negative prescription in that—like Fielding's *Jonathan Wild*—it is consistently based on the peculiarly English middle-class convention of Paradox by Inversion. For an eighteenth century artist, man was essentially a social being: so the first paradox is that 'of all animals of prey, Man is the only sociable one. Every one of us preys on his Neighbour, yet we herd together'. The thieves say they steal on behalf of a juster 'partition of the World'; Peacham, at once the thieves' agent and a government spy, explicitly relates his private activities to the public activities of those who rule the community ('Like Great Statesmen, we encourage those that betray their Friends' . . . 'Tis but fitting we should protect and encourage Cheats, since we live by them' . . . 'The Statesman, because he's so Great, Thinks his Trade as Honest as mine').

The second paradox by inversion concerns man in his domestic capacity. The only genuine emotion exhibited by anyone in the play is Polly's love for Macheath, which leads her to marry him. Of course, it is nothing like a grand passion; she merely follows her appetite, but she does so simply, straightforwardly, for no gain except her sensual pleasure. In her parents' view, however, she commits the unpardonable sin—not in giving herself to him, but in marrying him; and when she confesses she loves him, Mrs Peacham faints with horror ('I thought the girl had been better bred') and has to be recovered with a glass of Cordial. The only way in which the evil can be undone is for Polly to allow Macheath to be impeached, her parents keeping the ransom money: 'hang your Husband and be Dutiful'.

This subversion of the domestic institution of marriage brings us to the third, and fundamental, paradox by inversion: the equation of love with death. The seventeenth century metaphor that identifies sexual consummation with 'dying' (because it hurts and is desired, because it seems to take us outside Time) assumes, in *The Beggar's Opera*, a grimly realistic, rather horrifying form. The Highwayman, though he is outside social and domestic law, is subject to the arbitration of death; and the hangman's noose becomes an equivocation for the sexual act. Polly falls for Macheath because, as her mother points out, she prophetically sees him in the Cart:

> If any Wench Venus' Girdle wear,
>   Though she be never so ugly;
> Lilies and Roses will quickly appear,
>   And her face look wondrous smuggly.
> Beneath the left Ear so fit but a Cord,
>   (A Rope so charming a Zone is!)
> The Youth in his Cart hath the Air of a Lord,
>   And we cry, There dies an ADONIS.

Macheath is literally betrayed by sex—by the ladies of the town he cannot keep away from—and sings:

> At the Tree I shall *suffer with pleasure;*
>   Let me go where I will,
>   In all kinds of Ill,
> I shall find no such Furies as these are.

The outraged Lucy, to whom he had also promised marriage, sings

> When you come to the Tree
> Should the Hangman refuse
> These Fingers *with pleasure*
> Could fasten the Noose.

Even Polly says that 'Upon the Rope that hangs my Dear Depends poor Polly's Life'. All these death-wishes, whether sexually sadistic or masochistic, are the more scarifying because they carry a Christian overtone too. When Polly says 'I see him at the Tree' Macheath becomes Scapegoat; and the blasphemy lies in the fact that, far from having suffered for us all, he has never done anything that hasn't been motivated by the immediate gratification of his own appetites, however scrupulous he may have been in sharing out the plunder. In a sense far deeper than Gay intended, *The Beggar's Opera* became an exposure of the death-wish and the spiritual nullity to which materialism commits us; and Dr Johnson was strictly accurate—hitting the nail as firmly on the head as he always did when he could see the nail clearly—in describing the piece as 'a Labefactation of all Principle'. Compared with this resonant denunciation, later puritanic objections to *The Beggar's Opera* are frivolous.

There is a direct artistic consequence of the play's Paradox by Inversion: which is that the piece is, as the prologue explains, an Opera with no Music. At least, the theme implies a technique that destroys the basis of classical opera—the notion that human speech, uttered passionately, may be sublimated into song. The play is for the most part literary burlesque; and both the grand feelings that Macheath professes and the tender feelings that Polly expresses are deflated by being recognizable as parodies of conventions accepted in tragedy or romance. (Macheath is a great reader of romances; Polly utters a mock-pathetic lament when she has to send him into hiding—'The whole Circle are in Tears! Even Butchers weep! . . . and I bar myself from thy dear dear Conversation!') Though the humour consists partly in the fact that such types should express such feelings at all, the irony reflects on the feelings themselves; and the deflationary element extends to the music. In his Introduction the Beggar remarks 'I hope I may be forgiven that I have not made my opera throughout Unnatural, like those in vogue: for I have no Recitative'. The characters speak in 'modern' prose, for there are no heroic passions left, unless the swagger of the picaro may count as such. The theatrical situations, on the other hand, often treat the seedy goings-on in a mock-heroic manner, sometimes introducing topical allusions (the quarrel between the two girls over Macheath parallels the notorious fight between the opera singers Cuzzoni and Faustina), and leading us to expect a quasi-operatic set-piece. But when the characters do sing, it is not in the operatic language of heroism, but to Everyman's music, the tunes of the street. Some of the melodies to which the songs were fitted were real folk-songs, more were urbanized, eighteenth century popular tunes, a few were composed tunes by men such as Purcell, Jeremiah Clarke or even Handel himself. The one feature which all the tunes had in common was that they were well known: so that the piquancy of the situation came from the fact that the new words were often a satiric gloss on the implications of the familiar melody; sometimes, indeed, Gay rewrote the original words to suit his satiric purpose, as in the sequence of songs Macheath sings alone in the Condemned Hold, which transforms Chevy Chase into a drinking song to stimulate false courage, and makes Greensleeves, a love-song, an invitation to Tyburn. The point is that if everyone had his deserts, it would be hanging for everyone, not just for Macheath.

So the corrupt sing the language of innocence; and throughout the irony is always double-edged, and probably double-faced also. For the 'lowness' of the tunes ludicrously deflates the heroic pretensions of the operatic convention we have been led to expect: while the vitality and freshness of the tunes is denied by the shoddy, synthetic emotions they are called upon to express.[1] This complicated equivocation was probably the secret of the piece's success. Macheath's name became a household word, since everyone took vicarious pleasure in seeing himself as outlaw (Boswell fancied himself in the part and, in his cups, acted it for the delectation of two ladies of the town); Polly, originally played by a young woman of great personal charm, became 'everybody's sweetheart', her picture being embroidered or painted on fans, screens and snuffboxes. Yet Polly and Macheath became national figures only because their positive qualities of swagger, bounce, seductiveness, even pathos, were continually deflated by irony. One could enjoy their passions, while never being obliged to take them seriously. In this sense *The Beggar's Opera* represents the victory of the destructive cynicism inherent in Restoration society. In so far as it guys the conventions

[1] Gay intended the songs to be sung unaccompanied, like real folk-songs. Dr. Pepusch's continuo accompaniments were added at the suggestion of the theatrical management. Presumably the idea was that the songs would be more acceptable if garbed in contemporary fashion. The realizations weaken the irony of the tunes' innocence: but add another irony of their own—the disparity between popular simplicity and polite sophistication. Pepusch's overture—the only piece of specially composed music—is a more obvious example of this. In structure it is a conventionally heroic French overture, with a pompous double-dotted opening and a quick fugato in triple time. The latter, however, is in a somewhat skittish 12:8, like a jig: and so tends to deflate the opening's grandeur.

of aristocratic art and patronizes the tunes of the folk while understanding neither, it marks the beginning of British philistinism: of the belief that if art has any justification it is not because it helps us to deal more adequately with life's difficulties but because it makes us forget, momentarily, that such difficulties exist. The notoriously farcical, Hollywooden Happy Ending to *The Beggar's Opera* is only an explicit instance of a quality that is pervasive.

Emotional philistinism in *The Beggar's Opera* is mixed up with the social criticism and even with direct political satire, since jeers at the great (such as Walpole) usually imply, even when they are justified, a smug self-satisfaction. Dean Swift himself, writing in *The Intelligencer* in 1728, directly relates the artistic parody to the social criticism, pointing out that:

> this Comedy likewise exposeth with great Justice, that Unnatural Taste for Italian musick among us, which is wholly unsuited to our northern Climate, and the Genius of our People, whereby we are overrun with Italian Effeminacy, and Italian Nonsense. An old Gentleman said to me, that many years ago when the practice of an Unnatural Vice grew so frequent in London that many were Prosecuted for it, he was sure it would be a forerunner of Italian Operas, and Italian Singers; and then we should want nothing but Stabbing and Poysoning, to make us perfect Italians.

The victim of this barb is, as so often with Swift, somewhat ambiguous; but the ostensible point of the passage, so far from being peculiar to the misanthropic Dean, was a commonplace of contemporary journalism.[1] Certainly Gay would have said that

---

[1] Here is a lampoon addressed to 'Seignora Cuzzoni, on her return to Italy in 1725':

> Little Syren of the Stage,
> Charmer of an idle Age,
> Empty Warbler, breathing Lyre,
> Wanton Gale of fond Desire;
> Bane of ev'ry Manly Art,
> Sweet Enfeebler of the Heart,
> O too pleasing is thy Strain,
> Hence to Southern Climes again :
> Tuneful Mischief, vocal Spell,
> To this Island bid Farewell;
> Leave us, as we ought to be,
> Leave the Britons Rough and Free.

we had indeed reached the stabbing and poisoning; and that this was the responsibility of a corrupt ruling class that was in turn responsible for the vogue for Italian opera. Of course, his view was partial; and some people of sensibility took strong exception to it. 'Yesterday', wrote Mrs Delany to a friend in 1728, 'I was at the rehearsal of the new opera by Handel. I like it extremely, but the Taste of the Town is so depraved that nothing will be approved of but the Burlesque. The Beggar's Opera entirely triumphs over the Italian one . . . I am certain that, excepting some few, the English have no real taste for Musick; for if they had they could not neglect an Entertainment so perfect in its kind for a parcel of ballad singers.'

In different senses, both sides were right. Mrs Delaney was justified, of course, in approving of Handel's music, even in thinking the taste of the London public depraved. But Gay and Swift were right in seeing that the English vogue for Italian opera had never been more than superficial: that it was wrong because it was dishonest. The prosperous middle-class public would goggle over the spectacle and rave over the temperamental castrati; but the heroic concept that alone justified the opera's moral and material extravagance left them cold. The Italian opera—not opera in general—could be defined by Dr Johnson as 'an Exotick and Irrational Entertainment' because it was such if its apparent absurdities did not fulfil an artistic and ultimately moral purpose. The Beggar's Opera had no moral purpose: or at least being entirely critical and derogatory it had no positive morality. Yet its a-morality had, in its context of time and place, a kind of truth; and that is not affected by the fact that its prodigious success—more than a hundred imitations appeared between 1728 and 1738—was almost certainly attributable to the wrong reasons.

One might even argue that its a-morality was preferable to the new middle-class morality that took the place of the heroic ideal: though that morality is a direct development out of the Beggar's negation. Puritanic and prohibitive, it too was anti-musical: certainly it could not be complemented by the positive genius of a Purcell or a Handel. Thomas Arne, the most talented composer of the post-Handelian generation, is a sorry figure compared with his great predecessor; and the difference is one of moral stature as well as of technical skill. He is amiably pious and piously amiable; yet his morality is closer to the cynicism of *The Beggar's Opera* than it is to the Augustan *virtu* of Handel, because it is based on obliviousness of evil. At least in the social arts the consequence of the Beggar's negation is dedication to a morality of evasion and escape.

Let us examine, first, an early work of Arne, more or less contemporary with Handel's *L'Allegro*. In 1737 Paul Rolli, librettist of the Italian opera at the King's Theatre in the Haymarket, had made an operatic version of Milton's masque of *Comus*, which was unsuccessfully produced under the title of *Sabrina*. The failure of this opera did not deter John Dalton from making another version of *Comus*[1] in the following year. This was accepted by the Drury Lane theatre, where Arne was resident composer. Dalton's version is a rehash of Milton less disastrous than, but comparable with, the Dryden-Davenant rehash of Shakespeare's *Tempest*; a fair proportion of Milton's lines are preserved intact, but characters are added, usually in the interests of classical symmetry, and lines and scenes are interpolated to provide opportunities for music. The piece is described as a Musicall Entertainment, and the designation is accurate. Arne's music is often charming, the decor must have been pretty and the dancing graceful. But the additional spoken verse and incidental music destroys the dramatic significance of Milton's poem, so the piece is not an opera; nor is it a masque either, since it is a show, not a ritual.

The decay of the ritual element is revealed in the overture, which is a Handelian heroic piece with swooping scales and double dots—but completely without the inner harmonic tension that lies, for instance, beneath the grandeur of the overture to Handel's *Semele*. In the quick section the fugal order is elegant but perfunctory; the sequences make a pretty pattern but the pattern controls nothing. One is not aware of a tension between the public affirmation and the pressure of personal experience; so the public affirmation itself becomes no more than a gesture. The assertion of order does not impress because there is no real awareness of disorder. Lip-service is paid to the concepts of 'good' and 'bad' (as is not the case in the Dryden-Davenant *Tempest*); but the emptiness of the pretence is revealed in the

[1] Republished in *Musica Britannica*. Edited by Julian Herbage (Stainer and Bell).

un-Miltonic, non-Satanic nature of Arne's Comus. The most this Comus can rise (or fall) to is a polite salaciousness; the curtailed phrase on the words 'Tipsy dance and jollity' in 'Now Phoebus sinketh in the west' is slightly comic without disturbing the trotting symmetry of the jig rhythm, while the sequential modulations of the middle section suggest the opposite of abandoned chaos. (Compare what Handel does with sequential modulation in the hurly-burly chorus from *Jephtha*.) Other instances of Comus's songs are even more bathetic in their attempt to evoke licence. 'By dimpled brook' is a sentimental pastoral, with an intimate, stepwise-moving tune of delightful amiability about as remote from the night's lustfulness as could be imagined; clearly this girl is not, like Semele, in a longing condition. 'From tyrant laws and custom free' is an eighteenth century jig-ballad, 'low' as compared with Italianate heroism, but tied irrevocably to 'law and custom'. 'Why', the words ask, 'should niggard rules control.' No answer is proffered; and the rules' control remains absolute. Even the big choral number which Dalton added, inviting us to 'repair to Comus's court', carries no whiff of evil. The ubiquitous jig rhythm canters mildly along, and the 'Melting Fair' yields to sexual indulgence in the most conventional Handelian peroration. Either it doesn't really happen; or if it does, nobody cares, not even the participants. Arne's *Comus* is a victory for Society: whereas Milton's *Comus* is about the fight within the mind and without. (See Appendix D.)

Yet although Arne's *Comus* has not, in Milton's (or Handel's) sense, either public or private morality, it is not entirely without positive values. Its positive is the cult of sentiment: domestic, intimate, ignorant of evil and therefore, ultimately, of good, yet not for that reason the less touching. We have seen that Handel himself embraces this mode in parts of *L'Allegro ed Il Pensieroso* (for instance, 'Let me wander not unseen'). It became Arne's most characteristic manner; and there is no distinction in kind between the Comus song 'By dimpled brook' referred to above and the songs explicitly called 'Ballad' in the Dalton-invented third act. In all we find the gentle stepwise movement, the softly caressing appoggiaturas that create tender, not acute, dissonances, the simple binary structure, the 'anglicizing' and domesticating of Italian cantilena. Significantly, when this music does break through the 'rule', the public acceptance, it is to express not evil, but a slightly self-indulgent sentiment: consider, for instance, the saraband aria 'Now cold and denying', where an abrupt change to duple rhythm (bar 100) and some un-expected chromatic transitions (bar 116) express consent and complaint respectively. Sabrina, the water nymph, becomes her-self the apostle of Sentiment, being introduced by a most romantic un-Handelian passage of sequential sevenths. When the text returns from Dalton's words to Milton's, she sings a setting of 'By the rushy-fringed bank' in which the vocal line evades the complacent symmetries of the Comus music. Sabrina's cantilena is romantically sentimental, perhaps, in its very tor-tuousness. It is curiously difficult to sing; and its unfulfilment is a part of its romanticism—at least as compared with the canti-lena of Handel.

This water-nymph music is both exquisite and personal to Arne. A more ambiguous case is the Lady's Echo song, which begins as a tender saraband in dialogue between her voice and the fluted echo. The texture, melting in Arne's familiar suspen-sions, has a frail radiance quite unlike Handel; but the end, which refers to the Lady's translation to the skies, instead of ascending descends to bathos. The bouncing rhythm, the con-ventional modulation to the dominant, the ludicrous repetition of the rising arpeggio that is supposed to make 'Grace resound', the trite 6:5, 5, 1 conclusion[1] reveal that Arne is as incapable of ascending to the spirit's heights as he is of descending to the senses' depths. He can deal with the Sensibility of a young virgin or water sprite—and all his best music is in this vein of feminine sensitivity even when, as in the Handelian 'Now on beds of fading flowers', Dalton's words seem to be saying the opposite; but Comus is as far beyond him as is Milton's vision of eternal bliss. The moralistic final chorus is further evidence of this. As we read Milton's 'Or if Virtue feeble were, Heav'n itself would stoop to her' we are aware simultaneously of man's courage and of his dependence on God. Arne's music to the words, with its jogging rhythm, its unsullied symmetry, its always-expected

[1] Precisely the same formula does not sound trite at the end of a Haydn symphonic allegro or a Mozart operatic ensemble (though it is trite in a different way in many a rococo symphony) because it is, in context, part of the resolution of a sonata drama. It sounds idiotic in Arne's coda because it has no relationship to the mood and manner of the preceding air.

modulations, its stock final peroration, would make a cheery noise to introduce, or even accompany, the annual dinner of the city merchants.

So although Arne's *Comus* looks at first like a heroic piece, its positives turn out to be identical with those of his light operas which, without incorporating popular tunes, are in the tradition of English ballad opera. Consider the operetta *The Cooper*[1] which, written in 1772, belongs to the last phase of Arne's career. Arne himself translated the libretto from the French of Quétant, for which Gossec had written music in 1756; and the story, set in the world of the artisan, is common property to Italian opera buffa, French opéra comique and English ballad opera. It is, of course, anti-heroic; but in this case it is not merely the servant who gets the better of his aristocratic master, nor even the young artisan who triumphs over his old but not socially superior taskmaster. Fanny is ward to an old cooper, Martin, who falls in love with her. She loves Colin, the cooper's apprentice; and the young people have to find a way of making the course of true love run smooth without hurting the dotard, who is kind and lovable, if a buffoon. Their solution to the problem, typically enough, involves Money. Martin owes one Jarvis £50, which they know he cannot at the moment repay. Colin persuades Jarvis to enter the plot and to demand the immediate return of his money: whereupon Colin offers to pay off the debt if Martin will allow the young people to marry. So Jarvis becomes a middle-class (and very materialistic!) deus ex machina; Martin immediately agrees to the proposal and the lovers and the cooper sing a note-for-note trio in which Martin says he will solace himself with the bottle while the young people enjoy the pleasures of love. At the same time, all three promise to combine pleasure with 'labour'; if you work hard, you'll get rich, and if you are rich there are no more human problems. Thus everyone is basically Good; and any temporary difficulties that arise from conflicting human passions can be smoothed out by the application of £50.

Clearly this is, if comforting, also false; and the falsity is present in the music as well as the human situation. We may cite Fanny's 'Fly, time, with lighter pinions move', sung while she's

---

[1] Vocal Score, edited by Joseph Horowitz (J. & W. Chester).

276

waiting for her young man in the night, as a genuinely touching example of Arne's most typical manner. The falling fifths, the stepwise-moving quavers slurred in pairs, have a flavour of folk-song, in an eighteenth century, urbanized form; but the simple ternary structure (halfway between a da capo aria and a rudimentary sonata form), the symmetrically disposed modulations, and the grouping of the clauses in the middle section suggest the more conscious artifice of eighteenth century opera. The still more artful repetition of the phrases in the recapitulation, the pause on the high E on the word 'seem', turn the sentiment into sentimentality, a hint of melodrama that discreetly presages the Victorian ballad.[1] It is interesting that in moving, spiritually, from the theatre into the parlour the music becomes, in a sense, more not less 'theatrical'. There is something a little arch about such sentiment; without being exactly insincere, it becomes a game which one indulges in for its own sake. Fanny's siciliano in which she laughs (good-naturedly, of course) at the aged Martin's wooing shows a similar artifice in feeling. The soft appoggiaturas for his sighs, the Lombard snaps for his chuckles, are an amused exhibition, so that the effect is almost satirical—as is the intrusion of 'low' language ('gives my elbow a shove') into the prettiness. Even Colin's opening song, confessing his love for Fanny, with its skittish syncopations and intermittent (forte) yells of Zooks!, turns his passion into a self-indulgent prank ('when I catch her, then for pleasure'); and the game is later played out on the stage, in the kissing or rather non-kissing duet, which titillates, but does not satisfy. Interestingly enough, the exaggeration of sentiment and the deflation of it by satire tend to become synonymous; both spring from an incapacity for passion.

All the dialogue in The Cooper is spoken, as in a French opéra comique, and there are fifty-three minutes speech to twenty-two minutes music. There are, however, two scenes in accompanied arioso, both of which involve satire of heroic convention. The first of them presents Fanny waiting for her lover in the dark. The music she sings—especially her calls to Colin in falling minor thirds—is charming, even poignant. The 'concitato' comments of the orchestra, however, once more introduce an

[1] See Appendix C

277

element of artifice; we are encouraged simultaneously to accept her feeling and to laugh at it : which again is a way of being afraid. The other arioso scene occurs when Martin blunders about in the dark and gets scared by the apparently self-motivated barrel in which Colin is hiding. This is a straightforward parody of the 'arioso of terror', with shooting scales and 'horrid' diminished sevenths. Theatrically, the scene is quite funny; but the fear motive is not fortuitous and makes the sentiment we are supposed to feel for Martin the more difficult to credit, for there is nothing inherently sympathetic in the music he sings.

The ambiguity of sentiment that we have discovered in Arne's theatre music is to be found in his non-theatrical music also. His cantata *The Morning*,[1] for soprano voice, sopranino recorder, strings and continuo, is a curious example, conceived in the tradition of the Handelian solo cantata with obbligato instruments. The opening invocation to the sun begins grandly, with repeated quaver bass, dissonant appoggiaturas on each strong beat, and an expansive arpeggiated vocal phrase for the sun. This is all very resplendent, though there is an un-Handelian sense of strain about the vocal contours. This does not prepare us, however, for the footling, tootling coloratura that is supposed to make the sun glitter and rise, nor for the bathetic adagio cadence, which might be a prologue to the mayor's after-dinner speech, rather than a herald of dawn. This is an instance of the divorce of music from meaning; the musical cliché does not arise from the words; imposed on them, it renders them imbecile.

What actually follows is the appearance of the sopranino recorder, which inevitably sounds comic after the grandiose opening. The recorder turns out to be not a joke, like Polyphemus's flageolet, but a lark; and the music becomes not grand but graceful, in the manner of the bird pieces from Handel's *L'Allegro*. Again, however, there is an un-Handelian awkwardness in the vocal contours. This lark, buoyed up by sharp suspensions between recorder and violin, flutters a little breathlessly. He hasn't the ecstatic vitality of Handel's, and his relative frailty is his most Arne-like feature.

So far, the piece has manifested an odd ambivalence between the high baroque pretension of the opening and the half-comic,

[1] Schott & Co. Edited by Robert Salkeld.

278

half-romantic intimacy of the lark song. Despite the ambiguity, we are hardly ready for the grotesque comedy of the next arioso section in which the shepherd ineffectually 'tunes his pipe' in a stuttering recorder obbligato and then 'to the woodland hies' in a lurching dotted rhythm. Handel's physical and pictorial illustration may occasionally provoke mirth; but if it does, the satirical sense is usually latent in the words. It is typical of Arne's emotional dubiety that it is difficult to know whether this passage is meant to be funny or not. Either way, the effect is deflatory. Such naivety makes it impossible to take seriously the majestic opening, and it makes no difference whether Arne pricks the bubble intentionally or fortuitously. In any case, the deflation leads into Arne's real positive, his air of domestic sentiment. Heroic splendours and miseries are not for him and there are things about the heavenward-lilting lark he could never understand. So he gives us a saraband introduction in E minor, suavely Handelian in stepwise movement interspersed with leaping sixths, leading into a typical Arne andante, in which he says that he is unhappy because his Delia has left him and he's left alone with woods and vales. Yet the music breathes a quiet content; his vein of love can dispense not only with passion but also, apparently, with the beloved. The music, moving over a gentle crochet bass, with the habitual melting appoggiaturas, is very beautiful—some of the loveliest Arne wrote; yet it creates, again, a slightly ambiguous feeling which is not solely due to the (as we have seen) dubious context the air appears in. There is an element of preciousness in the way in which the folky pastoralism is modified by the artfulness of the sequential clauses in the middle section and by an extended operatic cadenza; and again there is an element of perversity in both vocal technique and in the treatment of language. The song, which is supposed to be simple and relaxed, is not grateful to sing (at least in comparison with Handel) because the feeling, though not contrived, is in part self-stimulated. As in *Comus* and *The Cooper*, the line between sentiment and sentimentality is wavery; and this is the beginning of the end—of a decadence in feeling and technique.

This 'decadence' is not merely a matter of the lack of a talent, for in natural endowment Arne was certainly not inferior to Matthew Locke who, seventy years earlier, was a 'progressive' rather than a decadent composer, in tune with the most urgent impulses of his time, which were soon to be fulfilled by Henry Purcell. Arne created an opera of domestic sentiment and hinted at a music of personal romanticism; yet in England neither came to fruition. On the continent, especially in Austria, the opera of common life became, in Mozart's fusion of traditional aria with sonata drama, a profound exploration of the desires, fears and aspirations of all sorts and conditions of men. Popular though Mozart's operas were in London, we could approach no closer to Mozart's musical and dramatic style than the operas of Storace; and though similarities between Storace and Mozart exist, the differences between them are more remarkable.

Born in England, probably in 1763, Stephen Storace was of Italian descent: which is perhaps why he could be, as Leigh Hunt put it, 'the golden link between the music of the two countries, the only one, perhaps, in which English accentuation and Italian flow were ever truly amalgamated.' He spent some of his youth in Italy, and also in Vienna where his sister Ann was prima donna. She sang the part of Susanna in the first performance of Mozart's *Figaro* in 1786; and Stephen himself produced an Italian opera to a libretto of da Ponte. It was hardly surprising, therefore, that on settling in England in 1789 he should consciously have attempted to infuse Mozartian musical and dramatic principles into the tradition of English ballad opera and the pastoral sentimentalism of Arne. Given the nature of Mozart's achievement and of Arne's, the attempt was bound, perhaps, to fail. How it failed is revealed in Storace's first English opera, *No Song, No Supper*,[1] produced at Drury Lane in April 1790.

The overture, scored for a small Mozartian orchestra, is curious. It begins *large maestoso*, in dotted rhythm, in what would seem to be an attempt at heroic style. Even the Allegro that follows is headed 'Chacone': though after the first few clauses it is no such thing, but a cheery rococo bustle, without Mozart's textural richness but with pliant, Mozartian lyrical contours. When the action opens we find two shipwrecked mariners on the coast of Cornwall. One of them, Robin, is asleep; the other, Frederick, sings an aria about 'the ling'ring pains of

[1] Republished in *Musica Britannica*. Edited by Roger Fiske (Stainer and Bell).

hopeless love'. Musically, this aria suggests that the (somewhat tentative) pretensions of the overture are to be justified. It is a very Mozartian piece, with a spacious, expressively decorated, appoggiatura-laden melody and a rich orchestral texture with panting repeated notes for the labouring heart and sizzling demisemiquavers for the sea's fury. Though there may be a hint of un-Mozartian melodrama at the cadential phrase when he asks for death as a release from sorrow, the aria is impressive; and if it were in fact by Mozart we would expect its mood of passionate authenticity to be maintained throughout the opera, however much it may be complemented by—even intensified by—ironic and risible contrasts.

In *No Song, No Supper*, however, passion is immediately deflated by a moral dubiety similar to that we commented on in Arne. The shipwrecked sailors disclose, in spoken dialogue, that they are both harassed by love-troubles which involve, typically, money and litigation. Frederick's Louisa has refused him because she is under the erroneous impression (fostered by him) that he is poor, and she doesn't want to embarrass her family. Robin has left his Margaretta because he is in fact poor, having been cheated by a lawyer, and knows that her father wants to marry her off to a rich dotard. Then we turn to the house of Farmer Crop, father of Frederick's Louisa. Mr and Mrs Crop are stock figures, marital bickerers. She sings a jaunty and unperturbed 'French air' (adapted from an unspecified opera), 'O George I can't endure you'; he sings an English air in the manner of Arne's urbanized folk-ballads, describing how happy he was before he submitted to the 'marital yoke'. (The opening of this song is, indeed, almost a quotation from Arne.) The ironic contrast between Frederick's passion for Louisa, as expressed in his first aria, and this picture of what married life is really like, might occur in Mozart: only with him the comic characters would not be merely comic, but would be involved in the same kind of music—and the same human situations—as the 'serious' characters. We wouldn't, in fact, be aware of any sharp differentiation between serious and comic. We would know that Frederick and Louisa might easily end up like Farmer Crop and his Dorothy; still more significantly, we'd know that Crop and Dorothy might once have been like the young people. In Storace's opera there is not, because there could not be, any real connexion between the Mozartian and the Arne-like elements; so the deflation of passion becomes an end in itself. Perhaps it was not an accident that, for the second quarrel song, Storace adapted a hit-number from Grétry; it didn't need any dramatic justification, only immediate recognition and appeal.

Margaretta comes in, travelling the country as an itinerant ballad singer, searching for her lost Robin. Her song, in a swinging dotted rhythm, is most refreshing, thoroughly English and open-air in feeling, yet quite without Arne's coyness; it deservedly became the most popular number in the show. She decides to ask for a night's lodging at the cottage she is passing: which of course proves to be Crop's house. An ensemble number —a trio—ensues when Dorothy and the serving maid Nelly deny admission to this 'gipsy'. Based on a number from Storace's first Viennese opera of 1784, this is a genuinely Mozartian ensemble which combines wit (the door-knocking motive in the orchestra, the women's peremptory dismissals) with pathos (Margaretta's 'imploring' suspensions). It is also musical drama in that it is a sonata-style movement wherein the development conveys, through modulations and rhythmic modifications, Margaretta's growing desperation and Dorothy's increasing annoyance. This is true dramatic and psychological action in music: which suggests that in innate talent, Storace was the composer English opera needed.

But nothing comes of the wit or the drama, any more than of the opening aria's passion. The ensemble is deflated by a return to the Crops' bickerings in English ballad style; and this in turn ruins the transition to the Act's finale. This is a Mozartian 'ensemble of perplexity', wherein the contrapuntal entries and the restless modulations are wittily used to suggest the lovers' feverish attempts to disentangle their relationships, while Margaretta's lyricism remains genuinely affecting. When the allegro reaches its climax everyone sings, homophonically, a hymn to Hope and Fancy, which 'calm the troubled heart'. It is a fine curtain; but the lyrical andantino tune is not good enough—compared with Mozart or even Gluck—really to bring balm to perturbed hearts; and it is not good enough because it does not grow from the allegro but is purloined from Storace's third Italian opera. And the reason why Storace had no compunction about such an act in such a context is, of course, that we have never been able to believe in the hearts' troubles; or at least as soon as we began to believe in them librettist and composer refused to allow us to. The difference between Mozart's 'recognition of other modes of experience that are possible' and Storace's deflatory irony is a distinction between two civilizations, as well as between talents.

Unsatisfactory as the first act finale may be, it is the closest the opera comes to musical-dramatic sense. The ensemble and coda unravel the emotional tensions, such as they are; but they don't unravel the action, so a second act is needed for this purpose only. That Storace had grown bored with the piece is suggested by the fact that the second act incorporates many more numbers from other composers—Grétry, Pleyel, Giordani and a Dr Harrington. Some of Storace's own numbers in the English ballad vein are genuinely comic, both English and personal to Storace: we may mention 'Across the downs this morning', and the opening sailor's song, with its blustering semiquavers that take a rise out of the ocean! As a whole, however, the second act is musical comedy rather than opera, complete with a Merrie Englysshe rout of rusticks to celebrate the marriages. This is a game of let's pretend; any hint of the Mozartian implications of the first act—the awareness of the realities of human feeling—has vanished.

And what happened to Storace's first English opera happened to English opera in general. Mozart's operas had dealt with the intrinsic natures and predicaments of the people who made up his society. Storace's opera gives up the attempt to create a mythology out of the conditions of life-as-it-was and turns into an operetta of escape. This tendency begins in the facetious pastoralism of the second act of No Song, is continued in The Pirates (1792) and still more in The Cherokee (1794), which was the first musical 'western'. From there it is only a step to the romantic dream-opera of Balfe; and from there it is another short step to the 'substitute living' of Edwardian musical comedy and The Desert Song.

The virtual disappearance, as a creative force, of both opera and drama from nineteenth century England is not fortuitous. On the contrary, it is a direct sequel to the negativism of The Beggar's Opera: which was in turn an extension of the cynicism inherent in Restoration society. In a world dedicated to trade and material prosperity, authentic creative activity went into the poetry of the inner life, as in romantic lyrical verse and land-scape painting;[1] or into the novel's imaginative commentary on a changing social milieu. The nineteenth century novel's amor-phousness was part of its integrity: prose discussion and critical interpretation could be a legitimate part of its creativeness. The immediately social arts of the theatre, on the other hand, could not lend themselves to exposition and disquisition: could not vitally prosper without an accepted scale of values and an ac-cepted stylization which would be the artistic equivalent of those values. Nor could the public arts of the theatre enter the romantic poet's private world: for a public inner life is a con-tradiction in terms. The romantic poet's retreat into the 'waking dream' was a search for reality within the mind, when public values seemed to have become meaningless; the theatre's public dream was an escape from reality, an acceptance of cliché—the lowest and commonest denominator as a substitute for living.

From this point of view serious or 'grand' opera became, in Britain during the nineteenth century, a pendant of the romantic ballet. Escape operas founded on the dream-worlds of Walter Scott's historical novels were, of course, a European phenom-enon; but only in England did the musical content of even the best of them degenerate to a vapidity that allowed for little distinction between the grandest opera and the most trivial musical comedy. By far the most successful of English romantic opera composers was Balfe, whose *Bohemian Girl* enjoyed inter-national, as well as local, esteem: and the essence of his romanticism was that it charmed, but did not disturb. His friend Barrett, attempting to explain the appeal of his work, signific-antly remarks that 'his melodies are of such a character that when the initial phrase falls upon the ear, the ear proposes the sequence'. The gipsy's abandon, that is, is conformable both to expectation and to social propriety; and Barrett goes on specifi-cally to relate his praise of Balfe's naturalness ('there is no ap-

[1] Apart from the minor instance of the Nocturnes of John Field, there is no British musical complement to our splendid efflorescence of romantic poetry. The reason cannot be that music is naturally a more 'social' art, for by its very abstraction it lends itself to the communings of the solitary heart. Perhaps the explanation is simple and practical: a disruption of tradition, such as we suffered in the eighteenth century, is more difficult to repair in a relatively artificial language such as music than it is in literature, which employs our normal means of communication.

parent effort of labour, no smelling of the lamp, no finding out of a strange chord and building up a passage to exhibit it') to Victorian morality:

> In not one of his operas is there any questionable situation or expression. The plots are all interesting and some are exciting, but their interests and excitement are not due to actions or motives of which right-minded men scarcely dare to speak to one another. On the stage Balfe was by predilection a moral teacher. There is no sensuous swim in his music, no association with doubtful actions, or connection with words of equivocation, to carry the soul to regions of impurity. All is honest, tender, manly, straightforward and true.

So the substitute-living of Balfe's romantic opera was really the Victorian prejudices writ large. It was an 'escape' in that those prejudices were themselves a falsification of experience. This explains both its immediate vogue and its subsequent eclipse.

Certainly *The Bohemian Girl* seems at this date neither true, nor straightforward, nor manly, though it was not consciously dishonest. The plot, turning on mislaid identity—the Fairy Prince and Princess brought up by gipsies, defying Fate through the purity of their love—was already a cliché; but it had not previously assumed so grotesquely synthetic a character. That quality it owes to the 'literary' language of Balfe's sublimely named librettist, Alfred Bunn, who can make gipsies blandly remark that 'the hot viands are served'. The most celebrated of all Balfe's songs—'I dreamt that I dwelt'—epitomizes precisely the synthetic element in the Victorian Dream. Arline, the aristocratic girl reared by the gipsies, dreams that she 'dwelt in marble halls, with vassals and serfs' at her side; that she had riches 'too great to count', and that she could boast of a 'high ancestral name'. Yet at the same time, she dreams that her Thaddeus, whom she believes to be a poor gipsy, loved her 'just the same': a supreme instance either of the British gift for compromise or of British greed (having it both ways), according to one's point of view. The implied link between democratic-domestic piety, snobbery and material prosperity, which we commented on in Arne, here takes on a nightmarish rather than dream-like character; and Balfe's music exactly fits the revolting morality. The basis is Italian bel canto in its post-Rossinian nineteenth century form, which was naturally more 'vulgar' (in the strict sense) than its heroic prototype. The vulgarity of Balfe's piece, however, is different from Verdi's passion or Donizetti's earthiness. A typical Victorian smugness comes into the way in which each melodic arch falls heavily and comfortably to its eight-bar period, with the first beat of the cadential tonic accented with the descending roulade that sounds almost like a parody of the Italianate sob. Expectation is monotonously fulfilled—'the ear proposes the sequence', as Barrett said; and the piece carries the Italian aria into the world of the Victorian drawing-room ballad. As in the ballad, the unreality is emphasized by the disparity between music and words. The habitual accenting of the second beat of the 3 : 8 bar—which makes her sing of serfs *at* her side, of rich*es* too gre-*at* to co*unt*—suggests a kind of gross exultation: while the musical repetitions of the final clause, mounting sequentially to an ornamented high G, exactly parallel the bathos of the words:

> But I also dreamed,
> Which pleased me most,
> That you loved me still the same.

On that 'which ple-*eased* me most' we can almost hear her licking her chops. There is something horrifying in the way the lilt, almost lurch, of the tune carries all before it; it's as though she were drunk with, hypnotized by, the vehemence of the wish-fulfilment.

English opera in the nineteenth century prospered materially but was hollow at the heart. The apparent exception to this —the comic operas of Gilbert and Sullivan—may not be an exception at all. It was a paradox that Sullivan—revered guardian of British musical respectability—should have achieved success in the theatre, which was wicked and French; yet it was also logical, for Gilbert's art was an art of paradox: which is in direct descent from the paradox of *The Beggar's Opera*. The Gilbert and Sullivan operettas, like the operas of Balfe, are essentially an escape art; and though they include social criticism they encourage, rather than offend, our basic social prejudices. Superficially, they deal with modern life: laugh at generals who know nothing of military affairs, admirals who have never been to sea, nobility who haven't enough money to live nobly. They laugh at parliamentary government as well as at social egalitarianism; ridicule Colonel Blimp as well as the *fin de siècle* Artist. But they never suggest that the Establishment ought to be other than it is, the rich less rich, the poor less poor; and their positives are based on the philistinism of the British middle-class. Meilhac and Halévy, and Offenbach, whom they took as their model, whom they wished to purge of 'crudity and artificiality', created an entertainment art which combined hedonistic zest with irony and even melancholy, for they were aware of the abyss beneath. For Gilbert and Sullivan there was no abyss, only an unsublime complacence; this is why so much of their humour consists of paradox and of musical parody— a *Beggar's Opera*-like guying of conventions which English middle-class materialism could not understand. It is significant too that though Sullivan was adept at characterizing in music groups of people—young girls, policemen, bumpkins and so on —he had little sense of individual characterization. He can see people collectively, in their public demeanour: but cannot encompass the flesh and blood reality of individuals. Like Arne, he has banished Comus; and you cannot do that and expect to see life whole.

Sullivan's musical roots were in Rossini and Offenbach on the one hand, the English cathedral tradition on the other. The catylist between these two unlikely partners was Mendelssohn, who offered both the exquisite dreamy elegance of his orchestral scherzi and also the portentous solemnity of his oratorio style. Sullivan uses both for risible effect; yet the humour is nearly always in the situation rather than in the music itself. We can see this in the admirable quartet 'In a contemplative fashion' from *The Gondoliers*. This is Sullivan's version of the Rossinian Ensemble of Perplexity. The 'contemplative fashion' is contained in a slow-moving chorale of churchy British respectability, not far from the idiom of *Hymns Ancient and Modern*; the perplexity is contained in the Offenbachian patter-song of the individual voices, expressing in turn and then together their personal anxieties and irritations. But the norm of respectability remains; there is nothing comparable with Offenbach's occasional unexpected harmony or modulation or rhythmic surprise. Though this is explicitly the point of the number, it has also a general significance.

Similarly Sullivan's marches have lost both the zip and the suppressed minatory venom that characterizes Offenbach's. They express rather the stolidified discipline epitomized in the Victorian Policeman; the prevalence of tonic pedals in the marches, anchoring the bass, is symptomatic. Something the same is true of Sullivan's dances, which are usually exotic or old-world. They couldn't be real, contemporary, happening at the moment—like Offenbach's can-can or Strauss's waltz—for Sullivan's London was not, mercifully, Offenbach's Paris or Strauss's Vienna.

The non-reality of Sullivan's gaiety points, however, to the non-reality of his heart. The soft centre of his work, and perhaps his most personal note, is the positive value of Charm he evokes from English Girlhood. It is interesting that in setting 'There was a time' in *The Gondoliers*—a song about Lost Love—Sullivan ignores the absurd situation that Gilbert plants it in, and composes a straight, nostalgic drawing-room ballad. The harmony relates it to Auber, Balfe, or the more sanctimoniously chromatic Gounod; the melodic contours and the texture suggest Mendelssohn of the Songs without Words; the drooping clauses are a little elegy upon a never-to-be-realized, ideal domesticity. In all Sullivan's pieces about young girls there is the same rather arch wistfulness: a more banal legacy from the archness we commented on in Arne. In Rossini and Offenbach there is an undercurrent of cruelty and of melancholy because they knew their hedonism necessitated a sacrifice of tenderness and compassion. Sullivan tried to preserve the tenderness by pretending the cruelty and melancholy weren't there. Being thus evasive, his art became at best wistful, at worst mawkish. The duet between the newly-wedded girls, at the end of Act I of *The Gondoliers*, is poised precariously between the two. The girls appeal to their husbands, off to rule their ruritanian kingdom, to be true to them. The floating semiquavers, with their gentle appoggiaturas, are unexpectedly subtle in their verbal accentuation; and this gives the music a frail reality that just counterbalances the archness. There is a similar quality in the unexpectedly abrupt modulation that leads back to the tonic for the final chorus. It's as though the girls are taken aback by the audacity of their own modulations in the middle section: as though they are pushing down a suspicion that they wouldn't mind toying with the naughtinesses they're warning their husbands against.

So the song's wistful authenticity may spring from the fact that it admits that the Victorian Dream of Domestic Bliss was based on unconscious hypocrisy. Unhypocritical hypocrisy, to coin a Gilbertian paradox, may be tolerable, for we all live in part on our illusions; and if Sullivan's myth of the English Rose is uncongenial to us in the mid-twentieth century it may not be any the worse for that. What is more serious, in his social-theatrical art, is that the false soft-centre has public as well as private implications. In *The Gondoliers*, for instance, from which we have taken our examples, the theme is a humourous treatment of social egalitarianism, with the moral that if everybody was somebody, nobody would be anybody. Of course this is true: or it would be if the paradox were practically realizable. But being a paradox, it is also an abstraction from reality: and becomes the means whereby Gilbert can dismiss the most urgent social preoccupations of his day. (The only thing that deeply moves him is the fact that a nobleman should be reduced to becoming a kind of publicity agent and impressario for the *nouveaux riches*). This is not to say that a public entertainer must possess a social—or even a moral—conscience; it is to say that he must be imaginatively aware of the reality upon which his dream-world is based. There is no reformatory zeal in the creations of Halévy and Offenbach; but there is an awareness that life is not really an eternal can-can: a mordancy in the satire, a hint of frenzy in the gaiety, that protect us from self-complacence. The death of an art, even of an entertainment, occurs when it loses all power to disturb.

It will be objected that, if this is so, the Gilbert and Sullivan operettas appear to be pretty lively corpses. But their survival-value, we may suspect, depends on extra-musical, perhaps on extra-dramatic, reasons. We like, especially if we have reached middle-age, to preserve a comforting illusion, and we cling to an art that helps us to do so; it is even possible that the superficially surprising popularity of Gilbert and Sullivan in the United States depends on the fact that they offer a period-illusion of what Americans think England ought to be. In any case it is significant that there have been no successors to the Gilbert and Sullivan operettas; a tradition that began with *The Beggar's Opera* and developed through the comic-sentimental operas of Arne, Linley, Dibdin and Storace, has here found its end. Since it was a tradition built on negation and evasion the end did not come too soon. While we do not yet know in what direction a recreated English tradition of musical theatre may develop, the very fact that composers in Britain are again writing vital works for the theatre may imply some more positive reorganization of our social and psychological lives.

APPENDIX A

It is interesting to compare with Byrd's Lullaby a Virgin's cradle-song of an earlier generation, Richard Pygott's Quid petis O fili[1], although this beautiful piece comes, chronologically, outside the scope of this book. Nothing is known about Pygott except that he was born about 1485 and died around 1550. On stylistic grounds one would hazard a guess that this piece was written about 1520. While it shows close kinship with the tradition of the medieval danced carol, and while it is not dramatic music in the sense that Byrd's Lullaby is dramatic, it shows (like so many nativity pieces) the development of a 'humanistic' approach within medieval mysticism.

Formally, it consists of a Latin refrain, interspersed with three stanzas in English alliterative verse; in effect it is a rondo in which, however, the episodes are variations on the theme. In so far as the lines of the four-voiced refrain move mainly by step or by pentatonic minor thirds they suggest—at least compared with Byrd—a mystical serenity, a remoteness from the physical. Yet even here the music acquires a speaking intimacy, asking its question Quid petis?—what are you seeking?—in a rising fifth, then fourth, then third, the parts moving in softly sensuous thirds or tenths. Moreover, the treble entry, tied over the bar, makes a diminished fourth with the alto's cadential F sharp: there's a hint of yearning in the query; and the (probably instrumental) melisma after the treble has asked his question seems to enact the babe's search for the nipple. Perhaps there is also a hint of agitation in the search, for the treble melisma bumps dissonantly into the alto melisma and the bass's rising B flat, before it fades out on the non-harmonic, modal flat seventh. The answering phrase ('mater dulcissima') is all lyrical, stepwise, upward-flowing, with four entries in fugato. This too, descending, turns into the physical gesture of a caress, as the mother coos to the child, ba ba. Both question and answer are then repeated, with longer, tenderer melismata, both for the child's seeking and the

[1] Stainer and Bell, the Fayrfax Series, No. 13. Edited by C. F. Simkins.

mother's kiss. The refrain ends, without finality, 'on' the dominant; both the child's and the mother's search goes on for ever, until Paradise.

The first episode renders the refrain music more overtly humanistic, since it grows out of the inflexions of the English language. There are many more repeated notes, following the speech-rhythm, and the leaping fourth motive becomes—in association with the words 'laughing in lap laid' and 'so prettily, so pertly, so passingly well apaid'—a bodily movement. In the phrase 'softly and full soberly' the flattened Es 'act' the tenderness and sobriety: while the 'and to her sweet son' phrase modifies the stepwise ascent of the 'mater dulcissima' refrain to create a stabbing suspended second on the word 'sweet'. The pathos of the dissonance gives the baby warmth and substantiality; and makes the return to the modal melismata, with flat seventh and re-sharpened sixth, the more heart-easing. Out of this gentleness, the refrain sings again, smoother, probably slightly slower, than the episode.

The second episode introduces another kind of musical humanism—the physical action of the dance. The rising fourth motive, followed by a descent down the scale, is still present, serenely suggesting the Virgin's 'lovely looking on our Lord'; but the skipping, instrumentally suggested dotted rhythm playfully expresses the child's agile movements, and changes the speaking rhythm of repeated notes into the more positive energy of a rising arpeggio (for 'the reson that I rede you'). The final melisma incorporates the skittish rhythm which, however, peters out in a modal, flat seventh undulation, and so carries us back into the rarefied remoteness of the refrain.

This scherzo-like episode is in two parts only. The last episode, which is in three parts, fuses together all the 'humanistic' intensifications we have so far encountered. Beginning close to the refrain-music, it introduces speech inflexions, passing dissonances, and even a false relation on the word 'pain', while the trebles (or an instrumental ritornello) remind us of the dotted rhythm dance. Though this music is rooted in medieval traditions which were not normally concerned with growth or 'Becoming', it is valid to say that in this episode the piece reaches its climax. And the climax is, significantly, harmonic: for when the text for the first time identifies divine and human, 'Gracious

God and good sweet babe', the voices sing repeatedly, in speech rhythm, a C major triad, low and resonant, occasionally oscillating to a G minor triad which is the modal tonic. In the context, this C major triad sounds like an inverted plagal Amen, with the stress on the subdominant *major*, rather than on subdominant minor as preparation for the tonic major. It suggests a darkly sensuous humanity: which makes the final repeat of the four-voiced refrain the more mysterious in its mystical tranquillity.

APPENDIX B

These *Hymns to the Trinity* by Henry Lawes are reproduced from an early printed copy in the British Museum, which is then transcribed into modern notation. The bass is left unfigured, as in the original, for its implications are clear enough. The occasional harmonic excitation (especially in the second Hymn) is commented on in the text of the book.

The beautiful recorded version of these songs (with continuo by Thurston Dart) is listed in the discography.

To God the Father.

Hou God the Father, hid from mortall fight, that cloath'st thy self with circumfufed

ght; thou King Eternall, with thy quickning raies, give life to my dead foul: clear all my daies with thy

bright prefence, my weak fpirit fill with pow'r not fubject to the Tempters will ; Giv me a

fil'all, not a fervile fear, let ev'ry fin be ranfom'd with a tear; forbid me to defpair, or to prefume,

left too much fear fhould my beft hopes confume ; and when my body in the grave fhall reft, may my

cleans'd foul in Martyrs robes be dreft.

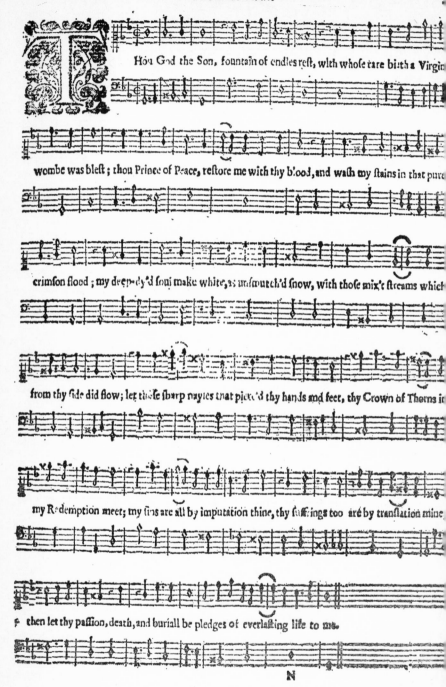

Thou God the Son, fountain of endless rest, with whose rare birth a Virgin wombe was blest; thou Prince of Peace, restore me with thy blood, and wash my stains in that pure crimson flood; my deep-dy'd soul make white, as unsmutch'd snow, with those mix't streams which from thy side did flow; let those sharp nayles that pierc'd thy hands and feet, thy Crown of Thorns in my Redemption meet; my sins are all by imputation thine, thy sufferings too are by translation mine, then let thy passion, death, and buriall be pledges of everlasting life to me.

N

296

Hou God the Holy Ghost, that spread'st thy wings o're wounded spirits, Bath me

in the springs of thy defusive joyes; and still impart fresh Oyle of Gilead to my bleeding heart; when

I am folded in the armes of Death, drop down, drop down thy dew on my expiring breath; let not a

doubt of one uncancel'd sin, dare to disturb my sweet repose within ; all clouds of fear, let thy bright

beames expell, that in my thoughts a serene calme may dwell : so shall my Rock of Faith unshaken

stand, in full assurance of the promis'd Land.

Hymns to the Holy Trinity
To God the Father

Thou God the Fa-ther, hid from mor-tal sight, that cloth'st Thy-self ___ with cir-cum-fus-ed light; Thou King E-ter-nal, with Thy quick-'ning rays, ___ give life ___ to my dead soul: clear all my days with Thy bright pres-ence, my weak ___ spir-it fill with pow'r not sub-ject to the Temp-ter's will; Give me a fil-ial, not a ser-vile fear, let ev-'ry sin ___ be ran- - -som'd with a tear; for-bid ___ me to des-pair, or to pre-sume, lest too much fear should ___ my best hopes con-sume; and when my bo-dy in the grave shall rest, may my cleans'd ___ soul ___ in mar- - -tyr's robes ___ be dress'd.

To God the Son

Thou God the Son, foun-tain of end-less rest, with whose rare birth a Vir - - gin's womb was blest; Thou Prince of Peace, re - store ___ me with Thy blood, and wash my stains ___ in that pure crim-son flood; my deep-dy'd soul make white as un-smirch'd snow, with those mix'd streams ___ which from thy side ___ did flow; let those sharp ___ nails that pierc'd Thy hands ___ and feet, Thy Crown of Thorns ___ in my re-demp-tion meet; my sins are all ___ by im-pu-ta-tion Thine, Thy suff-'rings too are by trans-la-tion mine; then let Thy pas-sion, death, and bur-ial be pled-ges of ev-er-last - - ing life to me.

299

To God the Holy Ghost

Thou God the Ho - ly Ghost, that spread'st Thy wings o'er wound - ed spir-its, bathe me in the springs of Thy de - fus - ive joys; and still im-part fresh oil of Gil-ead to my bleed-ing heart; when I am fold - ed in the arms of death, drop down, drop down Thy dew on my ex-pir - ing breath; let not a doubt of one un-can-cell'd sin dare to dis-turb my sweet re-pose with - in; all clouds of fear let Thy bright beams ex - pel, that in my thoughts a ser-ene calm may dwell; so shall my Rock of Faith un - shak - en stand in full as-sur - ance of the Prom-ised Land.

APPENDIX C

A link between Arne's sentimental songs and the Victorian ballad proper is provided by the parlour songs of a late eighteenth century composer such as James Hook. In 1796, for instance, he published a collection of airs, duets and part-songs under the title of *The Banquet of Apollo*. 'Glory' is a song sung by a girl whose young man has died in foreign parts. The Arne-like appoggiaturas express the girl's sighs and sobs; but the symmetrical disposition of the clauses, the operatic turns and trills, always in the expected places, 'theatricalize' the feeling. It must always have seemed an act, a tear-jerker, though it wouldn't have seemed risible, as it does to us. 'The Parents Lullaby' is a further stage on towards the Victorian ballad. The mother is bending over her babe and wipes away a tear when she thinks of the horrors that may be in store for its innocence. There is no longer any connection between the clichés of the words and those of the music. The pedestrian four-square tune, tied to its repeated notes, plods morosely on its way and the 'doubts and fears' that fill her bosom are verbal merely. This deficiency has more than technical implications.

Purcell had achieved the perfect equivalence between the poetic-dramatic and the musical image and rhythm: which was a manifestation of his awareness of the human situation. In Handel, or even in most of Arne, there is still a valid, if more generalized, relationship between the musical and the literary and theatrical convention. The disappearance of such a relationship is itself evidence of a lack of 'involvement' in human experience; the feeling has become synthetic, 'theatrical' in inverted commas. Of course, the medieval liturgical composer was not directly involved in words and in human experience either, as we saw in our comments on Dunstable's *Veni Sancte Spiritus* (p. 20). But he did not intend to be so involved: for he was involved in something else, which he believed to be more important.

There where the weeping rill dis-tills its wa-ters thro' the grove

where once with soft af-fections thrills I met the youth I love with

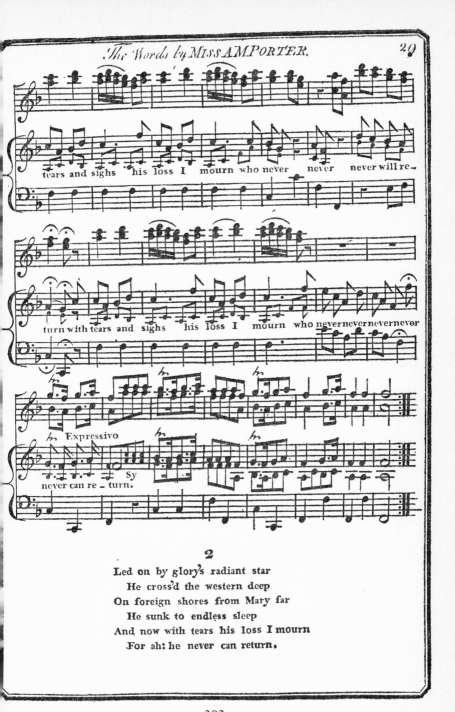

tears and sighs his loss I mourn who never never never will re-

turn with tears and sighs his loss I mourn who never never never never

Expressivo

never can re_turn.

Sy

2

Led on by glory's radiant star
He cross'd the western deep
On foreign shores from Mary far
He sunk to endless sleep
And now with tears his loss I mourn
For ah! he never can return.

THE PARENT'S LULLABY.

Andantino e Softenuto

O'er the new born in — fant

bending, as the mother views its charms doubts and fears, tho'

hopes at — tending, fill her bo — som with a — — larms yet she

The Words by Mr. HARRISON.

checks the tear the sigh, yet she checks the tear the sigh,

with her babes sweet lul_la__by yet she checks the tear the

sigh, with her babes sweet lul_la_by lul_la__by

lul_la__by. Dim⁰ PP

2

Cruel seems the world to beauty
Innocence has many foes
But my darling taught its duty
Heav'n will bless where e'er it goes
So she checks the tear the sigh,
With her babe's, sweet lullaby.

U

APPENDIX D

An amusing example of the denial of the Anti-masque—so much for the Satyrs—is produced by the following catch of Thomas Arne, here reproduced from the original edition in *Apollonian Harmony*. This copy (without date) is in the Music Library of the Barber Institute, University of Birmingham.

The second catch, reproduced from the same page, though not strictly relevant is similarly satiric.

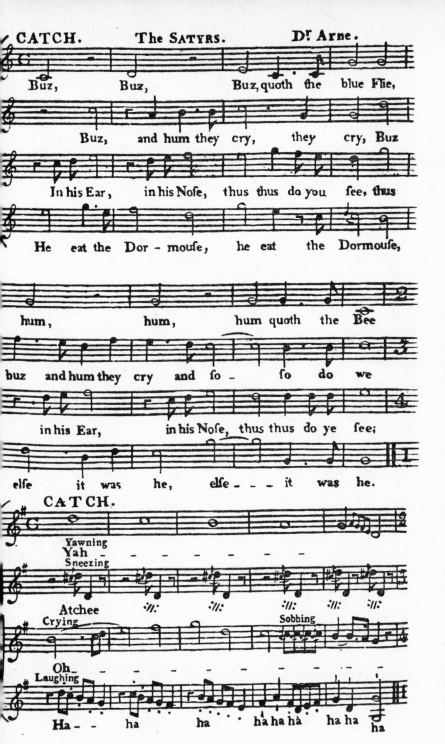

CATCH. The SATYRS. Dr Arne.

Buz, Buz, Buz, quoth the blue Flie,

Buz, and hum they cry, they cry, Buz

In his Ear, in his Nose, thus thus do you see, thus

He eat the Dor-mouse, he eat the Dormouse,

hum, hum, hum quoth the Bee

buz and hum they cry and so - so do we

in his Ear, in his Nose, thus thus do ye see;

else it was he, else - - it was he.

CATCH.

Yawning
Yah - - - - - -
Sneezing

Atchee ://: ://: ://: ://:
Crying Sobbing

Oh - - - - - - - -
Laughing

Ha - - ha ha ha ha ha ha ha ha

307

GRAMOPHONE RECORDINGS

The following list of selected recordings includes only records that have been issued in Great Britain. No attempt has been made to confine it to records in supply at the present moment; on the contrary, a number of deleted records are included, since these may frequently be obtained through dealers in second-hand or superseded stock. For the same reason, and because they provide so useful a format for intensive study, 78 rpm records have been added. Firms such as *Gramophone Exchange* of Wardour Street, London, W.1., keep large stocks of these.

Except where otherwise specified, records here listed are 33 rpm LP records. Stereophonic numbers have not been added.

Byrd
: *Agnus Dei* (Five Part Mass): Argo RG 226 (King's College Choir); Decca AK 1058 (78 rpm) (Fleet Street Choir).
: *Ave Verum Corpus*: Argo RG 226 (as above); Decca K 1081 (78 rpm) (Fleet Street Choir).

Gibbons
: *Hosanna to the Son of David*: Argo RG 80 (King's College Choir)—with other choral music by Gibbons; Columbia LB 92 (78 rpm) (King's College Choir).

Weelkes
: *O Lord, arise*: Columbia LX 1383 (78 rpm) (King's College Choir).

Byrd
: *Lullaby, my sweet little baby*: Brunswick AXA 4518 (Abbey Singers).
: *Though Amaryllis dance*: HMV C 3739 (78 rpm) (C.U.M.S.); HMV 7 ep 7169 (45 rpm) (Madrigal Singers).

Weelkes
: *O Care, thou wilt*: HMS HLP 8 (Elizabethan Singers)—with other madrigals, in HMV's History of Music series.

Ward
: { *Hope of my heart*
: { *Out from the vale*: HMV C 3747 (78 rpm) (C.U.M.S.).

Gibbons
: *What is our life?*: DG (Archive) APM 145056 (Deller Consort)—with other songs, anthems, and consorted music; HMV C 3744 (78 rpm) (C.U.M.S.).

Wilbye
: *Oft have I vowed*: Westminster WL 5221 (Randolph Singers).
: *Draw on sweet night*: HMV C 3742 (78 rpm) (C.U.M.S.).

Campion
: *Author of light*: Oiseau Lyre OL 50102 (Deller & Dupré)—with other songs by Campion.
: *When to her lute, Follow thy fair sun, It fell on a summer's day*: DG APM 14501 (Soames & Gerwig)—with other songs by Campion, Morley and Dowland (see below).
: *It fell on a summer's day*: Saga XID 5222 (M. Thomas)—with other songs by Morley, Jones, Dowland, Attey, Byrd, Weldon, Boyce, Purcell (see below).

Dowland   *Shall I sue*: Brunswick AXA 4515 (New York Pro Musica)—
with other songs and dances; HMV DB 5270 (78 rpm)
Schiøtz & guitar).
Flow my Tears: DG APM 14501 (Soames & Gerwig); HMV
DB 5270 (78 rpm) (as above).
I saw my Lady: DG APM 14501 (as above); Decca LW 5243
(Pears & Bream)—with other Elizabethan songs.
In darkness: Decca LW 5243 (as above); HMV C 3951 (78
rpm) (Deller & Dupré).
Come, heavy sleep: Argo RG 290 (Golden Age Singers)—
with other choral airs by Dowland.

Lawes   { *Sufferance*
Complaint against Cupid
Hymns to the Trinity: Oiseau Lyre OL 50128 (Watts)—
with other songs by Lawes.

Humphrey *Hymn to God the Father*: Alpha AVM 003 (English and
consort)—with other Baroque songs; HMV C 4144 (78 rpm)
(Deller & Jones).

Purcell   *The Blessed Virgin's Expostulation*: Top Rank 15/004 (45
rpm) (Cantelo & Malcolm); Nixa NLP 921 (Ritchie &
Malcolm); Saga XID 5222 (M. Thomas and M. Thomas).
Music for a while: Oiseau Lyre OL 50173 (Watts & Dupré)
—with other Purcell songs; HMV C 3890 (Deller & Bergmann) (78 rpm); HMV 7EP 7068 (Deller & Bergmann) (45
rpm)—same record.
Music in the Shakespearean Theatre: HMV ALP 1265 (Deller
& Dupré)—contains many of the pieces referred to.

Blow   *Venus and Adonis*: Oiseau Lyre OL 50004 (Ritchie, Field-
Hyde, Clinton, conducted Lewis).

Purcell   *Fancy no 4 in C minor*: DG Archive APM 14027 (Schola
Cantorum Basiliensis)—includes the complete Fancies of
Purcell.
Hear my prayer: Argo RG 365 (King's College Choir);
Columbia LB 93 (78 rpm) (New College Choir).
Dido and Aeneas: Nixa PLP 546 (Houston, Cummings, Leigh,
conducted Gregory); Oiseau Lyre OL 50216 (Baker, Clark,
Herincz, conducted Lewis); HMV ALP 1026 (Flagstad, Hems-
ley, Schwarzkopf, conducted Jones); HMV C 3471-7 (78
rpm) (Hammond, Noble, Baillie, conducted Lambert).
The Fairy Queen: Oiseau Lyre OL 50139-41 (Morison,
Vyvyan, Pears, Hemsley, conducted Lewis).
The Tempest: Oiseau Lyre OL 50171 (Excerpts only)
(Vyvyan, Herbert, Alan, conducted Lewis).

Handel   *Apollo e Dafne*: Oiseau Lyre OL 50038 (Ritchie, Boyce, conducted Lewis).

Acis and Galatea: Oiseau Lyre OL 50179-80 (Pears, Sutherland, Galliver, Brannigan, conducted Boult).

Semele: Oiseau Lyre OL 50098-100 (Vyvyan, Watts, Herbert, conducted Lewis).

L'Allegro ed Il Pensieroso: Oiseau Lyre OL 50195-96 (Pears, Delman, Morison, Watts, conducted Willcocks)—does not include *Il Moderato*.

Gay   *Beggar's Opera*: HMV CLP 1052-3 (Austin Version) (Cameron, Morison, Sinclair, conducted Sargent).

Arne   *Comus*: Oiseau Lyre OL 50070-71 (Ritchie, Morison, Herbert, conducted Lewis).

The Cooper: Saga XID 5015 (Intimate Opera Company, conducted Hopkins).

Balfe   *The Bohemian Girl*—'I dreamt that I dwelt': Decca MET 247-8 (Joan Sutherland).

Sullivan   *The Gondoliers*: HMV ALP 1504-5 (Evans, Young, Brannigan, conducted Sargent); Decca ACL 1151-2 (D'Oyly Carte).

INDEX

314

315

317